IMPROVISED NEWS
a sociological study of rumor

An Advanced Study in Sociology

IMPROVISED NEWS
a sociological study of rumor

Tamotsu Shibutani

UNIVERSITY OF CALIFORNIA
SANTA BARBARA

THE BOBBS-MERRILL COMPANY, INC.
Indianapolis • New York

ROBERT McGINNIS
Consulting Editor
CORNELL UNIVERSITY

Copyright © 1966 by The Bobbs-Merrill Company, Inc.
Printed in the United States of America
Library of Congress Catalog Card Number 66–29399

First Printing

PREFACE

This book deals with the problem of how people make up their minds in ambiguous situations; as such, it is a study of the genesis of ideas. Unlike many other inquiries along this line, however, little attention is given to ideas as they are explicitly formulated by some genius. While scholarly views are more readily available for analysis, they often differ considerably from the popular beliefs that actually underlie much of human conduct. What men do depends upon their own cognitive orientations, however naïve or misguided they may be, and interest here centers on the manner in which such views develop.

The manner in which popular perspectives are shaped becomes a question of crucial importance in periods of social upheaval. One of the characteristics of modern mass societies is that men face one ambiguous situation after another. They are constantly sensitized to news precisely because they have to get their bearings as they go along. Ours is also a generation in which manipulation of outlook through ingenious propagandistic devices is commonplace, where ruses, unsubstantiated testimony, and doctored evidence play decisive parts in local and national life. What makes decisions in such unsettled times so important is that crises are the crucibles out of which many innovations emerge; new modes of action often get their initial direction in attempts to cope with emergencies. In studying the manner in which people mobilize to act in such contexts we are trying to get at some of the processes whereby new social structures come into existence. The study of rumors is important, then, not only in itself but also in what it tells us about social change.

The development of reliable knowledge is a cumulative process, generally involving a division of labor. Since the behavioral sciences are still in their infancy, much preliminary spade work must precede systematic observation and analysis. Any serious inquiry into regularities in human behavior leads the investigator almost at once into a jungle of variables, and attempts at precise measurement and experimentation seem premature until at least part of this underbrush has been cleared. This study is therefore exploratory. Although the procedures used—case studies, comparative analysis, ideal types— are not uncommon in preliminary inquiries in the better established sciences, for some reason they have been used sparingly by sociologists during the past thirty years. The objective is to examine intensively a small number of concrete cases of rumor formation in order to identify some key variables, to restate problems, and to formulate hypotheses for subsequent testing, refinement, and eventual displacement. The investigation is obviously unfinished; the generalizations still require verification. It goes without saying that the case materials cited in this presentation are intended only as illustrations and not as evidence.

This undertaking began as a study of rumors as they are popularly conceived, but careful examination of data led before long to serious semantic difficulties. As the vocabulary of daily discourse was replaced by concepts somewhat less vague in signification, the inquiry was successively reconstituted until it became a study of the ways in which people caught in crisis situations develop a working orientation. A new way of looking at a long familiar subject has been developed in the hopes of clarifying what has been vague and of explaining frequently observed but hitherto puzzling facts. The central argument presented, though relatively simple, stands in sharp contrast to prevailing views on rumor held by laymen and behavioral scientists alike. Indeed, the contrast is sometimes so great that some may even find it difficult to see that the same subject matter is still under consideration. To those unfamiliar with the technical literature some of the discussions may appear quite obvious; what is evident has been spelled out, sometimes in painful detail, precisely because so much of the current research on rumor is predicated upon contrary premises.

Although this book is not written as a research monograph, it is the product of a fairly lengthy investigation, including some four years of field observation. The study began on December 7, 1941, with records of rumors among the bewildered Japanese in the San Francisco Bay Area, who suddenly found themselves suspected of being enemy agents. Observations were then made in a succession of unsettled contexts: evacuation of the Japanese from the Pacific Coast, days of confinement in relocation centers, mass migrations from the camps to the Midwest and East, an interlude in the U.S. Army, and Japan during the first year of military occupation. To make this study comparative, data have been drawn from many other sources; nonetheless a disproportionate share of the cases still deals with the fate of various categories of Japanese during World War II. Somewhat lengthy summaries of four of the original cases have been included; key insights were derived from them, and the materials are not available in any other published source.

In the course of the decades during which this book has been taking shape I have become deeply indebted to many persons. Without question my greatest debt is to Herbert Blumer, whose advice, critical comments, and encouragement have significantly affected my formulations. For their counsel I wish also to thank Kenneth Bock, Ralph Gundlach, Abraham Halpern, Everett C. Hughes, William Kornhauser, Frank Miyamoto, Sheldon Stryker, Anselm Strauss, Dorothy S. Thomas, and Louis Wirth. A preliminary organization of empirical data was made possible by a predoctoral training fellowship from the Social Science Research Council, and grants from the Research Committee, University of California, Santa Barbara, facilitated completion of the project. Sandra Gettman prepared the index, and Doris Kihara typed the final manuscript under somewhat trying circumstances. Most of all, I am grateful to my wife for so patiently maintaining optimal work conditions throughout the many years of the study.

TAMOTSU SHIBUTANI
October 1965

CONTENTS

1
ALTERNATIVE CONCEPTIONS OF RUMOR

Moments after President Kennedy was struck down in Dallas, rumors emerged. At first, verified news was meager: the president had been shot; a policeman had been killed; someone had been arrested in a theater. Newsmen, struggling desperately to describe the fast-moving events, disseminated every scrap of pertinent information. An unconfirmed report that Vice President Johnson had suffered a heart attack added to the gloom. Routine activities throughout the nation soon ground to a halt, and for the next few days, as the stunned populace huddled about listening to the radio or watching television, the glare of the world-wide publicity focused on Dallas.

Many elements of mystery remained. How had the crime been committed? Announcements by the police were immediately challenged by rumors. One man could not have fired three shots in the time allotted. Some shots came from the railroad overpass ahead of the caravan; rifle cartridges were found on the overpass; the windshield of the president's car was shattered. Who was Lee Harvey Oswald? Did he work alone, or was he part of a conspiracy? Many believed Oswald to be a hired killer; he had been trained in a special school for assassins in Minsk; an amateur photographer's picture, taken ten minutes before the shooting, showed two silhouettes at the sixth-story window. Others insisted that Oswald was connected with

1

the F.B.I. or the C.I.A.; because of his court martial in the Marines he could not have obtained a gun permit without influential help; Dallas police wanted to arrest him in connection with the attack on General Walker, but the F.B.I. intervened.

When Jack Ruby executed the accused assassin, more questions emerged. Who was Ruby, and why did he do it? Several insisted that just before death Oswald turned toward Ruby as if he recognized him. Rumors linked the two men with the slain policeman. Tippitt, Ruby, and Oswald lived within a few blocks of each other; Oswald was on his way up to Ruby's apartment when stopped by Tippitt; the three had met on November 14 at the Carousel Club; Ruby had lent Oswald money to repay the State Department for his return trip from Russia. According to another rumor, Ruby had been ordered by the Dallas police to silence Oswald. In the months that followed such accounts multiplied, and various investigative agencies trying to reconstruct the events of that fateful day were burdened with the formidable task of checking the accuracy of hundreds of rumors. Even the carefully documented report of the Warren Commission left many dissatisfied, still convinced that the truth was being withheld (Case 10).*

Just as the proliferation of rumors magnified the confusion in Dallas, unreliable reports at times of crucial decision compound difficulties and sometimes lead to disaster. Abortive insurrections have followed word of dissension among those in power. Exaggerated accounts of some offense have resulted in strikes, mutinies, lynchings, and riots. Men have been hanged on the basis of hearsay evidence, only to be exonerated by a subsequent confession. Talk of possible rationing has led to buying panics, and refugees flooding roads upon hearing of approaching invaders have hindered the establishment of effective defense. Information is necessary for planned action, but false intelligence is sometimes worse than ignorance. Special concern over the possibility of being duped arises in conflict, when contending parties fear being exploited by rumors deliberately planted by their adversaries; especially in time of war some control over rumors is felt to be imperative. But effective control requires reliable knowledge, and this requirement has led to scholarly interest in rumor.

* The appendix contains a coded list of cases referred to in this book.

The obvious starting point in any inquiry is the definition of subject matter, but for rumor this is not easy. Pioneering efforts in any field rest upon common-sense concepts, which are vague in reference and contain implicit value judgments. Popular beliefs are not necessarily false, but they are notoriously unreliable; ironically, popular beliefs about rumors have seriously hampered their study. Accordingly, the central focus of this chapter is to specify the identifying characteristics of the class of phenomena to be studied and to indicate some ways in which a fruitful investigation might be launched.

Distortion in Serial Transmission

Although warnings against apocryphal tales can be found in the folklore and literature of many peoples, it is only recently that they have become the object of systematic inquiry. Contributions have come from many sources: historians and jurists concerned with the reliability of testimony, psychologists studying accuracy of perception and recall, psychiatrists interested in the expression of repressed impulses in communicative acts, and sociologists involved in the study of collective problem-solving, public opinion, and reactions to disasters. Many of these studies, including some of the most extensive and careful investigations, rest upon the popular concept of rumor. It is therefore necessary to examine this concept in more detail to see how these studies came to be designed as they were.

The central attribute of rumor, as it is commonly conceived, is error. Rumor is ordinarily regarded as a false report, or at least one which is unverified and probably false. When an unverified report turns out to be true, no one notices its obscure source. When subsequent events reveal a report to have been unfounded, the item is dismissed as having been "only a rumor." It is also customary to label as "rumor" those reports that one is inclined to question. Thus, toward the end of World War II many skeptical Americans scoffed at the report of President Roosevelt's death as "another rumor" until they received confirmation through the mass media. Sometimes reports are labeled "rumor" by those who do not wish to believe them, such as individuals to whom a good friend has just been exposed as an imposter. Both popular and scholarly interest in the subject arises in contexts in which men are preoccupied with accuracy in communication, and "rumor" is one of the words used to designate falsehood.

A further belief concerning rumor is that it is a message transmitted by word of mouth from person to person. Indeed, *oral* interchange is frequently regarded as *the* identifying characteristic of rumor. Whereas news in print is fixed, in oral transmission some transformation is inevitable, for only a few can remember a complicated message verbatim. Psychologists conducting experiments on rumor under laboratory conditions have generally insisted that their subjects engage in oral discourse, while some historians have treated rumor together with gossip, myth, and legend—presumably because they all involve use of the vocal musculature.

Rumor is believed to become false through distortions introduced in the course of serial transmission, and this too is often thought to be an essential characteristic of rumor. A rumor is a message that is passed from person to person. The assumption is that the first speaker in the chain is an eyewitness whose report is accurate and that distortions are subsequently introduced in the relay. The account becomes distorted as each person in the chain of transmitters drops some items and adds his own interpretation. This popular conception is aptly put in the verse of Alexander Pope, who wrote in "The Temple of Fame":

> The flying rumours gathr'd as they roll'd,
> Scarce any tale was sooner heard than told;
> And all who told it added something new,
> And all who heard it made enlargements too.

In studying a phenomenon so conceived the problem logically becomes that of describing the distortions that occur under varying conditions.

Although fallibility of testimony had been discussed by various writers from the days of Thucydides, the first experimental study of distortion in the course of serial transmission was conducted by William Stern (1902, pp. 48–49). Although subsequent investigators have disagreed with some of his findings and interpretations, most have used his conception of rumor, his problem formulation, and his experimental design. The studies are designed to isolate regularities in faulty perception and inaccurate reproduction. The first subject in a series is either asked to describe a picture or given a predetermined message by the experimenter. He repeats the account to the next subject, who in turn passes on what he has heard. A careful record is made of what happens at each point of contact; additions and omissions are recorded and measured. Attempts have been made to formulate generalizations about changing length of reports, content of alterations introduced, direction of transformations, and the various correlates of these variables. In the first two decades after Stern's pioneering work an extensive literature developed in "forensic psychology"—much of it published in the *Zeitschrift für angewandte Psychologie,* a journal he founded—and then interest waned. Excellent summaries of the early studies have been prepared by Hösch-Ernst (1915) and by Gorphe (1927).

The work of Allport and Postman (1947) is the most comprehensive study of this kind. They summarize their findings in terms of three concepts: *leveling* designates the tendency of accounts to become shorter, more concise, and more easily grasped; *sharpening,* the tendency toward selective perception, retention, and reporting of a limited number of details; and *assimilation,* the tendency of reports to become more coherent and more consistent with the presuppositions and interests of the subjects. Their experiments not only confirm previous findings, such as those of Bartlett (1932), but have also been replicated by several others with substantially the same results. Repeated tests show, then, that testimony by serial transmission is rarely accurate, that most persons are unable to repeat verbatim what they had heard from others, that comprehension depends upon the frame of reference of the perceiver. These are demonstrated facts, and they have been explained in terms of limitations of human perception and memory.

In spite of the frequent and consistent confirmation of Allport and Postman's findings, some of their conclusions have been challenged by other investigators. Furthermore, some have asked whether the results are relevant to the study of rumors as they flourish in daily life. Do the experiments duplicate the natural circumstances in which rumors develop? Are the crucial variables actually under control? Among the early critics of experiments on serial transmission was Roretz (1915, p. 208), who contended that the artificial situation in the laboratory differs from contexts in which rumors form spontaneously in ways that encourage a higher percentage of omissions. Others, whose studies will be considered later (in Chapter 3), have repeated this objection. Allport and Postman (1945, pp. 67–68) recognize some of the differences: in the experiments subjects are instructed to be accurate; no opportunities are provided for asking questions; there is no lapse of time between hearing and telling; and subjects are not emotionally involved in the message. Nonetheless, they insist that their findings are relevant.

Another body of literature based on the popular concept of rumor has been developed by psychoanalysts, who have also been occupied with the problem of distortion. Since a person who repeats a rumor can claim that he is only passing on what he had heard, he can speak without assuming full responsibility for what he says. This provides another avenue for releasing repressed impulses, in much the same manner as Freud accounted for the content of dreams and jokes. In a pioneering study Jung (1910) analyzes a rumor in a girls' school about an affair between a teacher and one of the students. The rumor apparently started when a girl related one of her dreams to three classmates, who in turn repeated the story to eight others. Jung explains the dissemination in terms of the active participation of all the students; the girls had similar erotic interests, and the portrayal tapped something that was already "in the air." Rumors take shape, then, as individuals entertain and pass on reports that enable them to give vent to anxieties or hostilities they are otherwise reluctant to acknowledge. The method used by psychoanalysts is clinical rather than experimental, and interest centers upon the individual links in the chain. Many others have followed in this tradition—among them Hart (1916), Glover (1940), and Loewenberg (1943)—and their contributions are for the most part elaborations on the central thesis advanced by Jung.

Distortion is accounted for in the same manner as dissemination;

variations are introduced by participants whose personal needs are slightly different from those who preceded them in the series. The message is distorted by the projection of private interests. Jung deals with distortions as Freud handles secondary elaborations in dreams; gaps in continuity are filled by interpolations. Hart declares that distortions are due to repressed complexes, and several psychiatrists have suggested that the greatest distortions are introduced by those suffering from serious personal problems. What each individual contributes to the formation of a rumor depends upon his needs.

Many valuable facts have been uncovered by these inquiries, and their findings will be cited where pertinent. In general, however, this approach presents a number of difficulties. For one, studies of serial transmission rest on the questionable assumption that normal communication is necessarily accurate; the very use of the term "distortion" implies the existence of some objective standard from which deviations can be measured. The problem of accuracy in reporting is important, but it cannot be handled by fiat—by assuming that whatever the investigator happens to believe constitutes the truth. Is the testimony of an eyewitness necessarily accurate and objective? Do normal and healthy persons act only on the basis of verified propositions? The contention is absurd, for all men must act each day on the basis of unverified reports. Belief in a statement does not wait to be established; men believe implicitly in the truth of what they hear, unless there are special grounds for doubt or disbelief. Whatever seems reasonable at the moment is accepted, and most reports subsequently turn out to be sufficiently accurate for adequate adjustments. In the last analysis, the accuracy of any report is something that can be ascertained only with benefit of hindsight. It is therefore necessary to distinguish between the problem of accuracy and that of *credibility*. Truth and falsity are attributes of propositions; conviction and skepticism are attributes of a man's judgment. Men act on the basis of their beliefs, which are not necessarily demonstrated truths.

The theoretical model used is mechanical, with the report as the basic unit of analysis. Students of serial transmission implicitly distinguish between the *product* of social interaction and the *process* by which it is shaped; they see rumor as the product and are concerned with the character of the process by which it is formed. Perhaps because "rumor" is a noun rather than a verb, it is seen as a thing having a separate existence. It is treated as something that can be passed around from person to person—somewhat like a brick. It is an object that stimulates one person, undergoes certain modifications while passing through him, and then departs to stimulate someone else. In the experiments rumor has been treated operationally as a fixed combination of words which may be altered by additions and subtractions—as if one were manipulating a set of blocks. The implication is that a given word combination could be maintained if only men were more careful in handling them. If rumor is to be identified as distortion so conceived, then almost everything that men say would constitute a rumor, since verbatim reproductions are very infrequent. While the conception of rumor as a discrete entity floating about a community may be satisfactory for conversational purposes, it is unrealistic and inadequate as the basis for serious research.

The individualistic bias of most psychologists and psychiatrists becomes apparent in the explanatory scheme used. Persons involved in spreading rumors are treated as if they were disparate entities, each acting as an independent unit. What one contributes to a rumor is explained in terms of his ability in perception and recall and in terms of his motives. Rumor is recognized as a *social* phenomenon only in the sense that more than one person is necessarily involved; that human beings acting together in any enterprise are intertwined in a complex web of social relationships is ignored. In designing the experiments the organization of roles enacted by the participants— the claims and obligations that they have on one another—is a variable that is left uncontrolled.

Many investigators look upon rumor as a pathological phenomenon rather than as something to be expected of all men in given circumstances. If something is pathological, then special explanations are necessary to account for deviations from the normal. Instead of studying the conditions under which a recurrent form of communication takes place, investigators have been preoccupied with distortion of content, special defects of those who introduce error, neurotic traits of "rumor-mongers," and ways of removing obstacles to normal communication, which is presumably accurate. It appears that the uncritical adoption of a popular concept has brought in unexamined value judgments, and these have seriously hampered effective study.

Rumor as a Collective Transaction

A different approach to the study of rumor can be found in the writings of a number of historians and sociologists. They view rumor as a communicative pattern that develops when men who are involved together in a situation in which something out of the ordinary has happened pool their intellectual resources in an effort to orient themselves. They conceive of rumor as a collective enterprise that gets its organization and direction in the collaboration of a multitude of persons. To be sure, only individuals and their acts are involved, but the individuals are acting not as independent entities but as participants in larger transactions. They do not deny that rumors are sometimes inaccurate, but they have focused their attention on problems other than falsehood. Among the writers who have taken this position are Oman (1918), Dauzat (1919), Bysow (1928), Rose (1940), and Peterson and Gist (1951).

From this standpoint it is not easy to make a clear distinction between communicative processes and the product of communication. Rumor content is not viewed as an object to be transmitted but as something that is shaped, reshaped, and reinforced in a succession of communicative acts; as Turner (1964, p. 398) puts it, rumor is not so much the dissemination of a designated message as the process of forming a definition of a situation. In most cases one can speak of rumor content only heuristically. In the end some rumors do assume a stereotyped form that can be summarized in a single sentence; en route to this crystallized state, however, they are formed in a wide variety of verbalizations. Even after a fairly stable form has been attained, it is reaffirmed and reinforced in further communication. In this sense a rumor may be regarded as something that is constantly being constructed; when the communicative activity ceases, the rumor no longer exists.

That rumor is a collaborative process can best be seen by examining in some detail an actual case study:

Case 33. THE TRUNCATED TRAINING CYCLE. During the latter part of World War II the regular training cycle for infantrymen in the U.S. Army was 17 weeks; this included a two-week bivouac toward the end for putting newly acquired skills to use in the field. After that the recruits were given a 14-day furlough and then were sent to replacement centers overseas. After a few weeks of the rigorous training routine most men began to appreciate the awesome destructiveness of modern infantry weapons, the ease with which one could become a casualty, and how much there was to learn before developing proficiency as a rifleman. Before long most men became convinced that the more training one had, the better were his chances for survival. They knew that some of the enemy troops they would face had had many years of combat experience, and they had difficulty in seeing how, with only 17 weeks of training, they could possibly be a match for them.

In Camp Wheeler, Georgia, each battalion started its training cycle when its troop complement was filled, and the 10th Battalion began early in December 1944, just when the German Army was launching its last major offensive of the war. There had been a major breakthrough in Belgium, and American infantry casualties were mounting. As the German advances continued, trainees were told repeatedly that they would die on the Rhine unless they paid strict attention. On December 22, when a 35-mile German advance was reported, one of the companies was given a special orientation lecture in which this point was again emphasized. It was during this period that several rumors arose concerning the length of the training cycle.

"Hey, you know what some guy was saying at the P.X.? He said the 18th Battalion got only five days furlough and got sent to Fort Meade. Can you beat that? They only got five days at home!"

"No kidding? Only five days?"

"If that ain't just like the fuckin' Army. What the hell can a guy do in only five days? After 17 weeks of this shit I'll need a whole fuckin' month just to catch up on my sleep."

"Did the 18th Battalion pull out too? I heard the 6th Battalion got pulled out of bivouac and sent over."

"No shit! Didn't they even finish their cycle?"

"Nope; they got their ass yanked right out in the middle of bivouac."

During Christmas week, which was the fourth week in the 10th Battalion cycle, the men were given rifle practice and were later taken on an unexpected 14-mile hike. This gave further impetus to the discussions.

"You know, our cycle's been speeded up. That's why we're having rifle practice already."

"Yeah. In the 18th Battalion they didn't have rifle practice until the seventh week."

"Some guy said our cycle was cut to six weeks. I think that's a crock of shit."

"Six weeks!"

"Who said so?"

"Well, how come we're having a 14-mile hike this week? The most you have in training is 20 miles. That's what we're working up to. This is only our fourth week, and we're almost there."

"Maybe they did move it up a ways, but six weeks is too short. We don't know enough."

"Yeah, but they need riflemen bad. Sometimes they can use anybody who can pull a trigger."

On Christmas day the men were given a respite from their duties, but most of them sat about the barracks writing letters, sleeping, or talking about the shortened training cycle.

"Is it true that the 18th Battalion guys got sent out in their tenth week?"

"Ten weeks! Didn't they finish their cycle?"

"At least they got out of bivouac. That's something."

"I don't know, boy. I'd rather have it. The more you know, the better off you'll be."

"At least the 6th Battalion finished their cycle."

"The hell they did! They were only in their ninth week."

"I heard they were in the eleventh."

"Yeah. They were behind the 18th Battalion. I don't think them guys had their bivouac either."

Later in the same day there was another discussion:

"You know, the way things are going, we might not get a furlough."

"No furlough! They gotta give us a furlough."

"No they don't. If they need us, they can send us right away."

"What makes ya think we won't get one, Sherman?"

"Well, I heard the 6th Battalion was sent over in airplanes without any furloughs. They just sent 'em straight over, they needed 'em so bad."

"Aw, get out. Where'd you hear that?"

"No furloughs? Naw, they wouldn't do that. They might cut 'em, but they wouldn't take 'em out. Hell, my morale'd be shot. I wouldn't be no good if they did that."

"That's what you think, boy. When you get over there, and some bastard starts shootin' at ya, you're gonna be the best fuckin' soldier they ever saw."

The center of interest on Christmas day, however, was a rumor that the two-week bivouac had been eliminated from the 10th Battalion schedule and that this group would remain at Camp Wheeler for only 15 weeks. This was discussed avidly throughout the day with mixed feelings. Most men did not particularly look forward to bivouac, but they felt that the training might be invaluable later. Since the report was attributed to one of the training cadre, it was taken seriously, although guarded skepticism was not absent.

Throughout the first week of January 1945, the rumors persisted —with several variations. One was that the training of the 13th Battalion had been terminated during its tenth week; the men were flown overseas without a furlough, and some of them had to be called out of the post theater at 8:30 Sunday night. Another was that 22 men from the 10th Battalion (but presumably from another company) were being shipped to Fort Meade on the following day. Still another was that the 9th Battalion was going out to bivouac during its eleventh week, three weeks ahead of its original schedule. But the greatest interest centered on the length of the 10th Battalion cycle.

"Hey, the cut to 15 weeks is official!"

"How do you know?"

"Those guys who went to apply for O.C.S. found out. Right on the application blank they got the finishing date for our group. Webb figured it out. It comes at the end of the fifteenth week."

"Hell, yes, it's official. It was on the bulletin board, wasn't it?"

"I didn't see it."

"Aw, you're blind as a bat anyway, Schultz."

"Fuck you. At least I can read."

"When was it on the bulletin board?"

"It wasn't there, God dammit. I read that fucker every day, and I didn't see it."

"Well, one good thing. I hear the 20-mile hike was cut out of our cycle. That's supposed to come on the last week."

"Hell, they had to take something out."

The belief that the schedule had been altered was supported even in discussions that had nothing to do with it. For example, the following conversation was about a recruit who apparently was starving himself in an effort to get a discharge.

"I don't like this damn Army, but by God I'd feel like hell if I got discharged for not being able to take it."

"Bull shit! You'd be so damn happy you'd yell your ass off."

"By God, I'd just as soon get my ass blowed off here and get a discharge than go over there."

"Hell, yes! I'd give an arm to get out of here. Hell, you're no good dead."

"You're really not trained in 17 weeks."

"Fifteen weeks, you mean."

By the end of the week most men assumed that they would be leaving for overseas duty after 10 or 15 weeks of training, and rumors about the other battalions supported this belief. Checking on the accuracy of these reports was difficult, for recruits were kept too busy for visiting. The only opportunity for exchanging information with those in other battalions came at the post exchange or the theater on the two or three evenings a week that were open, and there information had to be accepted from total strangers. When the German advance was finally halted, interest in the subject faded. On January 13, a rumor developed that the 10th Battalion cycle had been restored to 17 weeks. Throughout this period not one official announcement was made on this subject.

From this record it becomes apparent that a rumor is a collective transaction, involving a *division of labor* among participants, each of whom makes a *different* contribution. A rumor exists only in the verbalizations of individual men, but it is a distinct whole for which the activities of the participants constitute only a medium. Each rumor has a history, but it cannot be discovered in the biography of any of the individuals participating in it. A line of action which is initiated in the behavior of one participant is carried on in the behavior of others and eventually completed in the behavior of still others. The participants are interdependent; no single person can perform the entire transaction alone. Futhermore, what is contributed by each performer constitutes only a small part of his own activity; except in catastrophes most persons cannot afford to spend too much time discussing the situation. Rumor, then, is not an individual creation that spreads, but a collective formation that arises in the collaboration of many.

The career of a rumor, unlike experiments in serial transmission, is not a process of unilinear development. As in the days following the assassination of President Kennedy, people who focus upon a common area of preoccupation talk things over. The participants are not robots who parrot automatically what they have heard. Some individuals introduce conjectures of what might have happened. Others speculate on what is likely to follow. Some are inclined to make comparisons with similar situations with which they happen to be familiar. A person with special contacts may add some real "leaks" of confidential information. Although deliberate lies are not common in human discourse, this possibility certainly cannot be ruled out. Some ask questions; they challenge statements and demand explanations. Out of this welter of verbalizations certain items of information gradually begin to stand out and enjoy priority in communication, and in this way a collective interpretation develops. Serial transmission is possible, but it is rarely found outside the laboratory.

Each person has a distinct personality and reacts in a unique way to each situation. Since no two persons enter a scene with identical vocabularies, perceptual sets, or interests, their contributions to a collective transaction differ, and each contributes what he does for somewhat different reasons. Therefore, the transaction *as a whole* cannot be explained in terms of individual motivation. Some persons pass on information, even when they know it is not verified, because they believe the group to be in danger; in disasters any available news is exchanged in the spirit of mutual assistance. Others may try to enhance their prestige by pretending to have access to "inside information." Those in important positions may conceive of themselves as focal points in communication networks and try to live up to their responsibilities by giving their views. As Glover (1940, p. 46) points out, a timid person may speak out of fear, hoping that a frightening report would be contradicted. The common objective is a satisfactory definition of the situation, which would provide gratifications of some sort to all the participants; the problem is to ascertain how a common definition develops in spite of the *diversity* of motives. Furthermore, the collective process apparently develops independently of the desires of any particular individual. Once a rumor is under way, it cannot be controlled by any one of the participants, any more than a lynching mob can be stopped when a few members change their minds.

The contribution made by each person varies with the character of his involvement in the situation and his relationship to the others. Participants in rumor construction enact various roles. Most obvious is the role of the *messenger,* the person who brings a pertinent item of information to the group. He usually sees himself as relaying something he has heard, even though he is reporting the information from an idiosyncratic standpoint. Another common role is that of the *interpreter,* the person who tries to place the news in context, evaluating it in the light of past events and speculating on implications for the future. The *skeptic* is the one who expresses doubt over the authenticity of the report, demands proof, and urges caution about using it as the basis for adjustment. When there are several possible interpretations or plans of action, the *protagonist* sponsors one over the others. Sometimes he is an individual who is personally affected, such as a relative or close friend of someone who has been victimized; if so, he may become an *agitator.* In rare instances a person who believes a report to be false may support it to encourage beliefs that serve his interests. The most frequently assumed role is that of *auditor,* often a spectator who says very little. Those who indicate their interest and merely listen, only occasionally raising a question, are nonetheless important, for their very presence affects the developing outlook. What each speaker says is organized in a manner designed to appeal to his listeners, and the attitudes imputed to those who pay attention affect communication content. A key role is that of the *decision-maker,* who takes the lead in determining what ought to be done. In many instances a person with specialized knowledge, an official, or someone of high status is expected to assume such responsibility. Sometimes a "natural leader," someone who is widely respected for his personal qualities, takes command. Such roles are not clearly defined in custom, as are the conventional roles of nurse in a hospital or judge in a courtroom, but these behavior patterns occur with sufficient regularity so that they are easily recognized.

Not all of these roles are found in each instance of rumor formation. The same roles are not always enacted by the same individuals; a person who is a messenger in one context may be a skeptic or a protagonist in another. Furthermore, in the course of the formation of a rumor a given individual may contribute in different ways as the situation changes, not from faulty memory but because he stands in a different relationship to the various persons he addresses.

Rumors exist only in the communicative acts of men, but they cannot be identified in terms of any particular set of words. What is identified as a "rumor" is usually a shorthand expression summarizing the general sense of many different verbalizations. A particular message may be stated as an affirmation, or it may be part of a question. It may be a direct statement, or it may be implied in what is said. In each universe of discourse certain things are taken for granted and need not be said at all. Synonyms may be used, and sometimes expressive movements—a look of dismay or a nod of assent—may be sufficient. A message may be implied in some overt act. Thus, the sequence of words differs for each speaker, for in rumor there is no standardization of word order as in slogans, proverbs, or ceremonial greetings. An observer is able to identify rumor content only by abstracting from dozens of communicative acts. Rumor is not so much distortion of some word combination but what is held in common. Without some central *meaning* a succession of discrete remarks by separate individuals could not be recognized as component elements of the same transaction. To focus attention upon words, then, is to misplace emphasis.

What appears to be transformation of rumor content—usually called "distortion"—is actually part of the developmental process through which men strive for understanding and consensus. Each participant ponders the meaning of what he has learned, integrates it into his own perspective, and thereby reconstitutes his own orientation toward the situation. That different words or phrases are used may or may not result in a significant change of direction for the transaction as a whole. But if something is actually added or dropped, this constitutes a reconstruction of the entire unit.

Although the primary concern of most writers on rumor in the past two thousand years has been the inaccuracy of reports transmitted by word of mouth, it must be emphasized that falsehood is not a necessary feature of rumor. As we shall see (in Chapter 3), there is evidence that under some circumstances a collective orientation becomes progressively more accurate as it is successively tested and revised. A report that is unverified may subsequently turn out to be either true or false.

In this book rumor will be regarded as a recurrent form of *communication through which men caught together in an ambiguous situation attempt to construct a meaningful interpretation of it by pooling their intellectual resources.* It might be regarded as a form of collective problem-solving. Rumors are found throughout the world in all periods of history. While the content is unique in each historical context, the action pattern itself is recurrent. This pattern, furthermore, does not depend upon any particular type of personnel; any individual, regardless of his level of sophistication, will take part when desperately trying to comprehend his environment. Engaging in this type of activity is certainly not limited to victims of mental disorders or other deficiencies. The reality to be studied, then, is not distortion in serial transmission but the social interaction of people caught in inadequately defined situations. To act intelligently such persons seek news, and rumor is essentially a type of news.

The Social Control of Communication

One useful route to a characterization of rumor is the behavioral approach: what is it that men *do* when they participate in constructing a rumor? Rumor is a collective enterprise whose component parts consist of some kind of cognitive and communicative activity. To specify further its essential features it is necessary to examine the manner in which communication is regulated in society.

Although we ordinarily regard language and other forms of communication as *devices* utilized for the transmission of ideas from person to person, they are primarily *modes of activity* used to influence the conduct of others. After all, a man who is talking is doing something; the sounds and bodily movements that constitute a language are forms of behavior—like walking, seizing, crunching, or pounding. Such movements and sounds become communicative only when they are used in the context of mutual assistance and direction, only when they facilitate the adjustment and readjustment to one another of participants in a common transaction. Thus, as Dewey (1926, pp. 166–207) insists, the heart of communication is not the expression of antecedent ideas and feelings, but the establishment of cooperation in an activity that involves partners, in which the contribution of each participant is modified and to some extent regulated by that partnership.

Because human speech occurs so spontaneously there is a tendency to regard the capacity to vocalize and gesticulate as instinctive, and few appreciate the extent to which communicative activities, like almost everything else that men do, are subject to social control. Although language is not ordinarily regarded as a social institution, it is a highly complex mode of action executed in accordance with conventional understandings and sustained through group sanctions. Each group has norms concerning the manner in which sounds are to be uttered, the proper order of articulation, and the meanings designated by each word; these norms are so well established that they are taken for granted. In addition to speech, bodily gestures may be used; indeed, any overt act may become communicative if it serves as an indicator of inner experiences. Like the vocal mechanism, the facial musculature is capable of producing a number of finely differentiated movements, and it is possible to communicate by winking, pouting, or wrinkling one's nose. Bodily gestures such as kissing the fingers, stroking one's chin, or drumming one's fingers are conventional; they differ from culture to culture.

While engaging in conversation each participant does two rather distinct things: he says what he intends to say through conventional words and gestures and reveals his individual feelings through the style of his remarks. One may distinguish, therefore, between *what* a man says and *how* he says it. Personal preferences, which are not always consistent with conventional obligations, are revealed through all kinds of expressive movements, of which the speaker is often unaware. Expressive movements are largely involuntary and always accompany deliberately organized acts; the more intense one's effort, the greater his tension, the greater is the likelihood that the expressive component of his behavior will be noticeable. Spontaneous facial expressions reveal fine nuances of changing feeling: the look in one's eyes, the changing position of his lips, jaws, or eyebrows, as well as the color and moistness of his skin. The quality of the voice is also important. If it is high in pitch, shrill, loud, or tremulous, it is regarded as indicative of anxiety. Sudden spurts or outbursts of words, the lack of pauses, the snapping of words, overtalkativeness, forced or inappropriate laughter, and rapid and shallow breathing are also viewed as symptoms of tension. A strained posture, forced motions, twitches, tremors, as well as the over-all rhythm and vigor of muscular movements also provide clues to inner dispositions. Men are delicately attuned to one another's expressive movements, for these involuntary gestures reveal each individual's actual inclinations to act rather than the conventional façade he usually feels obliged to maintain.

Expressive movements are biotic reactions and are not to be confused with conventional body gestures. They are outer manifestations of the internal transformations that occur in emotions; tears, grimaces, and the various involuntary sounds that accompany them are constituent parts of larger organic patterns that constitute fear, anger, or joy. Since expressive movements are instinctive, they are the same among all men. In his comparative study of emotional expression among Americans and Chinese, Klineberg (1938) found that expressive movements were identical: trembling, cold sweat, immobility, uncontrolled urination, and flushing of the face. But the Chinese used many conventional gestures that would be strange to most Americans, such as stretching out the tongue in surprise, opening the eyes in anger, scratching one's ears and cheek in happiness, and clapping the hands in worry or disappointment. Since rumors develop in situations marked by some measure of excitement, this aspect of communication assumes special significance. It is important to remember, therefore, that expressive movements are for the most part *not* subject to social control.

Content of speech is also regulated. Men are rarely free to say whatever they please. Each individual has his personal views, but whether or not he will reveal them depends upon the expectations he projects to his audience. In each standard context certain subjects are regarded as inappropriate topics for discussion. One refrains from making remarks that others would regard as implausible or offensive, just as he generally avoids doing other things that people ridicule or resent. Those who feel impelled to insult someone are usually required to inhibit their desire. The deference with which various persons are addressed depends upon extant social relationships, and norms exist concerning the extent of one's responsibility for the consequences of his statements. In many situations, therefore, men inhibit their impulses and formulate their remarks in conformity with group expectations.

Although psychologists are by no means agreed on the character of the cognitive processes, an increasing number are inclined to regard them as forms of activity; after all, a man who is thinking is doing something. Consciousness may be regarded as a form of communication; a man who is conscious of something is making indications to himself in much the same manner in which he might call it to the attention of someone else. Reflection consists of manipulating such designations in the course of solving problems. Thinking is private in the sense that others do not have access to one's thoughts, but it is subject to social control to the extent that it is carried on in terms of conventional symbols and cultural axioms. The use of words makes possible the organization and manipulation of otherwise inchoate experiences. Group norms necessarily become involved in thinking; even when one is talking to himself he must say things that "make sense." The human mind, then, may be regarded not so much as a substance but as a form of behavior—largely subvocal linguistic behavior. Those who participate in rumor construction are communicating with themselves as well as with others.

Theoretically any human being can speak to any other, but in fact there are many barriers to free intercourse. Each community has communication channels, which are integral parts of the established social system. The participants in recurrent transactions stand in understood relationships with one another, and information is exchanged during frequent and trusted associations. Every bureaucracy, for example, has its official channels. Stable networks are also discernible in the relations between different ethnic groups or between different classes; those in each stratum have frequent associations with one another while maintaining social distance from outsiders. *Communication channels,* then, are much more than mere points of contact; they consist of *shared understandings concerning who may address whom, about what subject, under what circumstances, with what degree of confidence.*

Institutional channels are well organized. Like other social institutions they are characterized by a stable set of rules, officers performing clearly defined roles, procedures so well established as to be followed by interchangeable personnel, and sustaining sanctions. There are fixed standards of acceptability, prescribed routes of transmission, verification procedures, and codes of reliable conduct. Since the participants are readily identifiable, they are held personally accountable for their performance. The fixing of responsibility, considerations of personal pride, and concern over one's reputation within the organization tend to temper the pursuit of personal predilections at the expense of accurate communication. In most communities the institutional channels are generally accepted as reliable sources of information.

In modern mass societies most institutional channels rely upon written or printed discourse. Because of the widespread tendency to confuse rumor with oral transmission and to assume that all such reports are unreliable, it must be emphasized that formal channels may be oral. Before the advent of the printed media much communication necessarily involved personal contact; even after the practice of printing had been established it remained for a long time the exclusive possession of men of large affairs, for the illiterate still had no access. Even in the twentieth century oral dissemination of news is not uncommon. In the Greek village studied by Stycos (1952), where the literacy rate is low, access to the mass media is meager. The established procedure is for the priest or the teacher to read at the village tavern newspapers dropped by bus drivers at irregular intervals. These men not only read the news but are expected to interpret and evaluate it and to provide advice on what to do about it. Firth (1956) reports that all communication in Tikopia is oral, but expressions such as "speech of the crowd" and "it is held that . . ." are used to convey derogatory judgment and to dissociate the speaker in advance from responsibility for the accuracy of his statement. Whether communication occurs through personal contact, writing, print, or some electronic device, if the channel is defined as authoritative, it serves as the standard against which reports attributed to all other sources are checked.

No matter how elaborate the institutional channels, they are invariably supplemented by *auxiliary channels*—the "grapevine." Informal networks are often built up around personal friendships which provide focal points of contact. The local barber shop, latrines of military units, and cocktail party circuits in capitals all become contexts in which significant exchanges occur. Every bureaucracy has ways of "cutting the red tape"; although personal ties that avoid formal channels are often discouraged or even prohibited, they nonetheless exist. Accidental contacts sometimes become exaggerated in importance: the foreman who is engaged to the manager's secretary or the recruit who comes from the same local community as the battalion sergeant major. Auxiliary channels are definitely supplementary; when "grapevine" information conflicts with official news, the latter is generally accepted.

Auxiliary channels arise to facilitate activities that are otherwise cumbersome—or in some cases illegal. If the formal structure of a hospital is unwieldy, views are exchanged during coffee breaks in a ward kitchen or in casual conversations between a doctor and attendants whom he happens to find congenial. Notorious among clandestine channels is the "grapevine" of the underworld; the whereabouts of various criminals are known along with their latest exploits, and the network reaches into prisons as well as high government offices. In occupied countries, where the populace distrusts official sources of news, special channels emerge. In resistance movements communication takes place largely through trusted individuals. During the Civil War Negro slaves kept well informed of movements of the opposing armies and of proposals concerning their freedom;

the latest news was announced at secret meetings on various plantations to which they could slip away at night.

The roles enacted in auxiliary channels are not fixed in custom nor defined in law. These sources are evaluated largely in terms of the personal reputation of the participants for honesty, knowledge, sound judgment, and "connections." Although the arrangements are informal, participants can be identified, for most of them know one another on a personal basis. Responsibility for the consequences of one's remarks is more or less fixed, and each must protect his reputation for intelligence and integrity. Although one can give vent to his feelings when discussing some trivial interest, his remarks must be tempered when purporting to give the best estimate of the situation at his command. The speaker's standing is at stake whenever he participates; were the others strangers, he might not care, but among those with whom one is in sustained association this becomes a matter of considerable importance.

As in all other forms of joint action, communicative activities vary considerably in the extent to which they are institutionalized, ranging from formal procedures to more informal interchanges to spontaneous expression. The distinctive characteristic of rumor as a collective transaction—what makes it different from other forms of discourse among men attempting to define an ambiguous situation— is the *lower degree of formalization* of many of its component communicative acts. There is a relaxation of conventional norms governing social distance, sources of information, verification procedures, subject matter, and sometimes even the use of gestures. Precisely because these transactions do not develop within an institutional framework there are opportunities for spontaneity, expediency, and improvisation.

The Situational Approach to Rumor

The basic unit of analysis becomes the *ambiguous situation,* and the central problem is to ascertain how working orientations toward it develop. If rumors are viewed as the cooperative improvisation of interpretations, it becomes apparent that they cannot be studied fruitfully apart from the social contexts in which they arise. They are not isolated reports but phases of a more inclusive adjustive process, and the analysis of symbolic content alone is not likely to yield adequate understanding. An appreciation of any rumor requires some knowledge of the sensitivities shared by the people and the manner in which they are mobilizing to act. Several interrelated rumors may emerge in the same situation, and they must be studied together. The focus of inquiry is thus redirected. Rather than asking how reports are distorted, interest centers on finding regularities in the cognitive and communicative behavior of men trying to cope with inadequately defined situations.

Unlike a great many inquiries in the social sciences today the design of this study is inductive and exploratory rather than deductive and experimental. The objective is the formulation of hypotheses rather than their verification. Since the situation has been adopted as the unit of analysis, the case method is used to preserve the unitary character of the context and to trace development over time. The prodecure followed—the successive reformulation of concepts and hypotheses through the comparative analysis of case materials—is roughly akin to what Znaniecki (1934, pp. 235–82) once called "analytic induction," although as Turner (1953) points out, his formulation is unnecessarily restrictive. Glaser and Strauss (1965) provide a more satisfactory description of the method.

Attention centers upon certain key questions about rumor. Each collective transaction has a career; this means that there is a beginning and an end. Accordingly, the first task is to ascertain the conditions under which rumors arise. Men do not always rely on rumors; in fact, they often challenge reports attributed to undisclosed sources. Under what circumstances, then, do they rely upon one another? Furthermore, in the study of any process we must also consider the problem of termination. What are the conditions under which rumors disappear? In many cases the communicative interchanges cease with the establishment of consensus, but even when this does not happen, rumors do not go on indefinitely.

Rumors vary considerably along temporal and spatial dimensions, and another problem is to account for these variations. Among strikers who have just watched the police escort "scabs" through their picket lines rumors develop almost instantaneously; on the other hand, several months may pass before a substantial portion of a community has heard the "latest" scandal about corruption at city hall. As Bysow (1928, p. 421) points out, some rumors are intermittent; they develop for a while, subside, and then emerge again. Furthermore, rumors differ considerably in the number of people who become involved and in their geographical distribution. What is commonly called "gossip" is generally confined to a relatively small number of persons who know one another, but millions scattered throughout the globe may become concerned over the possible use of nuclear weapons. How are these temporal and spatial patterns to be explained?

The key problem is to isolate regularities in the formation of rumor content. In studies of serial transmission this is relatively easy, since the initial report is assumed to have been accurate. Once this premise is rejected, however, we are confronted with a difficult question. If rumor is not a distorted version of the truth, how does it come to be organized as it is? Of particular interest are rumors that are inconsistent with already accepted beliefs. During World War II, for example, when Americans assumed that any sacrifice would be made for victory, it was entirely reasonable for recruits at Camp Wheeler to believe that, if needed, they would be assigned to combat duty overseas even before they were adequately trained. But the contention that the F.B.I. or the C.I.A. would become involved in a plot to assassinate the President of the United States flatly contradicts the presuppositions of most Americans. Yet, many seriously entertained the possibility that Oswald was a government agent. Such inconsistencies and the conditions under which they arise are of special interest, for if such rumors persist, they may form the basis for drastic innovations.

The contrast between these cases of rumor formation suggests the possibility of different developmental patterns. In this study two modes of rumor construction have been distinguished as polar types. Further investigation will no doubt disclose refinements or additional career lines, but at this stage of inquiry even this initial distinction proves useful.

Popular concern has centered on the consequences of rumor, and investigators working with mechanical models have formed hypotheses concerning "effects." Since they have regarded rumors as falsehoods, they have invariably found them deleterious. It would appear, however, that what follows the development of a rumor would depend upon its content; what people do or fail to do rests upon their definition of the situation. In addition, much depends upon the extent to which consensus is established; once men are agreed upon a particular interpretation, group sanctions arise to enforce it. But there is considerable variation in the degree of consensus that is achieved. In some situations a single definition prevails; in others a number of different versions arise, each with its partisan supporters; sometimes the different versions are all entertained simultaneously as possibilities, and the group is immobilized. Another important problem, then, is to ascertain the conditions under which consensus is established.

These problems have been investigated by examining case studies of 60 ambiguous situations in which some 471 rumors developed. In several of these contexts many more rumors emerged, but they were not recorded in sufficient detail to be usable in this study. Seven of the cases are based largely upon materials collected in field work during World War II; the rest have been taken from published sources. Rumors develop in extraordinary, often spectacular, circumstances; and historians, journalists, eyewitnesses, and social scientists have amassed extensive records, providing a vast reservoir upon which to draw.

Since only sixty cases have been subjected to close scrutiny, questions arise concerning the basis of selection. Because the objective was to construct hypotheses rather than to verify them, an effort was made to choose cases in which the key variables under consideration were likely to be maximized or minimized. Another criterion was fullness of detail. In published materials the particulars available differ from case to case, making comparisons difficult. Some cases were chosen for adequate coverage of those aspects of rumor construction under study. A third consideration was diversity. Since hypotheses were being formulated concerning the relation of rumor content to cultural axioms, care was taken to get some cross-cultural representation. Because of their easy accessibility most of the materials are on events in the United States and in Europe during the past hundred years, but almost one-third of the cases have been drawn from other parts of the world. An attempt was also made to include examples of each of the various types of contexts in which rumors flourish—sudden crises, sustained tension, impending decisions, boredom from monotony. The sources from which case materials have been drawn are not of uniformly high quality; because of the type and variety of data needed this unevenness is unavoidable. No claim is made of a representative sample, nor is there any particular significance in the total number of cases used. A sufficient number have been examined to make it unlikely that any generalization rests upon the record of a freak incident.

Several difficulties arise in collecting reliable data on rumors. First of all, in examining published sources, care must be exercised to pick out what is here defined as rumor rather than what is described as a "rumor." In many cases the latter consists of whatever the observer happens to find suspicious or does not believe. The descriptive material had to be recast in terms of the concepts of this study. Since rumors are elusive and ephemeral, accounts of them are often impressionistic. Eyewitness accounts are not objective, even when every effort is being made to be as accurate as possible. All human perception is selective and biased, and all that can be done is to guard against the pursuit of special interests to the point where descriptions are manufactured. As Killian (1956) points out, getting descriptions from different vantage points in a complex and rapidly changing situation is difficult. Especially when records are kept by a lone observer, much is necessarily lost. The matter of perspective assumes critical importance in considering accounts of conflict situations; rumors attributed to a group by its adversaries cannot be accepted at face value. In most cases what actually happened can only be ascertained in retrospect through a reconstructive procedure that Wallace (1956) calls the "jigsaw puzzle" method: carefully weighing available records, culling the testimony of those who played key roles, observing the consequences, and trying to fit together the different bits and pieces. Often the only information about a situation other than the rumors themselves is what the participants subsequently discovered to be true—sometimes from mistakes they made by acting on the basis of rumors. From the standpoint of reliability, then, these data leave much to be desired. Nonetheless, at this stage of inquiry we must use the best accounts available of real life situations. Where we are still groping for hypotheses precision must be sacrificed.

The problem of verification remains. These hypotheses have not yet been verified under controlled conditions. A few preliminary attempts at testing, however, have been made. In the comparative analysis it has been possible to take advantage of "natural experiments," situations in which the key variables were accidentally controlled. Furthermore, the generalizations have been checked through simple enumeration—the collection of confirmatory cases and a diligent search for negative cases. They are not contradicted by findings in the extensive research literature. A third type of provisional test is supplied by records of the political manipulation of rumors. Effective control of any phenomenon implies accurate knowledge, although procedures sometimes work for reasons the practitioner does not fully understand. If the generalizations have any validity, all techniques of control based upon them should succeed while those that contradict them should fail. Although the affirmation of consequences is not satisfactory proof in itself, it provides some measure of reassurance.

Summary and Conclusion

Underlying every investigation is a working conception of the phenomenon under scrutiny, and inquiry is directed by this initial conceptualization. The manner in which problems are posed and hypotheses formulated as well as the selection of research techniques all depend upon the assumptions made about the subject matter. If the initial assumptions are unrealistic, even the most careful research is not likely to be fruitful, for attention is not likely to be directed toward the significant variables. Many studies of rumor have been based upon the popular concept of distortion in serial transmission. Although studies of false testimony have been conducted with care and precision and have produced valuable findings on perception and memory, they have yielded little understanding of rumors. It appears that the development of more reliable knowledge has been impeded by one of Bacon's idols, and it has been necessary to begin this study with a semantic exercise. When rumor is viewed as a collective transaction, interest centers upon a type of communicative activity—intrapersonal as well as interpersonal—marked by a low degree of formalization and found among men caught together in ambiguous situations. Reorganization of inquiry along these lines means that many instances of accurate communication will be included and many cases of distortion will be omitted.

This reconceptualization will enable us to get closer to the actual difficulties that make rumor an object of concern and vituperation. We must distinguish between what is intuitively recognized as rumor, especially by those who feel they have been victimized by it, and popular beliefs about the phenomenon. Practical men of affairs are not concerned with the details of oral interchange but with collective beliefs that result in inexpedient action—and are subsequently adjudged erroneous. Such beliefs are thought to develop through serial transmission, but in fact they do not. The aim of this book is to go back to the original difficulty—the formation of collective beliefs—in hopes of formulating some generalizations that might eventually make some measure of effective control possible.

2
THE FAILURE OF FORMAL NEWS CHANNELS

Amid the smoldering ruins of razed buildings survivors of the disastrous San Francisco earthquake and the fire huddled together in parks and squares, confronted with the possibility of starvation, thirst, and death. It was April 19, 1907, after two days of a holocaust that had charred four square miles of the city, demolished 28,000 buildings, and left 200,000 homeless. At various encampments the exhausted refugees, separated from friends and families and dragging along their few belongings, made inquiries about lost persons and the progress in fighting the fire. Staffs of the three San Francisco morning newspapers moved to Oakland and on borrowed presses put out a combined *Call-Chronicle-Examiner,* which they distributed free. Their cars were almost mobbed. In the end the distributors had to drive along at full speed, throwing out the sheets as they went along, or they could make no progress at all. No bread wagon, no supply of blankets aroused as much interest as the arrival of news (Irwin, 1911).

In disasters one of the first things that men seek, after saving themselves, is news. Sometimes they become so desperate for such information that they get careless about its source. If sufficient news is not available, it may develop spontaneously. In an attempt to ascertain the conditions under which rumor construction takes place, then, a fruitful point of departure is the study of news.

Rumors of Environmental Changes

One type of situation in which rumors invariably flourish is a disaster. In flash floods, earthquakes, great fires, sudden epidemics, volcanic eruptions, tidal waves, tornadoes, severe bombings, or invasions by enemy soldiers the impact is sudden and drastic. Those who are caught must adjust quickly if they are to survive. Cases 11 through 20 are on disasters. The manner in which rumors emerge in such contexts can best be seen by examining a concrete case.

Case 19. THE BOMBING OF HIROSHIMA. By the beginning of August 1945, almost every major city in Japan had been leveled by massive B-29 bombing raids. As the number of untouched cities dwindled, Hiroshima seemed more and more a likely target, and the people were sick with anxiety. They had heard accounts of the raids on Kure, Iwakuni, and Tokuyama—all near by. Air-raid warnings were sounded almost nightly, for the B-29's were using nearby Lake Biwa as a rendezvous point. The frequency of warnings and continued avoidance of the city by enemy planes made the populace jittery. Some even speculated that the Americans were saving something special for Hiroshima.

On the morning of August 6 an air-raid alarm was sounded at 7 A.M., but this indicated only a slight degree of danger. It went off at the same time every morning when an American weather plane passed over the city. At 8 o'clock the "all clear" was sounded, and the daily routine got under way. There was no sound of planes; the morning was still, cool, and pleasant. Then, suddenly a tremendous flash of light cut across the sky. Few could recall hearing any noise, but each thought a bomb had landed directly on him. It was 8:15, and the world's first atomic bomb had been detonated.

Buildings were ripped to pieces. People were thrown about violently. Cries of agony arose from those trapped under collapsed buildings. Then, under what seemed to be a cloud of dust, the day grew progressively darker. Survivors struggled to get to the "safe" areas, and on their way they noted the extent of the devastation; houses were burning everywhere. Soon huge drops of water the size of marbles began to fall. Through the darkness they could see more collapsed houses; so many were dead, and the cries of those still trapped had to be ignored.

As the survivors gathered at the "safe" areas like Asano Park, speculations arose as to how the disaster had occurred. There had been no planes, and yet it was obvious that large segments of the city had been destroyed. One common theory was that the destruction had been wrought by a "Molotov flower basket," a self-scattering cluster of bombs. Another widespread rumor was that a single plane had sprayed the city with gasoline and then had set it afire in one flashing moment. All day more people poured into the park. All felt thirsty and drank from the river nearby, but they at once became nauseated and vomited. Those with no apparent wounds were suddenly dropping dead. Because of the strong odor of ionization many thought that they were sick from the gasoline the Americans were believed to have dropped. When it began to rain again and the raindrops grew abnormally large, someone shouted that the Americans were dropping more gasoline in order to burn those huddled in the park. By nightfall more rumors emerged—one that American paratroopers had landed in the area.

In the next few days the full extent of the damage became apparent. Although the Japanese radio announced that a new type of bomb had been used, the victims in Hiroshima did not hear the initial broadcasts. They continued to discuss the attack in terms of gasoline, a huge cluster of incendiaries, or parachutists. Another rumor was that the weapon was not a bomb at all; it was a kind of fine magnesium powder sprayed over the whole city by a single plane. This exploded upon coming into contact with live wires of the city's power system. One doctor, who was satisfied with this explanation, speculated that the new weapon would be effective only on big cities and only in the daytime when the tram lines were in operation.

About a week after the bomb was dropped a vague, incomprehensible report reached Hiroshima—that the city had been destroyed by the energy released when the smallest known particles were somehow split in two. The new weapon was called a *genshibakudan*, an "original child bomb." No one understood the idea; it was another interesting "rumor."

Whenever life becomes subject to the vicissitude of events over which individuals have little control, the events compel attention; unrelated matters are temporarily thrust aside. The victims become preoccupied with efforts to cope with the calamity. Should they run or remain where they are? What escape routes are available? What else needs to be done? Something must be done quickly, but intelligent decisions cannot be made without some understanding of what happened. Although information is needed badly for adjusting to the rapidly changing situation, institutional channels are frequently destroyed or impaired. The queries are answered by rumors. Sometimes survivors act on the basis of rumors, not because they believe them but because they cannot afford to ignore them.

Communication among disaster victims is facilitated by the disappearance of conventional social barriers. In grave danger men apparently gain comfort from not being alone. Describing the impact of the outbreak of World War I on England, Trotter (1917, pp. 140–42) notes that along with an immense, vague, aching fear was a heightening intolerance of isolation. Loneliness became unbearable, and each had an intense desire for the company of his fellows, a need strong enough to break down distinctions of class and to dissipate reserve toward strangers. Thus, people who undergo together a derangement of their way of life are drawn together; a spirit of camaraderie develops among the survivors, maximizing their sensitivity to one another. This creates ideal conditions for the emergence of rumors. Information, whatever there is of it, is quickly shared among equals.

Contrary to popular belief, men caught in disasters as a rule neither flee in wild panic nor become totally immobilized; careful studies reveal that the most common reaction is one of resourceful self-help and mutual assistance. After reviewing records of many disasters Quarantelli (1960) concludes that although pell-mell scrambles for safety by hysterical individuals sometimes occur, this is rare. Disaster victims frequently act on their own, sometimes contrary to recommendations of officials. Members of a family along with friends and neighbors who happen along form small groups. Generally they work out their own withdrawal arrangements from specific points of danger and cope with other problems that arise on their own initiative; they turn for help to relief agencies only as a last resort. Such groups also assist one another, and the sharing of information is part of this process of mutual aid. Reviewing the findings of the N.O.R.C. disaster studies, Fritz and Marks (1954) contend that the major problem in most disasters is not uncontrolled panic but lack of co-ordination among various groups and individuals, each acting on a somewhat different definition of the situation.

Environmental changes need not be so drastic. Any unusual event —anything uncommon, irregular, or unfamiliar—breaks the routine of life and often leads to the formation of rumors. The appearance of a stranger, the revelation of a miracle, the discovery of some precious object, a minor explosion, the unscheduled wailing of a siren, the failure of a policeman to arrest a lawbreaker—all such incidents arouse curiosity and start animated discussions. Cases 1 through 10 deal with such contexts, and the manner in which they are defined is revealed in the following account:

Case 8. DISCOVERY OF A CORPSE. Shortly before 9:45 one morning a woman went to her car in the parking lot of a venetian blind factory in a Los Angeles suburb. Wedged between the seats was the body of a man. She screamed and collapsed, and employees of the factory helped her back to her hotel next door.

As residents of the area began to gather and to mill about, a rumor developed: the car belonged to the owner of the factory, and the body was discovered by his wife. This was soon corrected by the factory employees.

Attracted by the excitement, passers-by and others living or working in the vicinity converged on the scene. Ownership of the car was soon established; it belonged to the woman's husband. To other hotel residents the man disclosed that he had worked late the night before and had left his car unlocked in a theater parking lot until about 2:00 A.M. He admitted the body might have been in the car when he drove home, for he had not looked at the rear seat. He denied knowing the victim.

As the crowd grew, the curious went from one circle to another gathering and exchanging details. The more courageous took turns rushing up to the car for a quick glance inside and then returning to describe the horrible sight. By this time most of those present believed the woman's husband to be the murderer; he had killed the man and hidden his body in the car. Some hotel residents recalled that there was "something queer" about him. When someone timidly suggested the possibilty of suicide, he was scornfully overruled: the body had been jammed into the back seat by someone else. Some thought the killing resulted from a drunken brawl, but others insisted it was premeditated murder. Some said the murderer had planned to appear surprised when the body was discovered; others believed that he had intended to get rid of it but had been trapped before he could do so. Questions arose concerning the woman's complicity, but the factory employees first on the scene insisted that her shock was too genuine. A few suggested that she might have collapsed not from seeing the body but from the realization that she was married to a killer.

When the police arrived, in several cars with screaming sirens, excitement reached its peak. As officers questioned the car owner, all the details were repeated for the benefit of newcomers. As the body was being removed, one man helping the police exclaimed scornfully and loudly, "Oh, hell! This is no murder. The guy's a lush!" His judgment was rejected. When the police departed, the crowd dwindled; only a few lingered on, hoping for more excitement.

Police subsequently disclosed that the car owner, the victim, and one or two others had gone on a drinking spree the night before. The victim, in a drunken stupor, had been placed in the back seat and forgotten. When an autopsy revealed that he had died of acute alcoholism, the case was closed.

By and large there is little personal involvement in such incidents; in most instances those who engage in rumor construction are more spectators than active participants. Although intensity of excitement varies considerably, in general there is no felt need to take emergency action. Such disturbances attract attention and arouse curiosity. Even if nothing can be done for the moment, an attempt is made to comprehend what has happened; understanding is a way of being prepared. Each individual builds his conduct from moment to moment on a pattern of normal expectations, and any departure requires some reorientation, however slight this may be. Conversations center on the unusual event. Some speculation occurs, but usually each item is considered judiciously. Since there is time to explore, various reports and opinions are sifted and compared. Those who contribute to the formation of rumors in such contexts usually retain their conventional social relationships and discuss new events within a familiar setting.

As long as a change in environment remains unaccounted for, Prasad (1935, p. 7) points out, it leaves a distracting sense of incompleteness, and attempts are made to understand the new situation by completing the incomplete. Nor can people wait until a thorough investigation has been made; the tension must be relieved quickly. Clarification requires a temporal location of the event; the present takes on meaning only when it is seen as a step between the past and the future. Events must also be explained in the light of known facts; Hudson (1954) shows how men react to ambiguity by projecting hypotheses, explaining the strange in terms of the familiar. One must know something of the implications of an event. Thus, rumors emerge after environmental changes to describe related events that are not immediately visible, to provide details, to explain anything that is not obvious, and to predict other occurrences. Although the temporal reference of rumors may be to the future or to the past, the subject matter always has present significance. Events of the past and future are of concern because of some decision that has to be made at once.

Crisis Situations and the News

Any crisis, however mild, arouses popular excitement and leads to the formation of a *public*, consisting of those who are in some way concerned with an event that has disturbed the routine of organized life. Although the term "public" is often used to refer to anything that is open and available to everyone, as opposed to the realm of the private, it will be used here in a more specialized sense of a "following." Events are thought to have consequences, and recognition of the possibility of being affected by them generates a common interest. Sometimes the anticipated consequences are sufficiently important to necessitate planning in order to guarantee results that are desired and to avoid those that are obnoxious. A public, as Dewey (1927) puts it, consists of *people who regard themselves as likely to become involved in the consequences of an event and are sufficiently concerned to interest themselves in the possibility of control.* It can be identified only in terms of its common focus of attention; the annual list of debutantes is of interest primarily to the social elite, just as the fate of the New York Yankees concerns only baseball fans. Publics vary considerably in size and in the spatial distribution of their participants. Each crisis generates its own public.

A public is not an organized group, except in those instances when a crisis happens to be confined to an already established unit. It does not have a fixed and easily identifiable membership, nor is there a formal organization of conventionally defined roles. As a situation changes and the same event comes to be viewed in a different light, the composition of its public changes. New people are attracted; others become bored and turn their attention elsewhere; or factions may be realigned. Even in areas with a continuity of interest—as in women's fashions, labor problems, or national politics—the composition of most publics is continuously undergoing change, and in a dynamic situation it is almost impossible to ascertain with precision the boundaries of any given public. Furthermore, a public is not to be confused with a community, for publics do not necessarily consist of the inhabitants of a particular territorial unit. Although the existence of a public implies a common universe of discourse, their boundaries are not necessarily coterminous; those who share a common perspective often develop somewhat different interests. Publics, then, as Dékany (1936) points out, are transitory groupings that can be identified only in terms of the temporary sharing of a common object of attention, and their size and composition vary with each event. This does not mean, however, that a public is merely an amorphous aggregate of individuals; each public that persists tends to develop some kind of structure, though usually at a low level of formalization. This inner structure, furthermore, is modified as the situation changes.

The reactions of those who make up a public are by no means uniform, for the participants differ in their involvement. Some become excited while others remain sober; some become highly suggestible while others remain critical. Those who are more strongly concerned with the event may attempt to organize in order to pursue their interests more effectively. If disagreements arise on what ought to be done, each faction may organize into an interest group. Often already existing organizations—labor unions, patriotic societies, political parties—may be utilized, but special voluntary associations may be formed to meet particular crises. Other persons, who are sufficiently concerned to follow developments but not sufficiently committed for direct participation, form a larger spectator-like body which serves as an arbiter in the struggle between interest groups. The passive segment of the public, as Lippmann (1925) shows, serves as the sanctioning body for whatever is done. Conspicuous activity is generally carried on by those with special interests, but the remainder of the public constitutes an audience whose reactions must be taken into account. Since its approval or acquiescence is required, the audience has an important influence over the course of events; it sets the conditions within which the activists perform. Action taken by publics varies considerably; as Clark (1933) points out, it is generally characterized by spontaneity and lack of formal action pattern. In many cases the people merely form opinions as they discuss the situation; should consensus emerge from these deliberations, however, some form of concerted action may develop.

Men whose plans have been altered by some unexpected event, who are dissatisfied or angry over what has happened, or who anticipate further changes become acutely sensitized to any information that will help them understand the changed circumstances. Being unable to act effectively, they experience discomfort and become responsive to anything of possible use in overcoming their frustration. They become preoccupied with those points over which there is uncertainty: the crest of the flood, the latest plans of their adversaries, market conditions elsewhere, the progress of relief trains. A public, then, becomes highly responsive to *news*, which is not mere information but information that is *important* to someone. As Park (1940) puts it, news gets its distinctive character from being a phase of interrupted activity; demand for news arises in situations in which action has been suspended temporarily for want of an adequate definition. Thus, news is about unusual events, extraordinary happenings that have broken the normal routine of life. It is not so much the intrinsic importance of an event but the existence of a problematic situation that converts what is otherwise ordinary information into news. Where the situation is ambiguous, where there are alternatives, where a decision has to be made, any item that might affect the outcome becomes "live matter." News is a phase of on-going action in that it enters at a crucial moment when something is still in process, when it is still unfinished and to be acted upon by a revision of opinions or a redirection of activity. News is that more or less urgent information that men need in making adjustments to changed circumstances; it is sought, even at great sacrifice, because of the necessity of getting one's bearings in a rapidly changing world.

Demand for news varies with the importance placed upon events. "Big news" affects a large public and is about matters that require immediate attention; it comes with an urgency that requires some kind of instant adjustment, even if it consists of nothing more than a change of attitude. There are, of course, different degrees of urgency. In acute emergencies a public becomes completely preoccupied with the shattering event. There arises among those who are involved a diffuse excitement that tends to envelop them like an atmosphere, giving direction to their interests. As collective excitement is heightened, the range of response is further limited, and at the same time the intensity of the impulses not thus inhibited is increased; exclusive attention to some things inhibits responses to others and limits the information to which individuals react. When people are similarly aroused—in hope of victory, fear of defeat, or hostility against a foe—rapid and efficient communication is facilitated by their mutual responsiveness.

On the other hand, there are crises in which the felt necessity of taking action is less urgent. Even when little can be done at the moment, however, one gains some comfort from knowing what has happened and from being able to make preparations for what appear to be reasonable eventualities. Other news items may not be taken seriously, but these contribute nonetheless to the formation or reinforcement of various beliefs. Thus, news of all kinds, from significant to trivial, constitutes the basis for maintaining a working orientation toward a changing environment.

Since news has immediate relevance to action that is already under way, it is perishable. This suggests that news is not merely something new; it is information that is timely. Even if it is about events long past, the information is necessary for current adjustment; it relieves tension in the immediate situation. For this reason news has an ephemeral career. Once a situation is understood, blockage is relieved, tension is reduced, and the accepted information is transformed into history—interesting but no longer pressing. Historical accounts may be as fascinating as news, but the events recorded have in general ceased to be important because nothing can be done about them. When nothing more can be done about events recorded in a newspaper, these items also cease to be news. This transient quality is the very essence of news, for an event ceases to be newsworthy as soon as the tension it has aroused has been dissipated. Once a decision has been reached, the quickening sense of urgency and importance disappears, and public attention turns elsewhere. As Park puts it, the significance of news is pragmatic rather than appreciative.

News is news only for those who make up an interested public, and much of what is reported in the media of mass communication as "news" is largely ignored by various segments of their audience. For example, when a girl in a small Midwestern town was selected in nationwide competition to appear on the radio with the New York Philharmonic, Bogart (1950) found that the matter was of interest locally primarily to the well-to-do and those with more sophisticated tastes. A study made three weeks after the announcement revealed that while 77 per cent of the college-educated knew of the event, only 27 per cent of those who failed to finish high school had heard of it.

The manner in which news is confined to a public is further illustrated in what is ordinarily called "gossip." Gossip is restricted to small local groups in which members are bound by personal contacts and concerns the private and intimate details of the traits and conduct of specific individuals. Apparently the most interesting local news deals with violations of moral codes; this information helps define status relations, a matter of considerable importance among those in constant association. Gossip seems trivial to outsiders, but within its public it plays an important part in ordering interpersonal relations and thus is an important means of social control (Blumenthal, 1937). If for any reason the details of someone's private life have consequences for those beyond the local group, such information concerns a larger public. A false step by an official may affect many who do not know him personally. Gossip about those in positions of power is always of general interest. Bysow (1928, pp. 425–26) points out that talk of the attentions of King Ludwig of Bavaria to his mistress reinforced charges of neglect of duty and added to revolutionary discontent in 1848, and gossip about the influence of Rasputin on the royal family did not help the Czar's cause in 1917. The conduct of professional entertainers is of such importance to their fans that gossip about them is published regularly in syndicated columns. Thus, an event that may appear trivial to the unsympathetic may under some circumstances attract a huge public dispersed throughout the world.

News is assumed to be accurate if it is attributed to institutional channels. In modern mass societies complex procedures have been established for the gathering, processing, and dissemination of news, and the world is encompassed by an intricate system of communication that provides news almost instantly. In most communities the media of mass communication have become established as the institutional source, and what is reported in newspapers or over radio and television is generally accepted as true, unless there are special reasons for doubt. Even if a news article is unsigned, there is a publisher or editor who is legally liable; therefore efforts are made to verify suspicious items. News disseminated through established channels is readily available for all to see, and anyone who wishes to check a report can trace it to an identifiable source. Furthermore, blatant error is easily exposed. In times of crisis people turn first to these channels, and they serve as the standard against which all other reports are checked. In every major crisis newspaper offices and radio and television stations are swamped with telephone calls. Within three hours after the death of President Roosevelt was announced, for example, the *New York Times* received 4,968 telephone calls asking for verification (D.C. Miller, 1945).

In mass societies many decisions are based on an understanding of distant events; men are more dependent on news agencies, and for most purposes these sources have proved reasonably adequate. Possibilities for deception are considerable, but the professional ideology of newsmen helps to maintain standards of reliability. The announced ideal in journalism is the clear, impartial, and accurate description of significant events. Rosten (1937, pp. 219–36) points out that staff members on the whole tend to be more "liberal" than the publishers who set newspaper policy. Publishers undoubtedly influence content, but they do not dictate it. After interviewing 120 American newsmen Breed (1955) reports that no explicit instructions are given to present news in any given way; staff men "learn the ropes" about an organization by reading the paper, by observing how their own contributions are edited, by reprimands they receive for flagrant violations of policy, from staff conferences, and from gossip about the views of the editor and the publisher. In most cases staff members comply, but they are not powerless. A reporter can "kill" a story; he can also place emphasis where he wishes by deciding whom to interview, what questions to ask, and which quotations to use; he may even "plant" a story in a rival newspaper and then submit his own version after the item has become too "big" to ignore. Journalists in the United States and England take great pride in their standards of fairness and accuracy; in spite of the appearance of cynicism, they evaluate one another's work in terms of these professed ideals. In his study of TASS, Kruglak (1962) notes that although the staff members are employees of the Soviet government who sometimes travel on diplomatic passports and may even engage in espionage, most of them are serious journalists who turn out reports usable in any country. News agencies throughout the world have standardized procedures that tend to maximize reliability.

Although some students of rumor write as if published news is always accurate, this is obviously not true. Some reports on institutional channels are outright fabrications, although this is not common. Even when every effort is being made to present an accurate account, objectivity is impossible. As the famous editor Frederick L. Allen (1922) points out, selection is inevitable. Too much material is made available by the wire services, and each editor must choose which items to include. There is often no time to verify suspicious items, and the temptation to present a "good story" is difficult to resist. During the autumn of 1945, for example, when all newspapers in Paris were limited to two pages because of an acute shortage of newsprint, editors had a wide margin for selection; anything could be omitted for want of space. Zerner (1946) classified thirty newspapers in terms of political orientation and checked their coverage of the reported illness of Premier Stalin. As expected, newspapers of the extreme left ignored the alarming news, and those on the right gave it highest preference. Because of time limitations selection is even more drastic in radio and television newscasts.

"Slanting" is a rather common procedure. This is not fabrication; an effort is made to create the desired impression through the omission of inconvenient items, the selection of details, and preferential placement—"featuring" some items and "burying" others. During the 1952 presidential compaign, for example, when Republicans were hitting at corruption in high government places, a startling revelation was made of a "private fund" operating for the benefit of Senator Nixon, the vice presidential candidate. Five days later some irregularities were disclosed in the use of campaign contributions for Adlai Stevenson. Rowse (1957) examined the handling of these two items in 31 of the largest newspapers in the United States, 28 of which favored Republicans and three Democrats. Of the 13 evening papers that received the first wire service reports of the Nixon fund only four printed the story on the front page; three of these were pro-Stevenson papers. Three others carried the story but "buried" it. Even when the item became too important to ignore, two were not able to find space on the front page for it until the fourth day. In contrast, all of the newspapers carried the Stevenson story on the front page from the very beginning.

Schramm (1959) compared 14 "prestige" newspapers the world over for November 2, 1956—the day on which Soviet troops and tanks crushed the Hungarian uprising and British, French, and Israeli forces attacked Egypt. The war in Egypt received far greater coverage; only the *Dagens Nyheter* of Stockholm gave more attention to Hungary. *Pravda* hardly mentioned the revolt, noting only that "bandit raids" had been conducted by "persons released from jail." Four other Communist newspapers were not unsympathetic to the Hungarians, but their coverage of the uprising was also meager.

Precisely because of the faith placed in institutional channels, if professional newsmen themselves become involved in rumor construction, they extend considerably the range of participation. In tense situations, as in the first hours after the assassination of President Kennedy, reporters and editors may become suggestible and provide institutional sanction for unverified news. Doubts often disappear when something appears in print or is announced over the radio. Although it was not actually a newscast, the Orson Welles broadcast on October 30, 1938, of the invasion from Mars illustrates what could happen. An estimated million persons all over the United States prayed, ran to rescue loved ones, telephoned farewells or warning, summoned ambulances and police, or fled to escape the Martians (Cantril, 1940). Such errors are sometimes costly, resulting not only in condemnation but also in law suits and even in retaliatory mob action; therefore, care is continually exercised to verify rumors. Not to publish information from private sources without substantiation or public notice of the source is one of the standards of the American Society of Newspaper Editors. But the task of journalists is not easy. As W. E. Hall (1936, pp. 165–66) and Mott (1952, pp. 67–88) point out, reporters constantly encounter rumors, for they must be alert for "tips" and "leaks." When the temptation to file a "good story" becomes too great, unsubstantiated information may be used. Such items are carefully labeled: "according to usually reliable sources," "unconfirmed reports that . . .," or "it is rumored that. . . ." That most readers pay little heed to such labels is well known, but they are scrupulously included to guard against law suits and to protect the reputation of the channel in the eyes of other journalists.

All communication channels, both formal and informal, are subject to repeated pragmatic tests, and their reputation for reliability depends upon adequate performance. Occasional lapses, especially on matters that concern only small publics, are overlooked if the source has proved generally reliable in the past. The frequent presentation of false information, however, discredits the channel. False intelligence leads to embarrassment and sometimes to disaster, and sources that prove unreliable are labeled and eventually rejected. In totalitarian states blatant use of the mass media for government propaganda leads to amused skepticism on the part of those in sympathy with the regime and outrage on the part of others. Communication channels of all sorts are constantly evaluated, and there is no substitute for reliable performance.

In the long run, then, all news agencies have a vested interest in providing reasonably accurate news. In capitalistic economies the mass media are generally commercial enterprises, where the primary objective is profit. Profits depend upon mass patronage, which in turn rests upon providing something that clients are willing to purchase. News may be "slanted" somewhat and special appeals may be made, but unless *most* of the news required by continually forming publics is provided with reasonable accuracy, the people will turn elsewhere. Even where news services are a government monopoly channels are still evaluated in terms of their utility. In a study of the Soviet Union, for example, Bauer and Gleicher (1953) show that many Russians in full sympathy with the regime rely on auxiliary channels for information on policy failure, adverse conditions elsewhere in Russia, opposition to the regime, and unsavory habits of prominent figures. Human beings are not gullible. Once a source is defined as unreliable for certain kinds of news, it is not trusted.

Rumors in Sustained Collective Tension

Rumors also flourish in situations characterized by social unrest. Those who undergo strain over a long period of time—victims of sustained bombings, survivors of a long epidemic, a conquered populace coping with an army of occupation, civilians grown weary of a long war, prisoners in a concentration camp, residents of neighborhoods marked by interethnic tension—become restless and dissatisfied. Combat troops, who face violence and abrupt changes that are often incomprehensible, develop intense insecurity. Discontent also arises among underprivileged persons who feel that they are being deprived of something that is legitimately theirs. After a succession of gradual changes in life conditions members of ethnic minorities or dispossessed classes develop self-conceptions that are incompatible with the estimates previously placed upon them. They then become increasingly dissatisfied with their lot, even when it is materially improved; they complain bitterly and demand immediate changes.

Blumer (1951, pp. 171–73) contends that whenever individuals experience impulses that cannot be satisfied within the existing social framework, they become restless. They feel balked, insecure, alienated, and often lonely. When those who are similarly frustrated come together, they exchange views and thereby reinforce and intensify one another's discomfort. When men are collectively dissatisfied, the customary is called into question, and those involved become acutely sensitized to possibilities of change. Restless individuals often wander about aimlessly, as if trying to find or avoid something without knowing just what it is. They become responsive to anything that might identify the source of their discontent or any object or program that is likely to bring relief. Restless people are mobilized to act, but in the absence of clear-cut goals, they have nothing in particular to do. As Shakespeare noted—in *Henry IV* and in *Macbeth*—under such circumstances rumors emerge at the slightest provocation.

Case 38. FAMINE IN TIKOPIA. Because the inhabitants are so polite and good-natured, Tikopia, in the British Solomon Islands Protectorate, is regarded by many as a Polynesian paradise. In 1952, however, it was struck by a hurricane, a famine, and an acute political crisis.

Although the island was governed by indirect rule, the traditional authority of the chiefs had been curtailed. Theft was ordinarily settled by the families involved; the only other sanction was derision. More serious offenders at one time had been sent out to sea, and legends recounted the wholesale banishment of commoners in time of crisis. Another custom was the *forau*, suicide by sailing into the sea without food, done in anticipation of banishment. The government and the Christian mission were known to oppose both banishment and the *forau*, and in recent times these measures had not been invoked. Furthermore, the priest had persuaded the people to abandon traditional population controls—abortion, infanticide, and limitation of marriage; as a result the population had increased from 1,300 in 1929 to 1,700 in 1952.

In January 1952, a hurricane destroyed the entire cocoanut and breadfruit crop and flooded parts of the island. A tidal wave inundated Faea, one of the two major divisions of the island. Seven weeks later two anthropologists arrived with the District Commissioner. Since complaining was impolite, no overt concern over the food shortage was shown. The anthropologists had brought a radio, and arrangements were made for them to keep in touch with the officials; in effect, they became representatives of the government.

As the food shortage became more acute, maintaining order became more difficult. In May, three investigating officials brought 500 cocoanuts and four tons of root crops; before the shipment reached shore, however, women and children pilfered the long boats. Equitable distribution of what remained was impossible, and considerable resentment developed. A month later the government sent 10 tons of rice and 1,000 cocoanuts. The *maru*, executive officers of the chiefs, were placed in charge of distribution; after the chiefs and the anthropologists had received their shares, the people could no longer be restrained, and a minor riot ensued. Officials who brought the food also asked whether there was any basis for a rumor among Tikopians working in plantations abroad that the chiefs were preparing a mass banishment of commoners.

As the food situation deteriorated further and the death rate rose, theft became a major problem. Almost nightly one could hear cries of "thief," and patrols were organized to guard the fields. Traditional sanctions against stealing were no longer strong enough to restrain the starving. A *fono*, a public forum ordinarily convened about once a year, was held almost weekly to discuss the difficulty. Leaders exhorted the people to stop stealing and to work harder in their fields; it was agreed that man and wife may fornicate only once a week; when a *maru* suggested that those without food should sit in their houses and die, others proposed that thieves should be sent out to sea. Formal hospitality, which involved the offering of food, was abandoned.

Late in August the High Commissioner ordered a large shipment of food. Locally it was agreed that one of the anthropologists should distribute it. To make arrangements he called a meeting in

Ravenja of all the chiefs and their aides. Residents of Ravenja knew what was happening, but in Faea a rumor developed that the anthropologists, the chiefs, and the *maru* had decided to send the commoners out to sea. When the representatives from Faea returned, they found excitement at fever pitch. Men had bound their heads with string, indicating readiness for violent action, and brandished clubs and spears. Everywhere women could be heard wailing. The anthropologist was quickly summoned. Shouting denials as he went along, he cursed and challenged the spirit medium to whom the rumor was attributed. It was some time before the turbulence subsided.

Seventeen tons of rice were distributed in October, but the famine persisted. Thefts continued, and people died at the rate of about three a week. Five suicide voyages were attempted, but all failed. More stringent measures against stealing were instituted, and plans were made for mass emigration. Before government permission could be obtained for the move, however, the newly planted crops began to grow, and the crisis subsided.

Since men under sustained collective tension are already aroused, attention is easily focused upon any object that is likely to provide direction. A public has already started to form, and a rumor quickly sharpens its boundaries. Unlike the unusual event that breaks an established routine, the incident that attracts attention in this type of situation strikes a spark that sets off already mobilized responses. No statistics are available on the incidence of rumors in various types of contexts, but this is certainly a frequent circumstance. Cases 21 through 40 are of such situations.

Collective tension may also be anticipatory. In a perceptive essay Morley (1919, pp. 174–80) notes that men are frequently able to "sense" momentous events in the making, basing their judgments upon stray, intangible clues dropped by those directly connected with the coming event. When a military coup is being planned, for example, preliminary happenings provide grounds for surmises and conjectures. Although one may not be able to put his finger on anything in particular, a correct impression may arise from such things as an unusual complacency or excitement manifested by a highly placed person who is "in the know." Those familiar with the arena are able to interpret these preliminaries, and many rumors turn out to be fairly accurate forecasts of coming events.

Expectant attention may be focused upon some scheduled event; the appearance of new automobile models in Detroit, a festival, or an election. Presidential elections in the United States have frequently been preceded by rumors; those formed during the campaign of Andrew Jackson were particularly vicious (Remini, 1963). Anticipatory unrest may also center upon events that are not definitely scheduled but can reasonably be expected to occur. Those suffering from severe illness, for example, know that it must sooner or later be terminated by recovery or death; anxiety-provoking rumors may develop on wards in which such patients are congregated (Case 42). When a war is about to end, many rumors arise. According to the U.S. Strategic Bombing Survey (1947, p. 52), in the early spring of 1945, after the German Army had suffered a succession of defeats and much of the country lay in ruins, many rumors emerged among German civilians of the collapse of military operations and of peace negotiations, usually with von Papen as the envoy. People who are waiting for something to happen become restless and especially attentive to anything thought to be connected with the anticipated event. As the deadline approaches, excitement is intensified and the public becomes increasingly preoccupied with the event. Especially in situations in which decisions must be made, demand for news becomes desperate, and men grasp at any information that will help them make up their minds. Cases 41 through 45 deal with such contexts.

Case 44. THE REPUBLICAN CONVENTION. As Republicans gathered in Philadelphia for their convention in the summer of 1948, they were confident of victory in November. Considerable uncertainty existed, however, as to who would be their standard-bearer: Stassen, Taft, Dewey, and Vandenberg were all strong contenders. No one would have a majority on the first ballot, in which most delegates were pledged, and a struggle began at once for votes in the second and succeeding ballots. It went on in hotel rooms, lobbies, and on the convention floor. Delegates and leaders of delegations had to act quickly. Supporting a winner would bring political rewards; on the other hand, backing the wrong man for too long could result in their becoming political outcasts.

Supporters of Governor Dewey were very active. On opening day rumors developed of rebellions in opposite camps; there were stories of desertions and claims of growing Dewey strength. Journalists helped the rumors along. Lobbies and bars were suddenly filled with startling, though unverified reports. Governor Green was going to deliver a portion of the 56 Illinois votes to Dewey in return for the vice presidency. Governor Driscoll, originally for Vandenberg, was going to deliver himself and at least part of the New Jersey delegation to Dewey for the same prize. Congressman Halleck was going to deliver Indiana for the same reason. Delegates were assailed with doubts about their candidates, and many became increasingly concerned about their own political fortunes. Were they missing the bandwagon? Would they go unrewarded when patronage was distributed after victory?

On the following day Dewey opponents were jolted when Senator Martin of Pennsylvania announced that he had withdrawn as a "favorite son" candidate and would not only vote for Dewey on the first ballot but would make the nominating speech for him as well. Martin's support for Dewey was well known, but it had been assumed that he had agreed with his Pennsylvania rival, Governor Duff, an opponent of Dewey, to hold the state's delegates until some strategic moment and then to make their bargain. When Dewey aides announced a press conference for later in the day, rumors formed that not only Martin but Driscoll would be there. Some seasoned delegates felt that the game was all over.

Next day four more blows fell. Halleck of Indiana, Driscoll of New Jersey, Ken of Missouri, and Bradford of Massachusetts all announced their support for Dewey. Stassen, Taft, and other opposition candidates met with their aides; they accused Dewey supporters of spreading stories so rapidly that by the time one was checked another had emerged. They charged that the delegates were being stampeded.

Just before the first ballot a rumor developed that the Michigan delegation was about to desert Vandenberg. The story appeared in the *Philadelphia Evening Bulletin* under an eight-column headline and confronted delegates hurrying into Convention Hall. Just before the voting began, Governor Sigler got up and angrily denied the report; he insisted that Michigan was still behind Vandenberg.

On the first ballot Dewey drew 434 votes; and on the second, 515, only 33 short of the nomination. The opposing candidates still would not give in and asked for a recess. While the official count was being tallied, tension mounted on the floor. Restless delegates from opposition states saw the Dewey bandwagon rolling past their door. Should they switch to him now? Hurried, private conferences were held on the floor. The opposition collapsed.

Communities split by internal dissension provide another common context for rumor formation. Intramural conflict frequently evokes more acute tension than wars against external foes. In war the entire community is mobilized for concerted action, and the wholehearted contributions of each participant enjoy collective support. When struggles break out within a community, however—in strikes, inter-ethnic tension, revolutionary uprisings, or military mutinies—men who are interdependent and often bound by ties of friendship are forced to take sides against one another. In war hostile acts are expected; in internal strife they are highly resented as unethical. As tension mounts minor incidents break out, compounding the difficulties of leaders urging moderation. Each side prepares for defense and becomes increasingly sensitized to negative traits of its adversary. As cases 46 through 60 show, rumors flourish in such situations.

Case 58. THE "MAU MAU" EMERGENCY. Soon after World War II Nairobi became the center of widespread discontent. African war veterans, back from overseas duty, found tribal life too dull but no market for their skills in the city. In September 1946, Jomo Kenyatta returned after fifteen years of study and agitation in England, and soon political activities took on sharper focus. Although the Kikuyu had many grievances, their demands centered on the question of land. When European settlers first arrived in Kenya, they had purchased land from whomever they found on it. They had worked long and hard to build up their holdings; under European law the land was theirs, and they were not going to be dispossessed. Under Kikuyu law, however, land could not be sold without approval of the extended family to which it belonged; hence, it had been expropriated. Most settlers concluded that on this question the

Kikuyu were incapable of logical reasoning and that negotiation was impossible.

By 1947, settlers and officials working closely with the natives sensed that something unusual was happening, but they were unable to find out just what it was. Only a few had learned the Kikuyu language; hence, even though political agitation was being carried out openly, they were unable to understand the speeches or to read the mimeographed pamphlets. Rumors arose that a secret society known as the "Mau Mau" had been formed and that many Africans were saying that all the wrongs they had suffered would soon be rectified by the slaughter of all white men. Members of the Mau Mau were said to have taken an oath not to reveal anything about the organization; because the Kikuyu believed in the killing power of a broken oath even the friendly could not disclose its secrets. Another rumor was that many were being forced to take the oath against their will, some by threats that only members would benefit in the coming redistribution of land and others by threats of violence against themselves and their family. Rumors also tied Kenyatta to the organization; it was charged that he was supervising the oath ceremonies. These reports could not be confirmed; Africans either did not know or were not talking. A general view developed among the settlers that while most of the Kikuyu were happy, agitators and rabble-rousers were fanning the flames of discontent, and some vicious thugs were forcing the innocent and ignorant into their fold.

Kikuyu political leaders realized that their strength lay in unity of numbers, and the movement of the oath was devised to consolidate this weapon. The first oath was one of unity in the Kikuyu's struggle for land and independence. Members of the brotherhood who proved reliable were then administered the second, a fighting oath. This was a blood oath that included the promise to kill, if necessary, even members of one's own family in the struggle for freedom. In this way an effort was made to develop a sense of solidarity among those who had to face overwhelming enemy strength. The organization initially had no name. It was labeled "Mau Mau"—a meaningless expression sometimes used in children's games—by some Kikuyu who opposed it, and this title of abuse and ridicule stuck. Since one of the oaths required swearing allegiance to "the unity that is mocked with the name of 'Mau Mau'," the members, in effect, adopted the name under protest.

Many Kikuyu opposed the revolutionary movement. The chiefs, who enjoyed their position through the colonial policy of indirect rule, and others who were well established were against it; and in January 1952 a campaign of terror began against these "white stooges." Harassment was initially by arson, but in September, 14 Africans suspected of giving information to the police were killed and mutilated. On October 21 a state of emergency was declared; 83 political leaders, including Kenyatta, were arrested; and various military units were moved into Kenya. A week later the first European settler was cut down by night raiders. Although the killing of Europeans attracted world-wide attention, rebel activity was directed primarily against Kikuyu who remained loyal to the government. Throughout the emergency only 32 European civilians were killed by the Mau Mau, compared to 1,826 Africans. Since unity was their most powerful weapon, collaborators and traitors had to be silenced. When the Kikuyu Home Guard was organized to help hunt down terrorists, the rebels retaliated. On March 23, 1953, they raided Lari, a loyalist area that had provided many recruits for the Home Guard; 200 huts were destroyed, 84 were killed, 31 others were mutilated, and 1,000 cattle were maimed. The settlers were astounded that the Mau Mau could attack its "own kind" with such ferocity, and many concluded that it was a protection racket to finance the bid by Kikuyu, who made up only one-fifth of the population, to dominate all Kenya.

Even with military mobilization effective measures could not be instituted for want of information. Many settlers became convinced that the Kikuyu were by nature suspicious, secretive, and masters of double talk. As the police worked desperately to get information, sometimes resorting to torturing prisoners, many rumors developed among the settlers. By this time Kenyatta was assumed to be the leader of the Mau Mau, and one rumor was that the members were required to swear personal allegiance to him. Others were that the Kikuyu were forced to pay 60 shillings to have the oath administered, that each night a motorized oathing team went out from Nairobi to the reserves to speed up the forcible recruiting, that 800 were given the oath at one time.

As the terror continued, rumors emerged about the character of the attacks. According to one, the Mau Mau invariably split open the stomachs of pregnant women. In 1953, when government forces went on the offensive, the rebels—now called the Land Freedom Armies—were forced to hide in the forests; before long, they became desperate, hunted men. Additional rumors developed about their oaths. Dedan Kimathi, leader in the Aberdares forest, had ordered his oath administrators to devise more and more horrible oaths. Some men had been forced to take as many as 14 oaths, each more disgusting than the last. Oath-takers had to swallow seven times from a foul concoction; the elements varied according to rumor—ingredients from menstruation or masturbation, putrefying flesh taken from graves, still warm brains of women and children just murdered. Other rumors were that copulation with sheep, donkeys, bitches, or goats was part of the ceremony. Thus, the fight against the Mau Mau became a campaign against inhuman beasts.

By this time officials realized that well over 90 per cent of the Kikuyu stood behind the movement and supported it by providing information, supplies, and weapons. But the rebels were now on the defensive; in the first 14 months of offensive operations 3,064 guerrillas had been killed and another thousand captured. Prisoners were interrogated relentlessly for additional information, and rumors developed among the Kikuyu of the methods being used to extract confessions. According to one rumor several men had been castrated for refusing to talk; another was that bottles of soda water were pushed into the uterus of women to make them confess. On April 24, 1954, in Operation Anvil, Nairobi was surrounded and then searched area by area. Extensive use was made of hooded informers, former rebels completely covered but for eye-holes—called "little sacks" by the Kikuyu—to identify those who were active in the movement. By May 8, 30,000 Kikuyu had been screened; of this number 16,538 were detained and their dependents sent back to the reserves. This move cut the supply lines to the forests. The trickle of information from Africans soon became a flood, and the movement collapsed. Of the rebels—estimated at 12,000 fighters supported by some 1,000,000 Kikuyu—10,527 had been killed. In 1956, when the state of emergency was lifted, 38,449 were still in custody. From the standpoint of the settlers the area had been cleared of savage terrorists; from the standpoint of the rebels a fight for freedom had been brutally suppressed.

Rumors also develop among people who are weary of a monotonous routine. Men doing boring work, civilians and rear-echelon troops in time of war, idle members of privileged classes—all find talking about the "latest" a way of relieving their tension. In his discussion of rumor LaPiere (1938, pp. 176–83) writes primarily of this type of context. He refers to rumor as a "fugitive pattern," a by-product of rivalry for leadership in congenial situations in which each vies to tell a good story. Rumors in such contexts differ from others in that a larger proportion of the participants do not take seriously what they are saying; they frequently label their own remarks as "rumor" and speak for the amusement of their audience. Similar activities can be found among men under severe tension in situations marked by a surfeit of rumors disproved one after another by subsequent events. They become weary of rumors and sometimes make them the butt of humorous jibes. In her account of the Bacolod Internment Center on the Philippines, where civilian prisoners were kept by the Japanese during World War II, E. S. Vaughan (1949, pp. 133–35) indicates that wholly unreliable and humorous rumors broke the monotony of camp living and gave it some zest. Similarly, the Japanese interned in relocation centers as the United States sometimes referred to their unsettled way of life as *dema-kurashi*, literally "existence through rumors," but pronounced "democracy" in a heavy Japanese accent. U. S. Navy men speak lightly of the latest "scuttle-butt," and Army personnel make similar references in somewhat less delicate terms.

This suggests that for some individuals participation in rumor construction may on some occasions be more cathartic than instrumental. Rather than making a serious effort to define the situation, they are merely relieving their tensions by giving vent to inner dispositions. Situations in which such facetious contributions are discernible have not been set up as a separate category of case studies, however, for rumors that some individuals regard lightly are taken very seriously by others.

Conditions of Rumor Construction

Although students of rumor disagree on other matters, a high degree of consensus exists among them concerning the general conditions under which the phenomenon is found: rumors emerge in ambiguous situations. Oman (1918), Prasad (1935), Rose (1940), R. H. Knapp (1944), and Carrard (1953) are among those who have specified that rumors develop when there is an unsatisfied need for information. In a discussion that is quite unrelated to their experiments on serial transmission, Allport and Postman (1947, pp. 33–34) have tried to formalize such observations in a widely quoted formula: $R \sim i \times a$—"the amount of rumor in circulation will vary with the importance of the subject to the individuals concerned times the ambiguity of the evidence pertaining to the topic at issue." Although the exact relationship designated has never been demonstrated, the formula does point to important variables.

Examination of the various contexts in which rumors develop reveals that they have one element in common; they are all problematic situations. In spite of the diversity of the circumstances in other respects they are all marked by a discrepancy between mobilization to act and overt action. The public, whether it has already been formed or develops with the rumor, is balked; men are unable to carry out their activities for want of accurate, up-to-the-minute information. They turn first to institutional channels; if it is available there, they use it as the basis for collective adjustment. If adequate information is not available from established sources, the problem remains unsolved; if anything, there is even more frustration. Those who are thus deprived of news are much like a driver who cannot see through his rain-obscured windshield; he must still find his way. If enough news is not available to meet the problematic situation, a definition must be improvised. Rumor is the collective transaction in which such improvisation occurs. As Vansina (1965, p. 20) notes, rumor is a form of news; it arises in situations of tension when ordinary communication channels are not operating adequately.

These observations may be summarized in a hypothesis: *if the demand for news in a public exceeds the supply made available through institutional channels, rumor construction is likely to occur.* The proposition is stochastic; the existence of this condition does not necessarily result in rumor, although the probability is high. *Demand for news* is variable and theoretically measurable; at this stage of inquiry, however, we must be content with gross estimates. The greater the *unsatisfied* demand for news, the more likely it is that rumors will develop. Demand for news, furthermore, is positively associated with intensity of collective excitement, and both depend upon the felt importance of the event to the public. Rough tests of this hypothesis can be made by manipulating the variables.

Given demand for news, if supply is for any reason cut off, situations are very likely to be defined through rumors. During the German seige of Paris in 1871, for example, the city was completely cut off, although a French relieving army was no farther away than Orleans. In the French provinces there were encouraging rumors of successful sorties and of breaches in German positions. Within Paris a multitude of rumors developed about events in the outside world, and none of them could be contradicted until the next balloon succeeded in getting over the lines (Oman, 1918; Kranzberg, 1950). Accounts of revolutionary uprisings all indicate the extent to which rebels must rely on rumors and couriers, for the institutional channels are generally controlled by defenders of the status quo. Another context in which demand for news outruns supply is the stock market. As Rose (1940, pp. 160–93) points out, profit depends on anticipating changes before others know of them; hence, speculators in particular need information before it is reported in formal channels. They often act on the basis of rumors. It is of interest to note that procedures for the orderly collection and distribution of news were originally developed to facilitate market transactions (Wright and Fayle, 1928; Merrill and Clark, 1934).

If the news in demand is of the sort not expected in institutional channels, reliance is placed upon rumors. Matters regarded as being in poor taste, such as the sex habits of community leaders, are discussed surreptitiously; it is understood that potentially libelous material cannot be published. News of concern only to a very limited public rarely appears in the mass media; professional men frequently exchange gossip about the latest escapades of fellow specialists, and members of small ethnic minorities rely upon their "grapevine" for intramural news. Before 1856, when rise of the frankly sectional Republican party led to open fears of slave revolts, Southern newspapers made a practice of never mentioning the subject of Negro insurrections. The ante-bellum South was plagued by hundreds of rumors of such uprisings, and these occasionally resulted in harsh retaliatory measures against innocent slaves (Carroll, 1938, pp. 202–12; Wish, 1939). In high government affairs many key decisions must be veiled in secrecy. In Washington, D. C., and in capitals throughout the world rumors have become an invaluable source of information, and Rosten (1937, pp. 14–15) shows how newsmen have learned to use them in their analyses. Many news items from "usually reliable sources" are rumors being seriously entertained by the press corps.

When institutional channels are discredited, the supply of reliable news is cut off. When a previously accepted source is redefined as the tool of special interests—enemy occupation forces, "big business," or some political party—news thought to be of interest to those in control is dismissed as propaganda. During the German occupation in World War I, for example, Belgians jeered at official bulletins. Even when a newspaper was published in the French language in which a special effort was made to demonstrate impartiality and independence of the German government, the only printed source that was trusted was a clandestine underground bulletin, the *Libre Belgique;* otherwise, the people got their information from one another (Millard, 1938). Again in World War II German occupation forces were confronted with the same problem. In the spring of 1945 even the German people lost faith in government sources, and many rumors developed that contradicted official news: exaggerated casualty figures, forecasts of new attacks, dissension among the leaders (U.S. Strategic Bombing Survey, 1947, pp. 98–99). In the period just preceding its overthrow in 1960, the Menderez government in Turkey prohibited press coverage of most subjects debated in the Assembly. Thus, many people first learned of various incidents when headlines announced a ban on publication of news about them! Details had to come from other sources, and especially in Ankara and Istanbul the people relied on rumors (Case 60).

There is widespread agreement that known or suspected censorship increases the incidence of rumors. Institutional channels are then not fully trusted even when the censor is identified as a party with allied interests; as Oman (1918) points out, the public invariably credits the censor with gratuitous stupidity. In time of war the necessity of maintaining secrecy over certain operations is well understood; nonetheless, people speculate over what has been omitted. Hence, a flood of rumors develop even among those in complete sympathy with the

war effort. Just before the attack on Pearl Harbor, George Creel
(1941), who had directed the Committee on Public Information during World War I, appealed against censorship on these grounds.
While some secrecy is essential, he argued that the need was exaggerated beyond the bounds of common sense. Since people who know
that something is being withheld often became convinced that a
great deal more is being hidden than is actually the case, he argued
for relaxation. His appeal went unheeded.

Schöne (1936) notes that the availability of news does not preclude
the development of rumors if the supply is inadequate. Describing
the emigration movement that swept Sweden with epidemic intensity
from the middle of the nineteenth century, for example, Lindberg
(1930, pp. 46–64) shows how hunger for news about America was met
in peasant communities. What was published was not enough. Letters from those who had gone ahead were devoured by the recipients,
their relatives, and their friends; then they were copied and distributed further. Returnees were swamped with questions. At the
peak of "America fever" children were educated to migrate, and
religious leaders who warned of dangers and privations were dismissed as uninformed.

Spectacular events with possible consequences for millions result in
a sudden increase in demand for news that cannot be satisfied even
by the most efficient press service. News of the attack on President
Kennedy was on the wire services only nine minutes after the shots
were fired; after that, the incident received unprecedented coverage,
virtually monopolizing all of the major news media. But this was
simply not enough. As D. C. Miller (1945) indicates in his study of
how Americans learned of the death of President Roosevelt, when
news interest is high, limitations of the formal media are overcome
through oral interchanges. Similarly, when a spectacular crime cap-
tures public attention, as in the "Jack the Ripper" murders in London in 1888 (Case 2), the institutional channels cannot possibly carry
enough details to satisfy the inflated demand.

In an experiment conducted in a small preparatory school for girls
Schachter and Burdick (1955) to some extent controlled demand for
news. One morning the principal went to four different classrooms,
interrupted the work, pointed a finger at one girl, and asked her to
get her belongings and to leave with her. Such action was unprece-

dented and aroused much excitement; the teachers were harassed with questions. A few days before this incident eight girls—four of them from classes from which a student was withdrawn—had been asked in a counseling session if they knew anything of a missing examination. In the afternoon a team of twenty interviewers questioned all the girls; all but one had heard of what had happened. The classes were divided into three categories: those from which a girl had been removed and where a "reason" had been planted, those from which a girl had been removed without such planting, and those in which planting occurred but from which no girl was removed. Tabulations indicated that twice as many exchanges occurred in classrooms of the first two categories as in those of the third. Furthermore, in these classes about 70 per cent of the girls reported discussing other possible reasons for the removal, whereas less than 15 per cent of the girls in the third category of classes had considered other possibilities. These results support the hypothesis.

When demand for news is diversified, when a public is divided into factions, some rely on rumors and others do not. Since a given event may have different consequences for various segments of the populace, there is differential sensitivity to news. Furthermore, various groups place different estimates on the reliability of institutional channels. As R. H. Knapp (1944, p. 27) suggests, the extent to which demand for news can be satisfied through institutional channels varies in different parts of the public. During World War II, for example, most English-Canadians followed developments through institutional channels, but many French-Canadians were suspicious of these releases. Especially in Quebec many rumors developed that were openly hostile toward England: that the British were sending men of military age to Canada for "soft" civilian jobs, that Canadian troops were being mistreated in England, and that French-Canadian soldiers were being forced to "volunteer" for hazardous duty (Irving, 1943). The previously cited study of informal communication in the Soviet Union by Bauer and Gleicher (1953) reveals that while those in positions of privilege are more inclined to participate in rumor formation, they use this information as a supplement and corrective to what they find in the official media. Although fewer members of the lower classes participate, those who do rely more heavily on the rumors. In the United States members of ultraconservative circles have little faith in the press services and rely largely upon their own communication networks. Their demand for news can no longer be satisfied by the established communication system on which most other Americans depend.

Summary and Conclusion

Rumor is a substitute for news; in fact, it *is* news that does not develop in institutional channels. Unsatisfied demand for news—the *discrepancy* between information needed to come to terms with a changing environment and what is provided by formal news channels —constitutes the crucial condition of rumor construction. Demand for news may arise in an effort to cope with an unexpected event or in sustained collective tension, when men are mobilized to act but have no clear-cut goals. Supply of news depends on quite different considerations. When activity is interrupted for want of adequate information, frustrated men must piece together some kind of definition, and rumor is the collective transaction through which they try to fill this gap. Some of the different ways in which this is accomplished may now be considered.

Far from being pathological, rumor is part and parcel of the efforts of men to come to terms with the exigencies of life. This suggests that an understanding of the phenomenon has significance that extends beyond the subject matter itself. One of the central problems in sociological inquiry is ascertaining how social structures are transformed. What are the unchanging processes of social change? The analysis of social structures, while valuable in itself, can reveal little of how they come into existence or are subsequently modified; it is necessary to examine situations in which change is actually under way. Significant transformations often follow changes in intellectual orientation; with the development of perspectives more in line with altered life conditions new social patterns emerge. As Dewey (1938) argues, knowledge is not a final result outside of inquiry, but an instrument that permits life to go on in spite of problematic occurrences. The study of how consensus is formed in crisis situations, then, is an investigation of one of the ways in which societies undergo change.

3
PROBLEM-SOLVING THROUGH DELIBERATION

During the early phases of any inquiry an investigator is over-whelmed by variety, and even a casual glance at actual cases of rumor formation discloses many different ways in which working orientations toward changing environments may arise. Men may act precipitously on the first proposal offered, or they may engage in calm deliberation as to what should be done. They may procrastinate until the last possible moment and then in desperation grasp at a solution. Or they may argue so vehemently among themselves that each faction becomes more concerned with winning the argument than with getting out of the predicament. Each rumor has a career, and one fruitful approach is to isolate typical career lines. To expedite analysis of diverse patterns of development ideal types will be constructed of two different ways in which crises are resolved: *deliberative* and *extemporaneous*.

The central concern in Chapters 3 and 4 is the formation of rumor content. If most rumors are not derived from eyewitness accounts, how do they take shape? They are not planned and organized; the transactions develop spontaneously. Are there any regularities in their formation? Use of a simple typology provides a helpful beginning for work on this problem. It must be emphasized, however, that these constructs do *not* designate classes of phenomena, for individual cases cannot be subsumed under them as instances of a category. They are intended as depictions of extreme poles of a continuum, and specific cases of rumor construction can only be characterized as to the extent to which they approximate these ideal patterns. Such typologies only facilitate description and result in low-grade generalizations, but they constitute an important step in the development of scientific knowledge. They focus attention upon certain empirical regularities, make essential distinctions and clarify seemingly contradictory observations, and stimulate effort toward the invention of more precise conceptual apparatus. Eventually criteria will have to be developed that will make possible an ordering of all cases of rumor construction from one pole to the other. As Hempel (1952) points out, once such criteria have been adequately specified, the polar types become unnecessary.

Evolving Preoccupations of the Public

Every crisis situation is extended over time, and coping with it consists of a *succession* of collective adjustments. Situations become problematic either when discontent becomes unbearable or when some dramatic event is perceived. Exploratory discussions usually lack focus, but inchoate dispositions gradually crystallize, and step by step more specific interpretations emerge. Problems and proposals are formulated with increasing clarity. Issues may arise as alternative formulations are studied, debated, and perhaps abandoned as unfeasible. Information thought to be relevant is considered and evaluated. In the course of these interchanges outlook is successively modified, and as new orientations evolve, the participants become sensitized to other events that may become relevant. Since this activity is not prearranged, fortuitous events play an important part. Sensitivity to news, then, is sequential; as the situation develops, demand for news changes.

Rumors, which usually develop in interrelated clusters, reflect and reinforce the developing preoccupations of a public. An area of preoccupation is one that is unstable and only partially organized; a preoccupation represents a mobilization to act that has been interrupted. Attention is focused on those areas where impulses are still striving for some kind of gratification. The initial selection of topics of conversation occurs on the basis of shared interests; comments that reflect the common focus of attention tend to enjoy priority in communication. The test of whether something is worth discussing is whether it is listened to by others. Men do not gather together willingly to hear about commonplace things of their daily routine; what is uninteresting is selectively eliminated. When a spectacular crime has been committed, the community is full of talk elaborating the details. In factories rumors are of changes in working conditions, new supervisors, promotions, and possible layoffs; on the battlefield rumors deal with impending operations, personnel changes, casualties, diseases, and rotation. Thus, rumors are always timely; they are usually a better index of the preoccupations of a public than most other forms of verbalization.

Rumors always reflect shifts in preoccupation. In a changing situation, where dramatic occurrences follow one another in rapid succession, the newer events progressively gain attention even if previous problems have not yet been successfully resolved. As preoccupations shift, rumors are displaced. The coincidence of rumor and preoccupation is shown in the following record of what happened to persons of Japanese ancestry in the San Francisco Bay Area during the first six months of World War II. These rumors were collected in two Japanese barber shops—one in Oakland and the other in Berkeley.

Case 29. FROM PEARL HARBOR TO EVACUATION. Although the attack on Pearl Harbor was a stunning shock for all Americans, nowhere was the impact more jarring than among persons of Japanese ancestry residing in the United States. For them the attack initiated a period of acute insecurity, conflicts of loyalty, misunderstandings, and persecution. Everything that could be vaguely identified with Japan was denounced as having a partnership in the treachery, and innocent groups were suddenly discovered to be spy rings or schools for saboteurs; "Jap-baiting" became a safe and profitable pastime for politicians. Between December 7, 1941, and the time of their evacuation from the Pacific Coast hundreds of rumors about their pending fate emerged in the Japanese communities in the San Francisco area.

Rumors of physical violence against Japanese persisted throughout the six-month period. Other rumors, however, flourished only briefly. During the first month of the war many questions arose concerning the regulations governing enemy aliens, and the status of American citizens of Japanese ancestry was not clear. Among those anxious not to do anything that might conceivably be misinterpreted by authorities as an act of disloyalty many rumors arose about what was proscribed. One was that Japanese were not permitted to drive across the San Francisco Bay Bridge; another, that no Japanese was allowed to travel on buses or trains; and still another, that no one could sell his belongings unless he had a birth certificate proving that he was a citizen. Toward the end of December, when one of the Japanese language newspapers that had been closed at the outbreak of war resumed publication, some of the questions concerning what could and could not be done were clarified. Although many queries remained unanswered, within a few weeks the people became preoccupied with another threat.

The relative calm that characterized the first few weeks of the war was broken toward the end of December and early in January by a succession of attacks by Filipinos. Japanese and Filipino immigrants, who occupied somewhat complementary positions in the farm structure of California, had gotten along only superficially, and reports of enemy atrocities on the Philippines touched off long smoldering antagonisms. The most violent outbreak came in Stockton on Christmas day, when a Filipino gang broke windows of numerous stores, assaulted those caught in the streets, and killed a garage attendant as he stood talking to a friend. The open city of Manila was bombed on December 27, and the violence continued in spite of immediate police action; a few days later another man was shot in Sacramento. The Japanese became preoccupied with the problem of dealing with Filipino gangs. The prevailing view was that Filipinos were "uncivilized" and incapable of understanding that immigrants in the United States had nothing to do with an enemy army invading the Philippines. Since rational appeals were thought to be useless, little could be done, and the people cowered in fear. Whenever they got together, the attacks and details that presumably had not appeared in newspapers were discussed, and most of the rumors during this period dealt with Filipinos. One was that the Filipinos of San Francisco, reinforced by those from Stockton and Sacramento, would attack in force on New Year's Eve. There were other rumors of shootings, murder, beatings, knifings, arson, breaking of windows, and especially of rape. People remained indoors at night, took extra precautions, and gingerly kept their distance upon encountering Filipinos on the streets. By the middle of January open violence was curbed through the efforts of Filipino leaders and drastic police action. The Japanese continued to be fearful, but by the middle of February rumors about Filipinos virtually disappeared.

In February attention was focused upon F.B.I. raids. That Japanese were being arrested was not surprising, since the incarceration of suspicious enemy aliens was to be expected. Excitement over the raids, however, did not coincide with the timing of the arrests. Raids on Japanese homes and establishments began almost immediately after the outbreak of war and continued until the evacuation; however, relatively few rumors about them developed during the first two months of the war. It was not until sensational stories about spies and saboteurs were printed in newspapers that the preoccupation arose. Although published accounts of spy rings, huge stores of firearms and ammunition, and disguised Japanese admirals were frightening to those outside the Japanese communities, to the people within the charges were so preposterous that questions arose as to what constituted the *real* reasons for the arrests. The reasons given in the newspapers were patently absurd; then, why were people being arrested? Answers were provided by a flood of rumors. One widespread belief was that many had been arrested for possession of contraband, and a variety of objects were rumored to be forbidden—Bibles printed in Japanese, radio transmitters, cameras, Japanese flags, knives longer than eight inches, Japanese literature or phonograph records, photographs of airplanes, field glasses, maps, photographs of the Emperor of Japan, and dozens of other objects. All Buddhist priests and fencing instructors as well as teachers in Japanese language schools were thought to be on the "wanted" list, even though many such persons were still free. Those who thought they might qualify for arrest packed their suitcases and stoically made preparations for jail. Others desperately destroyed anything, even Bibles, that might conceivably be regarded as evidence of disloyalty.

Although the F.B.I. raids continued in March, rumors about them declined, for the people became increasingly preoccupied with the possibility of mass evacuation. Popular demands for the removal of Japanese from the Pacific Coast did not become vocal until late in January, and even in the middle of February federal officials were still declaring that wholesale movements were not contemplated. On March 3, however, the Army designated the western half of California a military area and announced that various categories of persons *might* subsequently be ordered to leave. A series of conflicting statements followed, and no one could be certain what would happen. Were the Japanese to be evacuated from their homes, or would they be permitted to remain? Would everyone have to go to camp, or would American citizens be exempted? Would families be separated? What procedures were to be followed? Some persons moved eastward on their own initiative, and soon rumors emerged of the horrible fate they suffered. Toward the end of March it was rumored that evacuation could not begin until autumn because constructing the camps would take much time, that persons with sons in the U.S. Army would not be evacuated, that farmers with crops planted would have an opportunity to harvest them. But another widespread rumor was that contracts for building the camps were for completion by April 15. Most other matters were forgotten, and these rumors persisted until the evacuation program actually got under way. Then, attention turned to more specific questions of the kinds of facilities available at the centers.

During April people were so preoccupied with preparing for their new lives in camp that everything else became secondary. Virtually all rumors during this period dealt with camp conditions. What should be taken, and what should be sold? What would be provided by the government, and what would have to be furnished by the evacuees? As the movement got under way, reports began drifting back from the vanguard, and rumors emerged of inadequate food supply, thick dust storms, mud, absence of recreational and educational facilities, inadequacy of showers, low salaries for work, typhoid epidemics, and sexual immorality among the young. Some, taking these rumors seriously, arrived in camp with huge hoards of food. As one locale after another was evacuated, many arrived at the centers with a sigh of relief; at last the uncertainty was over.

Situations are defined through a syncretic process. Rumors tend to build on each other. Once a plausible start is made, it is supported through a variety of other material. Reports about other matters thought to be relevant are often treated as though they constituted evidence in support of the developing interpretation. As Janis, Lumsdaine, and Gladstone (1951) show, earlier choices provide a selective base for all subsequent items. Rumor construction, then, involves much more than the simple passing on of information. Every item of information is evaluated, compared with other items, digested and interpreted, and those that survive usually support each other in the construction of a unified definition of the situation.

Popular definitions are usually oversimplifications and are often couched in stereotyped terms. In the course of development certain objects and symbols begin to stand out and become the focus of special concern. Such objects may become rallying points. Tracing the background of the 1943 riot against Mexicans in Los Angeles, for example, Turner and Surace (1956) point to the manner in which attention was increasingly focused upon the "zoot suit." An examination of the use of the term "Mexican" in the *Los Angeles Times* over a ten-year period shows that for the most part the traditionally favorable references persisted. In the period just preceding the riot, however, there was a sudden increase in references to "zoot suiters" rather than to "Mexicans," and these references were all unfavorable. Those who wore this uniform were characterized as a breed of human beings outside the moral order—draft-dodgers and thugs who were responsible for gang attacks and sex crimes. It became a symbol that elicited unrestrained hostility on the part of others. Thus, in each context certain events and objects come to stand out, and the situation is eventually defined in these terms.

Any public that persists for any length of time develops some kind of incipient structure. The structure evolves from the way in which a succession of events affects different segments of the community and the manner in which each faction successively redefines its position. Bucher (1957) provides an illustration in her study of the public outcry following three plane crashes in Elizabeth, New Jersey, from December 16, 1951, to February 11, 1952. Some persons were deeply concerned, while others dismissed it as a freakish coincidence. Only those who were concerned remained in the public; in the discussion that took place among them some concluded that airplane accidents are inevitable and that airports should be moved away from heavily populated areas, and others thought only that aircraft should be serviced more carefully. Of the former faction only those who were convinced that officials would not make necessary corrections on their own initiative demanded action. Thus, as the issue was debated, the composition and alignment of the public changed, and in the end only a small proportion of those who were originally shocked by the accidents were making demands. The internal structure of a public also depends upon the network of communication channels that develops within it.

The over-all pattern of development of a rumor reflects the evolving structure of the public. This is certainly true of the range of its dissemination. *The spatial distribution of a rumor depends upon the size and geographic disposition of the public, limited by the availability of communication channels.* At any given time the total number of persons making up a public constitutes the potential number of participants in rumor formation; actual participation is limited by physical and social barriers to effective communication. When the public is very large and widely dispersed, the developmental pattern may turn out to be very complex.

If a public becomes divided, this internal differentiation is likely to be reflected in diverse versions of the same rumor or in the formation of different rumors on the same event. Cleavages among those with similar preoccupations may arise from differences in presuppositions, from diversity of other interests, or from participation in communication channels that remain separated. As diverse segments of a public develop somewhat different sensitivities to news, their perspectives evolve separately. As different branches are formed, definitions tend to proliferate. Of the 60 cases under scrutiny 26 have more than one public.

Rumor Construction through Discussion

If unsatisfied demand for news is moderate, collective excitement is mild, and rumor construction occurs through critical deliberation. Differences of opinion arise over what ought to be done. As efforts are made to resolve these differences through discussion, participants generally become acutely self-conscious, for each becomes more cognizant of his own interests in relation to those of the others. Whenever there is disagreement, however minor it may be, deliberation takes on a more rational character. Contentions must be defended and justified; opposing proposals must be reviewed. All this requires critical judgment. This also places a premium upon facts, for facts will stand up under examination. Men who are seriously attempting to interpret a situation in which they are involved are not gullible; they carefully examine available information, appraise it for plausibility, make attempts at verification, mull over alternatives, and consult one another. The first and more common form of rumor construction is *deliberative*. In it men who are caught in an ambiguous situation pool their intellectual resources, examine each item critically, and arrive at some decision through rational discussion.

Meeting a crisis by critical deliberation is a form of collective problem-solving, and as Clark (1933, p. 313) indicates, group thinking has many of the characteristics of individual reflection. Whenever something happens that cannot be settled by habitual response, a problem arises. Tension grows as activity is delayed, and attention is increasingly focused upon relevant objects. Group discussion corresponds to the "inner forum" of which Dewey (1910a) writes. Thinking is an imaginative rehearsal of alternative ways of meeting a problem; the individual weighs each program of action in the light of probable consequences, and eventually makes a selection. Mentality is the capacity for pretesting solutions in advance of overt commitment; rational conduct involves foresight and planning and is marked by this controlled quality. In their comparison of group and individual problem-solving, Moore and Anderson (1954) also found many similarities, although efficiency varied considerably among individuals and among groups.

Whenever existing social relationships are retained among those involved in a crisis, new interpretations arise through already established auxiliary channels. In their study of the adoption of a new drug by doctors in four American cities, for example, Coleman, Katz, and Menzel (1957) found that physicians who were active in professional circles were the first to adopt the drug; next came those who had friendship ties with these men; last were the patient-oriented doctors who learned of it from medical journals or from representatives of pharmaceutical firms. This points to the importance of informal communication networks, for those integrated into a professional community for the most part learn of new techniques from each other. Three studies of rumor formation, all in situations characterized by mild collective excitement, also show the operation of auxiliary channels. Festinger and his associates (1948) studied a rumor about the alleged Communist affiliation of a community worker who had been active in planning a nursery school for a housing project. Interviews conducted six months after the incident revealed that 62 per cent of those with children from one to five years of age remembered the rumor, whereas only 28 per cent of those without children of nursery-school age could recall it. Furthermore, 71 per cent of those participating actively in the program knew of it; 46 per cent of those with other family members participating had heard it; but only 29 per cent of those not involved at all could recall the rumor.

In an experiment at another housing project Festinger, Schachter, and Back (1950, pp. 114–31) planted a report that one of the project's special activities was to receive nationwide publicity. They found that this information was conveyed in the main to individuals who had taken a prominent part in the activity. Dissatisfied with studies based on retrospective interviews, Back and his associates (1950) placed seven participant observers in an organization of fifty-five people at five authority levels. The observers were to record the rumors they heard and to ask each speaker for the source of his information. Nine items of information were planted over a period of four months, and a record was made of their dissemination. Two of the reports were about matters of concern only to members of a six-man committee. One of these reached the whole committee in fifteen minutes, but even four days later only one outsider knew of it. The second item reached all committee members but one within an hour; outsiders never did learn of this one. The remaining seven items concerned all company personnel, and they were not confined to any segment of the organization.

To the extent that rumors constitute conscientious efforts to define situations as realistically as possible, *accuracy* becomes a primary consideration. Efforts are made to secure confirmation from institutional channels, and unverified reports are considered seriously only in the absence of reliable news. Each item is related to the generally accepted facts, compared with other reports, and evaluated. Even items regarded as plausible are accepted only tentatively, often labeled as "rumors," and these are dropped as soon as more plausible accounts are formulated. Since each item is subjected to examination, development occurs at a slow or moderate rate. Since definitions constructed in this manner are regarded as hypothetical, any action that is based on them is usually tentative and marked by considerable hesitation.

Questions also arise about the reliability of sources. Information from all persons is not given equal consideration; acceptance depends upon each person's past performance and reputation. Hovland, Janis, and Kelley (1953, pp. 19–55) found that when a message is fully accepted on its own merits, the source to which it is attributed does not matter. But when a message lacks this compelling quality, is inadequately substantiated, or is incompatible with existing attitudes —conditions frequently found in rumor formation—evaluation of the source becomes decisive. Sources are evaluated in two ways: in terms of competence and in terms of trustworthiness. If either expertness or motive is questioned, the message tends to be discounted. For example, Kriesberg (1949) studied a French labor union known for the Communist leanings of its leaders but located in a predominantly Catholic area. He was surprised to find that few members were even aware of any inconsistencies or cross-pressures. Union leaders were just regarded as fellow workers who were no better informed than themselves; if any were labeled as Communists, their remarks were discredited. Interest in political issues was not strong, and most men were skeptical of both Church and Party as reliable sources. A number of other studies show that acceptance of information depends on credibility of sources; among these are Hovland and Weiss (1951), R.A. Bauer (1961), and Aronson, Turner, and Carlsmith (1963). In January 1941, Ambassador Grew reported from Tokyo a rumor that the Japanese Navy was planning a surprise attack on Pearl Harbor. It was attributed to the Peruvian Embassy, regarded as a "not very reliable" source. Everyone, including the ambassador, labeled the rumor as fantastic. The date, however, coincides with the inception of the Yamamoto plan (Wohlstetter, 1962, pp. 368, 386).

The critical procedures used by those involved in rumor construction of this type resemble those formalized by jurists, historians, and others concerned with accuracy of testimony. Does the reporter have any special interest that would be served by the dissemination of such information? Is his personal integrity beyond question? Could he be biased through force of circumstance, sympathies, vanity, or deference to popular views? Or could the person, though speaking in good faith, have been mistaken? Is he really in a position to know? Is the information from personal observation or from some other source? Such standards are not explicitly stated in rumor formation, of course; they are only intuitively felt. But these are precisely the questions that professional historians raise in their "internal criticism" of primary sources (Langlois and Seignobos, 1898, pp. 155–90).

If publics persist and contacts are repeated in a number of transactions, newly formed channels tend to solidify and become increasingly more reliable. In his study of informal communication among American soldiers in the South Pacific during World War II, Caplow (1947) indicates that once channels are established, diffusion occurs over a relatively small number of well-defined routes. A limited number of contacts are available to any individual, and available news items are transmitted only where others had been received with appreciation. Those who find one another congenial form new friendships, and as people come to know one another better through sustained association, personal responsibility for reports and views becomes fixed. When passing on unverified news, one must either disclaim responsibility by labeling the report as apocryphal or risk the consequences. As auxiliary channels solidify, then, unreliable parties are either eliminated or labeled; as with Aesop's boy who always cried "wolf," the remarks of a discredited person are treated with skepticism and sometimes discounted even when plausible. Highly personalized interpretations thus become rare. Only when auxiliary channels collapse are such individuals again taken seriously. On the other hand, each time a rumor is verified by subsequent events, substantiation adds respectability to a newly formed channel; such occasional confirmations give added credibility to the source. Thus, auxiliary channels are successively reconstructed until a satisfactory arrangement is reached.

Caplow contends further that rumors through auxiliary channels tend to become more accurate as they develop, especially when sources are available for checking. In his study many of the rumors of future troop movements turned out to be accurate forecasts of what actually happened. A selective process favored the accurate items, for military secrecy did not forbid the denial of false speculation. Soldiers constantly asked officers for confirmation of reports and eliminated those that were denied. They then pieced together their definitions from what remained. Furthermore, the same items were heard several times and from different persons, and this comparison of experiences apparently led to corrections of mistaken views. Thus, where careful deliberation is taking place, more esoteric variations tend to be eliminated. Apparently errors in transmission are also compensated for and corrected by selection. Whenever circumstances allow enough time, then, constant repetition and discussion tend to eliminate variations. Buckner (1965) notes that when participants are critical in their deliberation, their views become involved in a feedback chain, thus increasing chances for accuracy.

Studies of disasters that have aroused widespread interest show that reports are often less accurate at a distance, where possibilities of checking are diminished. In March 1952, a rabies outbreak in eastern Pennsylvania received extensive coverage in the mass media. Diggory (1956) interviewed 300 persons—100 in the affected county, 100 in an adjacent county, and 100 in a county far to the west where no cases of rabies had been reported. He found that there was less tendency to exaggerate the seriousness of the threat among those who were closer to it; the closer the threat, the greater the number of sources of information—including details by word of mouth. Inaccurate impressions could be corrected by frequent communication. During the spring of 1954, when mass hysteria developed in Seattle over unusual pitting in automobile windshields, Medalia and Larsen (1958) found that the persons they interviewed included believers, the undecided, and skeptics. Of the skeptics 94 per cent owned automobiles. This suggests that those closer to the vehicles were better able to check for themselves as well as to discuss the matter with men who serviced cars. Similar findings have been reported by Larsen (1954) and Vansina (1965, pp. 117–118). Among the best-known cases of this kind are the rumors of treachery and sabotage allegedly committed by local Japanese during the attack on Pearl Harbor (Case 18). In Hawaii the official denials were accepted, for the people could see for themselves and could talk to various defenders of the islands. On the mainland, however, the rumors persisted and were apparently an important consideration in the decision to evacuate all persons of Japanese ancestry from the Pacific Coast. In May 1943, Hawaiians were astonished when they were asked once again for an official denial of rumors they had long since dismissed (Lind, 1946, p. 45).

This does not mean, of course, that rumors developing through critical deliberation are necessarily accurate. On the contrary, even in the most careful discussion results may turn out to be in error, especially when no sources are available for denying false reports. Students of forensic psychology have demonstrated that even the best efforts often fail. Thus, Binet (1900) shows that even the most precisely given testimony is often incorrect, and that witnesses are just as certain of their incorrect statements as they are of correct ones. Borst (1904) demonstrates that careful testimony under oath, given with personal conviction, is inaccurate; and Whipple (1909) shows that eyewitness accounts are inaccurate even when perception and reporting are going on simultaneously. Furthermore, there is some evidence that testimony may become less accurate under interrogation, although here contradictory evidence has also been presented. Such findings, along with what students of serial transmission have presented, all point to the difficulties involved in oral interchanges. Yet a surprising number of rumors turn out to be accurate.

Rumors as Plausible Extrapolations

Even when opportunities for verification are not available, those who are left to their own resources do not accept anything that happens to be suggested. As a public acquires structure, rumor content tends to become progressively more circumscribed by considerations of *plausibility*. Much of any crisis situation is already defined; a certain number of particulars are available, and these constitute the know facts of the event. Only the missing gap is supplied by rumor. There are many possible relations among these facts, and one is selected from among them. Events are not disjointed affairs, but chapters in a united outlook; hence, an interpretation becomes understandable only when the gap is filled in a manner that makes it an integral part of an ordered conception of the world. The definition most likely to be accepted is one that fits in with presuppositions held more or less in common within the public. Sometimes accidental events, actually unrelated to each other, are combined. By piecing together disparate but seemingly related events a total picture may be constructed that is quite inaccurate, but highly plausible. As Oman (1919) puts it, definitions that emerge in such deliberations are often nothing more than "reasoned expectations"; many rumored incidents that are subsequently found to have been falsely reported are such that they might very conceivably have happened. A careful examination of the 60 case studies reveals that of the 225 rumors that developed through auxiliary channels in situations marked by mild or moderate tension only 12 are inconsistent with cultural axioms.

Even when a rumor seems bizarre to an outside observer, it is quite plausible from the standpoint of the public. Diversity of outlook explains many of the "wild" rumors that become the object of dismayed comment; rumors provoke amazement only on the part of those who do not share the perspective of the participants. During the spring of 1946, for example, Americans on occupation duty in Japan were astonished to learn that many Japanese believed General MacArthur to be of Japanese ancestry! A closer examination reveals that this was not entirely unreasonable.

Case 36. GENERAL MACARTHUR'S ANCESTRY. In August 1945, the Japanese people were horrified at the prospect of their homeland being occupied by units of the U.S. Army. Throughout the war countless atrocities had been attributed to American soldiers; one had even mailed the skull of a dead Japanese home to his sweetheart. Americans were generally depicted as lewd and lustful, and one widespread belief was that feminine companions were provided for the crews of B-29 bombers. Had not the body of a woman been found in one of the planes shot down over Japan? The fire bombing of cities and the use of two atomic bombs were regarded as further proof that Americans were barbarians. When it was announced that General MacArthur would command the occupation forces, the people were aghast. He was the man their armies had defeated, the man they had scorned as the coward who had deserted his troops in Bataan. It would be a vindictive occupation; stoically they prepared for the worst.

Much to their surprise Americans neither raped nor plundered. The soldiers were on the whole quite friendly, and American officials introduced a far more humane government than the underprivileged classes—the vast majority of Japanese—had ever known. The cumbersome educational system was modified to make possible more training for the poor; the common practice of beating subordinates was abolished; young people were given legal rights to oppose their elders; women were allowed to vote for the first time and given access to court action when seduced or raped; the practice of selling daughters into prostitution, long hated by the poor, was made illegal. The *Kempeitai,* the dreaded national police, was disbanded. Thus, Americans forcibly enacted many social reforms that had been long advocated; they accomplished what Japanese politicians, representing the privileged classes, had refused to do.

The most telling impression was made by the distribution of American food in the spring of 1946. Although the amount each family received was so meager that it made little difference in their diet, the very thought of relief supplies being sent by a nation that had so recently been a bitter enemy was overwhelming. Most Japanese declared frankly that they would not have done the same thing for Americans, had their fates been reversed; they felt that they did not deserve such "kindness." The militarists had dismissed humanitarianism as effeminate, but to people who were starving it took on a different significance. Many concluded that they had been duped by the militarists. What came to be regarded as the American way of life presented a sharp contrast to the harsh program required during the war, and in less than a year after the beginning of the occupation there developed a mass adoration of all things American. American style clothing virtually displaced the *kimono;* American slang expressions were adopted; American movies attracted record audiences.

The symbol of all things American was General MacArthur. He came to be worshipped by many as the one man who did more for Japan than any one else in history. All his orders were obeyed without question. The general was viewed as the champion of the common people against conniving and inefficient Japanese politicians, and instances of local corruption were immediately exposed and reported to him. Instead of cruel vengeance he had given them more than their own leaders; this was taken as an indication of superhuman greatness. Pictures of the general appeared on walls side by side with those of the Emperor, and when a plot to assassinate him was uncovered, many Japanese were infuriated. Among the hundreds of rumors that emerged during this period the most widespread were those concerning the background of General MacArthur; from May to July 1946, the subject was discussed heatedly throughout the islands. One set of rumors concerned the general's ancestry: his grandmother was Japanese; his mother was a Japanese woman born in Kyoto; he was the son of a Japanese concubine but was reared by his legal mother, an American. Another set of rumors did not question his ancestry but tied his childhood to Japan: the general was brought up by a Japanese wet nurse; he was born in Kyoto; his mother, an American, was born in Japan.

That the general's father was a U.S. Army officer who had spent much of his time in Asia was well known. Since high-ranking Japanese officers sometimes had concubines, it seemed natural that an American officer might have done the same thing. All the rumors identified the general with Japan, either genetically or through childhood experiences, and this seemingly made other things more intelligible. It had been assumed that all Americans hated Japanese, and the general was one man who had special reasons for doing so. Yet he had done so much for the people. This was difficult to understand. But if the general were part Japanese, everything would fit together; he would not be an outsider at all. Japanese intellectuals, who were embarrassed by the rumors, often challenged them, but to no avail. When believers were asked why the story had not appeared in published sources, one frequent reply was that such delicate matters could not be discussed openly. Thus, for many Japanese the general came to be identified racially with the nation. He was a living god; he controlled the destiny of Japan, and yet many felt absolutely safe.

Similarly, the beliefs of ultraconservative Americans strike most of their countrymen as fantastic. Many are firmly convinced that their way of life is gradually being stifled by a gigantic Communist conspiracy. To those who believe that enemy agents are everywhere, it is not unreasonable that fluoridation is a plot against health, that the post office zip code is an attempt to number everyone in preparation for totalitarian control, or that federal agents have become involved in a plot to murder their own president. Given this perspective the following incident becomes more understandable:

Case 40. OPERATION WATER MOCCASIN. Early in 1963 the U.S. Army began a series of unusual training maneuvers at Fort Stewart, Georgia. The objective of Operation Water Moccasin was to teach the latest anti-guerrilla, counter-insurgency techniques to 2,500 American soldiers and a small group of officers from 17 friendly nations—including 4 officers from Liberia. Before long rumors developed of a plot to seize Georgia as a prelude to turning the whole country over to the United Nations. Co-conspirators in the crash program to disarm and conquer the nation were N.A.T.O. and the U.S. Arms Control and Disarmament Agency. The attack would begin when 20,000 Congolese, supported by 30,000 Mongolians, swept through Georgia. Furthermore, 35,000 Chinese soldiers were already deployed in a staging area in Mexico, awaiting orders to attack San Diego. These reports were disseminated throughout the country by the press and radio of ultraconservative groups, and Congressmen were soon flooded with letters from frightened constituents. The outcry became so intense that the Army had to alter its plans, and finally Senator Kuchel made a public address, lashing out against "fear peddlers."

If a public is made up of persons drawn from different cultural backgrounds, each faction develops a somewhat different definition of the same event. Plausibility is the basis of credence, but what is plausible differs from one universe of discourse to another. In a divided public, then, some people will accept a given rumor without question; others will regard it as a definite possibility; while still others will ridicule it as ludicrous and question the intelligence of those who take it seriously. The diverse ways in which an event may be interpreted is illustrated in the following case.

Case 22. THE EXECUTION OF PUGACHEV. On January 10, 1775, a public execution was held in Moscow of Emelyan Pugachev, who had organized a rebel army that seriously threatened the government. By order of the Empress Catherine II, he was to be drawn and quartered and only afterward to be beheaded. Thousands gathered in the square to witness the spectacle; the roofs of all nearby houses and stores were covered with spectators drawn from different social classes. Many there were sympathetic to Pugachev, who had claimed to be Peter III, husband of Catherine, who had escaped her assassins and was trying to regain his throne. They hoped that a decree of pardon would still come. Most of the noblemen, who gathered in large numbers in the square, hated Pugachev, although a few of them were actually deserters from his seditious government. Among the troops present were Pugachev's countrymen, loyal Cossacks who had fought on the side of the government but who were nonetheless inclined to regard him as the rightful Czar. Finally, there were many curious spectators in the square who were not concerned with the political significance of the event.

The execution did not occur in the expected manner. Instead of cutting the prisoner into several parts the executioner struck off his head with a single quick movement. Eyewitnesses standing near the scaffold claimed they heard an official cry to the executioner, "You scoundrel, what have you done?" Then, "But now quickly, the arms and legs." There was agreement on certain basic points: a decree was read ordering Pugachev to be drawn and quartered; instead of doing this the executioner beheaded the prisoner immediately; and an official scolded him loudly for disobeying the command.

Rumors emerged immediately, and different interpretations of the event came to be accepted in different strata of Moscow society. One rumor was that Empress Catherine, moved by pity, had given a secret order not to torture the criminal. Therefore, the executioner had put him out of his misery quickly. This explanation was widely accepted in court circles, consisting largely of admirers of the Czarina, and it was apparently promoted by Catherine herself.

Among the noblemen unfriendly to both Catherine and Pugachev two rumors emerged. One was that the executioner was inexperienced, performing for the first time in his life; he had become confused and had lost control of himself. Another rumor was that the criminal adherents of Pugachev had bribed him so that their leader would not be tortured any longer than necessary.

Among the Cossacks who were present at the square a different rumor developed. Since a Czar, even a rebellious one, could not be exposed in such a shameful execution, secret commands were given to the executioner. This rumor was regarded as being in bad taste and took on a clandestine character; people looked around for possible informers before discussing this possibility.

Still another rumor formed among the troops from the Urals and Pugachev's loyal followers. Since a Czar could not be executed, an ordinary criminal had been substituted in his place. At the last moment, when the criminal was about to reveal that he was dying in place of the Czar, the executioner had to hurry in order to decapitate him before the secret escaped. The real Czar was still alive in Petrograd.

If a report is not plausible, it is ignored, contradicted, or attributed to persons of questionable integrity. It may be rejected even if it comes from institutional channels. Soon after the bombing of Hiroshima an official announcement was made of a new type of bomb; although eminent scientists were quoted, the victims did not take it seriously because it did not "make sense." Sometimes reports that are rejected as implausible subsequently turn out to be accurate. The following incident shows how two newsmen missed an opportunity for a sensational "scoop" primarily because they were such well-trained journalists.

Case 37. MARSHAL GÖRING'S SUICIDE. On the night in October 1946, when the major German war criminals were scheduled for execution, only eight especially chosen newsmen and representatives of the Allied Control Commission were permitted to witness the hangings. Hermann Göring had cheated the gallows by committing suicide, but the eight newsmen were kept incommunicado and not allowed to contact their colleagues outside who had access to the wire services. As the reporters outside waited anxiously for an official announcement, one of the American guards called out to a friend working for the *London Evening Standard* and asked, "Hey, have you heard that Göring committed suicide?" She had known the soldier since childhood, but she had heard rumors before, and she let the matter pass. Another guard told a representative of the Mutual Broadcasting Company, but when the latter was unable to get official confirmation, he also refused to send out the report. He commented, "A man could ruin himself in five minutes by broadcasting a silly report like that." It was not until three and a half hours after the final hanging that an official announcement was made that Göring had indeed cheated the gallows.

The consternation that arises when implausible accounts are presented on institutional channels is revealed by the virtual immobilization of Communists throughout the world by disclosures of the excesses of the Stalin regime. On February 25, 1956, Premier Khrushchev made his "secret speech" at a closed session of the Twentieth Congress of the Communist Party in Moscow. No official announcement was made, but within a few days rumors of the speech were all over the city. Although foreign Communists were barred from the meeting, they participated in the Moscow discussions and were able to report to their respective organizations. On June 4, the U.S. State Department published a text of the speech. Some Communists immediately dismissed it as propaganda; but others were more restrained, for the text supported reports from their own delegates to Moscow. British Communists complained of the absence of an official report, necessitating dependence on sources hostile to socialism. Despite misgivings about the channel, indications are that Communists the world over studied the text carefully; soon they complained to Moscow of inconsistencies, unclear distinctions, and perplexing questions left unanswered. They were stunned. Many parties failed to respond promptly. Factional quarrels broke out, some condemning fellow Communists who were slow in supporting the anti-Stalin campaign. In the United States the *Daily Worker* not only published letters to the editor written from standpoints both for and against Stalin but also acknowledged its "blind and uncritical" attitude of the past. It was not until June 30 that official confirmation came from Moscow, and on July 2 a text of the speech was finally published in *Pravda* (Russian Institute, 1956).

Since rumor construction is a cumulative process, content may be successively reconstituted as the situation develops. If so, the account tends to become increasingly more plausible. Once the general direction of interpretation is set, it tends to be supported by additional clues. Seemingly relevant facts are introduced. Similar incidents in the past may be recalled. Details are added, names and specific references to places also increase credibility. People become sensitized to other occurrences that they believe relevant for testing their earlier hunches; events that are quite unrelated may therefore serve to reinforce the developing orientation. As Bernheim (1920, pp. 97–108) indicates, motives may be assigned to various characters to make a story more effective; thus a report that might otherwise be incomprehensible or likely to be misunderstood is rounded out. Little by little what was problematic becomes more meaningful.

Peterson and Gist (1951) studied the public excitement in a Missouri town over the slaying of a fifteen-year-old girl. The prime suspect was believed to be a man who had employed the victim as a baby-sitter, and soon subsidiary rumors developed about his absence from a party he was supposed to have been attending, his strained relationship with his wife, and other items presumably suppressed by the police (Case 7). They note that numerous details accumulated to elaborate on the central theme. Similarly, in his study of a landslide in Darjeeling, Sinha (1952) found that rumors tended to elaborate on what took place. These findings contradict Allport and Postman's contention that rumors necessarily become shorter as they develop. The discrepancy arises, of course, from the use of different conceptions of rumor. Under conditions of the experiments on serial transmission reports tend to become shorter because of limitations of human memory. As Avigdor (1951, p. 8) points out, subjects in the experiments were instructed to be as accurate as possible; hence, they were not likely to elaborate. But in actual crises, developing definitions tend to be supplemented by additional information. Several studies support Vergil's view that *fama crescit eundo*.

In critical deliberation speakers are constantly confronted by skepticism. Many rumors acquire the appearance of increased authenticity in the course of construction through the efforts of supporters to justify their views. Often some authority is cited to back a report, and this inspires more confidence. In his description of rumors in Tikopia, Firth (1956) notes that the anthropologists' radio was often cited as the source of tales of disaster to Tikopians working away from the island, of the arrival of ships, or of moves contemplated by the government. Remarks are formulated for the benefit of some audience, and a speaker is generally aware of the interests, sensitivities, and beliefs of those whom he addresses. People ask questions; they sometime challenge the accuracy of reports. Men resent doubts, and their answer to skeptics often becomes more positive and detailed. When faced with silence or skepticism, as Dauzat (1919, p. 66) notes, the narrator may make his account more plausible—to himself as well as to others—by citing additional material. Some individuals may purposely exaggerate or invent for effectiveness. Sometimes others who feel they know what happened prompt the speaker. Human beings do not think and talk in fragments; they seek a full and coherent account, and what is missing is often supplied by speculation.

Even under the artificial conditions under which serial transmission has been studied reports have been found to change in the direction of greater plausibility. Thus, Allport and Postman (1947, pp. 99–115) stress the tendency toward assimilation to a principal theme; a story becomes more coherent, plausible, and well rounded. Particularly revealing are the results obtained with the subway scene —a picture containing a white man holding a razor while arguing with a Negro. In over half the experiments with adult subjects, the razor was transferred to the Negro. When the experiments were conducted on children, however, this shift did not take place (pp. 130–31). To youngsters who had not yet acquired the stereotype of the Negro, such a change would not have enhanced plausibility. In her replication of Allport and Postman, Avigdor (1951) found that items of particular interest to the subjects, facts that confirmed their expectations and helped them to structure a story, were the last to be leveled out and often were retained to the very end. Transformation of content thus brings about a better closure. Earlier, Bartlett (1932) and E. H. Moore (1935) had noted similar tendencies; Bartlett explained his observations as an "effort after meaning."

When rumor construction takes place through auxiliary channels, interaction tends to be critical, and content tends to be consistent with the presuppositions of the public. When collective excitement is mild, men try to interpret ambiguous situations by projecting reasonable expectations and then becoming sensitized to other items that tend to support them. Definitions are constructed by piecing together what is plausible. This hypothesis is consistent with the results of recent studies of perception. Postman and Bruner (1952), for example, indicate that perception is not a passive process of recording what is "out there." Men project expectations into their environment and then become selectively sensitized to sensory cues that are relevant to them. The better established the expectations, the fewer cues are needed for confirmation. The principle is also illustrated in the account of Wohlstetter (1962) of the failure of American officials to prepare for the attack on Pearl Harbor. The attack was presaged by a variety of warnings and signals; even the secret Japanese diplomatic code had been broken, providing access to all kinds of detailed information. Yet it achieved complete surprise. One difficulty was that no single agency had access to all the indicators, but even more important was that American officials were not expecting an attack. The manner in which signals are read depends upon expectations, and this possibility was not considered seriously; it was too improbable. Thus, the extent to which any report is accepted depends upon whether or not it appears plausible. As William James once noted, disbelief is not the opposite of belief; it is a negative belief. Those who scoff at a rumor actually believe something else that contradicts it.

Wish-Fulfillment in Rumor Content

One rumor recorded on several occasions during World War II is that of an American prisoner in Japan who wrote home that he was being treated well. At the end of his letter he asked that the stamp on the envelope be saved for his collection. When the stamp was soaked off, his family found written beneath it, "They have cut out my tongue." This and similar tales are apparently recurrent and ubiquitous. This particular rumor was reported during World War I, the victim being a captive in Germany (Harvey, 1915), and H. H. Smith (1943) has found similar rumors during the Spanish-American and the Civil War. Atrocity stories develop in all intense conflicts, and Loewenberg (1943) indicates that rumors of well poisoning and rape are found the world over among people caught unprepared in catastrophes. As Hughes (1940, pp. 184–216) points out, such accounts have also been published as human interest stories at various times and places. Can they be regarded as independent inventions? So many details coincide. Bonaparte (1947), presenting a collection of such tales from various parts of Europe, contends that while the possibility of diffusion cannot be excluded, they can be explained in terms of the unity of the human mind. Certain complexes haunt the human psyche, and in critical moments they manifest themselves in such stories. Thus, following the tradition of Freud, Abrahams, and Riklin, psychoanalysts account for the widespread distribution of these tales in terms of universal needs.

Indeed, psychoanalysts have attempted to explain all rumors in these terms. They suggest that desires and interests, especially those that are forbidden in a group, gain indirect expression in rumors; according to writers like Hart (1916), Glover (1940), Roos (1943), and Colombo and Moccio (1961), participation in rumor formation is essentially a cathartic process. Where private views conflict with sanctioned communication, various forms of speech do provide opportunities for the camouflaged expression of suppressed attitudes. Jokes provide opportunities for giving vent to one's feelings. In a rigidly stratified society, where it would be dangerous to criticize the rulers openly, the underprivileged are often able to deride their taskmasters in covert tales. For American Negroes, for example, the best jokes are those in which a Jim Crow practice backfires on a southerner, when a Negro who had been treated as a "darky" subsequently is discovered to be incomparably superior to the white man. A gnawing sense of inadequacy is transformed temporarily into a vision of triumph. As Powdermaker (1943) points out, such stories mock the foibles of those in power; their avowed intention is to entertain, and there is no personal responsibility for the content. Thus, a man may gain gratifications from vocal activity to the extent that he says something that verifies his suspicions, voices his alarms, or amuses him at the expense of someone he does not like. Furthermore, men are responsive to ideas that justify their deeds, give expression to emotional dispositions, or placate their conscience. Such symbolic acts do make some kind of tension-reduction possible.

Rumors may similarly provide a camouflaged means of expressing one's feelings. Although personal responsibility for accuracy is fixed in institutional or auxiliary channels, in many rumors the source is obscure, if not anonymous. Many participants in rumor construction disclaim responsibility for what they say, insisting they are merely passing on what they had heard. This is a matter of crucial importance, for many persons are far less inhibited in situations in which they are not liable for the consequences of their remarks. Thus, fears of which men are ashamed, suspicions that cannot be voiced openly, and forbidden hopes may appear in disguise in rumors. Cornetz (1919, pp. 608–09), for example, points to the utility of rumors of treason in time of war. When some loss is explained through treason, calm is reestablished, for one can believe that it was not the fault of his heroes. National pride is safeguarded; the heroes are withdrawing after a magnificent defense, unconquerable except by unfair tactics.

But catharsis is an individual experience. As Prasad (1950) protests, rumor is a collective transaction, and what is projected in expressive communication is individual. The problem is to ascertain some of the conditions under which such individual contributions become important in shaping a collective product. *Expressions that are primarily cathartic are not likely to become current unless the emotional dispositions are shared by a substantial portion of the public.* The mere fact that someone says something satisfying to himself does not mean that it will be taken up by others. Especially apropos is the discussion of confabulation by Weinstein, Kahn, and Malitz (1956). This form of speech is found among victims of certain types of brain damage, and it somewhat resembles participation in rumor formation in that it is a narration of events about one's past life. But the accounts are often false and internally inconsistent; a patient may deny having been in an accident or give a fictitious account of how it occurred. Although some of the recitals are grandiose, most are modest and quite plausible, and psychiatrists believe that these stories are expressive of hidden motives. But they do not become rumors in the hospital—precisely because the interests are private and are not shared by the audience.

Are there other conditions under which wish-fulfillment may become prominently involved in rumor construction? Strongly felt inclinations may gain currency, of course, if they are consistent with shared conceptions of what is plausible. Where several reports are equally plausible, the most satisfying item is likely to gain currency. But what of expressive rumors that are not plausible? Most of them emerge in situations characterized by intense collective excitement, and they will be considered in Chapter 4. In the 60 cases, however, 12 rumors developed in publics under moderate tension that were both highly expressive and inconsistent with the presuppositions of many of the participants. All 12 are found in three cases, which may be examined in more detail.

Case 25. THE OPENING OF RUHLEBEN. On November 6, 1914, a bit more than three months after the outbreak of World War I, all British subjects in Germany were arrested and sent to a deserted race track on the outskirts of Berlin. No newspapers were available in Ruhleben, and the internees were suddenly cut off from the rest of the world. As they settled down to their new life, many rumors emerged concerning the progress of the war and their eventual fate. There was much speculation over the possibility of being transferred to other camps and of being exchanged for German prisoners in England. During the early days most of the rumors were optimistic. Among them was one that 250,000 Germans had drowned at Dixmuiden, and another was that a German warship had been sunk by the *Queen Mary*. On November 20 a rumor developed that everyone in camp would be repatriated to England within a week. As the war wore on and camp existence became a dreary routine, the optimism gradually faded.

Case 26. THE MONS RETREAT. During the spring of 1915 a rumor swept through England that angels had intervened in behalf of British troops fighting on the continent. Although there were several versions, the most popular was that during the Mons retreat German cavalry had gotten around the left wing of a retiring British unit and threatened it with disaster. Suddenly, a whole row of shining white figures arose between the advancing horsemen and the tired infantrymen. The Germans stopped like dazed men and remained standing until the British had escaped. According to another version the German horses swerved and stampeded when the angels arrived.

The rumor led to a heated controversy between those who objected to "superstitions" and others who felt that it did not hurt for people to believe that God supported the British crown. An investigation revealed that British officers were puzzled over an unusual incident. On the morning after the battle of La Cateau the enemy had refrained from pressing the flank of the retreating 2nd Army Corps. The men who were trapped appreciated their danger in the most acute way, for they were tired and realized that they were in no condition to fight. Then, the Germans stopped. The survivors did not speak of angels, however; they insisted that a French cavalry unit had covered their flank and then had disappeared mysteriously when the crisis was over.

The incident was not explained until after the war. On that day the Germans had suffered so severely that they simply did not have the necessary resources to continue their assault.

Case 27. PRESIDENT ROOSEVELT'S CONDITION. In 1935 the nation was well on its way to recovery from the worst depression in its history. As Congress enacted one piece of social legislation after another, questions were raised in conservative circles of the dangers of changing too quickly and of pampering the poor. At this time several rumors about the Roosevelt family arose among the very rich. One was that Mrs. Roosevelt planned to succeed her husband as president and to hold office until one of her sons was ready to take over. Another was that the Roosevelt family was always drunk. According to other tales the president was insane; he was on the verge of collapse, physical and mental, and his associates constantly feared his making a spectacle of himself. When he heard that the Supreme Court had invalidated parts of the N.R.A., he had a violent fit. Since the hatred expressed was so bitter, some observers suggested that the president, himself born to great wealth, was regarded as a traitor to his class.

Particularly suggestive is a study by McGregor (1938) on the manner in which personal preferences affect forecasts. He cites two significant variables: degree of ambiguity of the situation and ego-involvement. If either ambiguity or importance of the forecast to the individual is zero, the influence of personal preferences is also zero. This also appears to be true of the twelve rumors. In Ruhleben there was no way of getting new information or confirmation; the men could only continue speculating. No solution to the Mons mystery was possible until the termination of hostilities, and the wealthy could not understand how one of their own kind could "soak the rich" for the welfare of the poor. *If a situation remains ambiguous even after attempts at definition, opportunities arise for personal intervention.* No fixed expectations stand out, and one possibility becomes as plausible as another. In a study of autokinetic effect, for example, Sherif and Harvey (1952) found that the more uncertain the situation, the fewer definite anchorages there were, the wider the range of individual judgments, and the more accentuated the differences among individuals. As William James (1897, p. 11) noted long ago, passion may decide between propositions, if the option cannot be decided on intellectual grounds.

McGregor's second variable is ego-involvement. The situation must not only be ambiguous, but ego-involvement must be low. That is to say, accuracy of the information is not important to the individual. *Indirect expression of emotional dispositions is facilitated in situations in which nothing can be done.* Where action is impossible or not seriously contemplated, accuracy of definition is not decisive, and people may say things that please them. Especially if strong impulses have been aroused, speech may become cathartic. Should action subsequently become necessary, the situation can be redefined at that time. Thus, both the internees at Ruhleben and British civilians at home were helpless; there was nothing they could do to affect the outcome of the war. Similarly, wealthy Americans could do little about the popular president whose party controlled both houses of Congress. In prisons and concentration camps, among the unemployed during depressions, among the bored in large-scale production much discontent develops, but nothing can be done about it; in such contexts aroused feelings are often expressed in rumors. In his discussion of "gallows humor" Obrdlik (1942) notes that victims of hopeless and dangerous situations often tell jokes about their own miseries; this is their last refuge, for there is nothing else they can do. Such catharsis is also found in gossip. LeGallienne (1912), Lomer (1913), and Lanz (1936) all point to the expression of personal feelings in such talk; again, in most instances little can be done. Similarly, in many congenial situations no strenuous effort is made at achieving accuracy. Firth (1956) notes that Tikopians often acted on rumors of the arrival of a ship even when they did not believe them. Such rumors provided sanction to do what many of them wanted to do anyway—to stop work and to go out for a joyful boat ride to greet a ship. Even if none appeared, this was a pleasant interlude. Under some conditions, then, men enjoy verbalizations that may not be accurate; they may even resort to what Coleridge once called the "willing suspension of disbelief."

Even in studies of serial transmission experiments show that distortion is kept to a minimum on matters of direct importance to the individuals concerned. Higham (1951) repeated the Allport-Postman experiments on some students, using somewhat simpler stories, and included a report in which ego-involvement would be expected—a conversation between two faculty members concerning a forthcoming examination. On the Allport-Postman type of material his results replicated the original experiments; on the ego-involved story, however, fewer details dropped out, and the main sense of the account was not distorted. The developmental pattern differed from that of emotionally neutral materials. P. Chaudhuri (1953) performed a similar experiment in India, and his results confirm Higham's findings. In the previously cited experiment by Schachter and Burdick (1955) the rumor that four students summarily removed from their classrooms were connected with some missing examination papers was not distorted. In every case it was reported to the interviewer in the original form. Brissey (1961) did a serial transmission study on a movie on hit-and-run drivers; he found a marked decline in the amount of information transmitted, but the important items were retained to the very end. These studies deal with distortion, which may not involve the intrusion of personal feelings; what they reveal, however, is that when accuracy is important to those participating in the experiment, there tends to be little distortion of *any* kind.

Thus, in some contexts rumors are a better index of the actual interests of the people than other verbalizations. Especially in situations marked by pluralistic ignorance, where people support one another openly on views that many of them do not hold privately, rumors may be inconsistent with avowed beliefs. As long as men feel obliged to say what is deemed proper, a general impression is created that everyone shares certain views, when in fact they do not. For example, in many American communities making hostile remarks about ethnic minorities and using epithets is regarded as indecent and uncouth. Since most adults conduct themselves in accordance with egalitarian norms, a superficial impression of harmony arises, and those who experience aversions sometimes develop guilt feelings. In some locales only a small number may actually believe what they say, but no one can be sure of this; it becomes apparent only in a crisis. Similarly, the Kinsey reports have revealed among other things that certain segments of the American population have supported one another, somewhat ostentatiously, on sex mores that they no longer practiced in private. Under such circumstances rumors may consistently support the dispositions that everyone ignores or denies. In his account of life in Ruhleben, for example, Ketchum (1965, pp. 58–75) states that an unwritten law developed among the internees to keep up a "front" of cheerfulness. Individually many prisoners felt depressed, but they did not dare show it; they took tremendous pride in being British. During the first six months, when many of the younger prisoners saw camp life as an exciting adventure, about nine-tenths of the rumors were optimistic. As the war wore on, however, the men sobered; even though they kept up appearances, an increasing proportion of the rumors became unfavorable.

Whenever a serious attempt is being made to define a situation, however, wish-fulfillment is definitely secondary. When perplexed men are trying to develop a realistic orientation toward their environment, pragmatic considerations come first. Some individuals may become hysterical, but their remarks are discounted by others. Those who are overly responsive to interpretations that justify their feelings find themselves challenged by others who demand supporting evidence. Implausible remarks, however pleasant they may be, do not gain currency. Jones and Kohler (1958) compared the reactions of persons favoring segregation and those opposing the program to statements for and against it, some plausible and others implausible.

They found that prosegregation subjects learned plausible prosegregation and implausible antisegregation material with less difficulty than plausible antisegregation and implausible prosegregation material. The reverse was true of those who were against the program, and subjects who were neutral made intermediate scores. Although the results are inconclusive, the study shows that even under conditions of the experiment autism is limited by considerations of plausibility. So long as men retain their critical ability, then, desire is not the father of invention.

Summary and Conclusion

Rumor formation always involves some measure of relaxation of conventional norms governing social interaction, but the manner in which definitions develop depends upon the type of social regulation of communicative activity that prevails in a situation. As a starting point a distinction has been made between two types of rumor construction—deliberative and extemporaneous—and this chapter has been devoted to the first. If unsatisfied demand for news is moderate, collective excitement is mild, and rumor construction takes place through critical deliberation. Social control is then informal. Interchanges take place through auxiliary channels; most of the participants retain their critical ability; reports are checked for plausibility and reliability of sources; and the definitions that eventually emerge tend to be consistent with cultural axioms. The personal preferences of individual participants may at times affect rumor content, but only when the situation continues to be ambiguous and when concern over accuracy is low.

Although only a few seem to realize it, most ambiguous situations are resolved through joint deliberation, and most of the decisions one makes in the course of each day are predicated upon unverified reports. Men rely to a large extent upon what they "hear" from others, and they generally find such information sufficiently reliable for meeting the exigencies of daily life. Such definitions are not called "rumors," the term being reserved for those accounts of which one is suspicious; most of the information upon which men base their lives, however, cannot meet high standards of verification.

4
SUGGESTIBILITY AND BEHAVIORAL CONTAGION

In medicine a contagious disease is one that is communicable by contact, and in sociology the term *behavioral contagion* may be used to designate the relatively rapid dissemination of a mood or form of conduct, generally through direct interpersonal contact. Affective communication generates in each situation a pervasive mood, a *Stimmung*, which colors the thought and behavior of the participants by facilitating some acts and inhibiting others. Emotional atmospheres vary in intensity, and behavioral contagion may be regarded as that type of transaction in which collective excitement is extreme. Examples include aggressive mobs, suicidal infantry charges, stampedes at bargain counters, collective hallucinations, bank runs, and dancing manias. Under the influence of fervid passion men do things that they would otherwise inhibit. Much of the concern over rumors is elicited by spectacular instances of the most amazing credulity on the part of otherwise sensible people, resulting at times in disastrous consequences. This pattern of development, more rare than critical deliberation, involves the uncritical acceptance of information without serious attempts at verification. The second type of developmental pattern, then, consists of rumors whose component communicative acts are subject to a form of social control based upon the reciprocal reinforcement of emotional reactions.

Widely held beliefs concerning behavioral contagion have been crystallized in the classic study of LeBon (1896), still one of the most perceptive accounts of this subject matter. LeBon's problem is posed by the common observation that a person in a crowd feels, thinks, and acts quite differently from the same individual when he is alone. Individuals seemingly surrender their inhibitions in the crowd situation; the "thin veneer of civilization" appears to wear off, and in many respects they behave like savages or wild animals. Participants in a crowd lose their self-consciousness, their critical ability, and their self-control. They develop a sense of invincibility and dismiss the notion of impossibility. The improbable, says LeBon, does not exist for a crowd. In the study of how rumor content is formed in contexts marked by intense collective excitement it would be worthwhile to examine LeBon's contentions critically to see whether they provide an adequate explanation for rumors that are inconsistent with cultural axioms.

Intensification of Collective Tension

If unsatisfied demand for news is very great, collective excitement is intensified, and rumor construction occurs through spontaneous interchanges. The social regulation of communicative activity is relaxed, for both institutional and auxiliary channels are inadequate. Since reports must be accepted from almost any source, they tend to be anonymous, and personal responsibility is minimized. While some discussion takes place, it tends to be hurried. As excitement is heightened, thinking becomes more confused, and there tends to be more autism. As a sense of desperate urgency develops, an increasing proportion of individuals are disposed to fall back on imaginative constructions which are not clearly distinguished from what they perceive. Tension also puts people who are similarly upset into rapport; men become suggestible, and new definitions sometimes emerge with remarkable speed. For want of a better term this mode of development might be designated as *extemporaneous,* in contrast to deliberative.

The term *collective excitement* does not refer merely to an aggregate of separately excited individuals but to a condition that emerges in social interaction. Those who are similarly disposed to act—to attack some hated object, to flee from danger, or to anticipate something with great enthusiasm—communicate their feelings, not only in what they say but also in their expressive movements. As a result there develops a common mood, which is experienced by the participants as something that is "in the air." Actually this impression is created through their perception of one another's expressive movements and the projection of their own feelings. As Blumer (1951, pp. 170–77) points out, expressive movements tend to elicit imitative reactions; the response of one participant tends to reproduce the stimuli emanating from the other, and in being reflected back to the first person reinforces his feeling. To the extent that the same dispositions are mirrored in the gestures of all participants, such circular interaction further enhances the feelings of each. As Park (1933) puts it, a developing crowd assumes the character of a closed circuit, each individual responding to his own excitement as he sees it reflected in the attitude of his neighbors. Each participant contributes to the construction of an affective milieu to the extent that he reveals his own feelings through his expressive behavior. Each is affected by the common mood to the extent that he detects such feelings on the part of others and modifies his conduct accordingly. He inhibits impulses that are contrary to the general mood and supports those that tend to reinforce it; in doing so his own feelings are further reinforced. Such mutual support is of crucial importance in maintaining excitement. If alone, an upset man may recover from his shock. When feelings are constantly reinforced by others, however, they are not only sustained but will probably become intensified. Furthermore, a single excited man who engages in impulsive behavior soon becomes acutely self-conscious, if others around him do not respond sympathetically. But the perception of others around him also engaging in unconventional acts reinforces his own dispositions.

Some measure of collective excitement is found in all situations, and what men think and do is colored by the emotional atmosphere. In a solemn religious ceremony or in a funeral, for example, there is no room for levity; even those who do not feel serious pretend that they are. In a congenial party personal reserve tends to break down; there is gay chatter and banter; mild flirtations occur, and other acts take place that are inhibited elsewhere. Such moods also develop in crisis situations through the milling of aroused individuals, as in the ugly mood of men who are muttering protests against some frustrating incident. Indeed, the various forms of crowd behavior may be regarded as extreme cases, in which excitement has been intensified to the point where it supersedes conventional norms as the basis for joint activity. Rumors often develop in situations in which people are so upset. Since expressive movements play a conspicuous part in the communication that occurs in such contexts, these rumors often cannot be understood exclusively in terms of words alone. The flash of the eyes, the whisper of a syllable, or the glance over a shoulder may be far more revealing than verbal content. Unfortunately, such gestures are difficult to record, and data in this regard tend to be superficial.

Because men are acutely sensitized to indications of feelings on the part of others, once collective excitement gets under way, it tends to be cumulative and progressively more difficult to control. Escalation occurs through positive, deviation-amplifying feedback (Maruyama, 1963). The electrifying atmosphere in which mob action takes place develops through milling. Mobs begin to take shape when disgruntled men gather to discuss what ought to be done. As they mill about and talk excitedly to one another, they become further preoccupied with their object of concern. Of course, not everyone relaxes his critical ability, but those who continue to raise questions seem out of place. Persons who have doubts or are only mildly interested drop out; long before a lynching gets under way, for example, anyone inclined to question the suspect's guilt departs. He may argue for a time, but finding his efforts futile, perhaps even dangerous, he leaves or remains quietly on the fringe. As an increasing proportion of the public comes under the influence of the developing mood, intolerance of differences increases, and those who are not in accord either withdraw or are driven out. The self-selection of personnel, then, is continuous. With intensification of excitement more and more participants lose their sense of individuality, and self-discipline in terms of conventional norms is gradually relaxed. As LeBon points out, intense collective excitement imposes a form of social control. Men are no longer free to do as they wish; they must comply or suffer the consequences. Although no satisfactory measuring device is now available, it is possible to make gross estimates of intensity. Anyone who has ever been in an angry mob would have little difficulty in contrasting that atmosphere with the levity of a pleasant gathering of friends. In all sixty cases it has been possible to rate intensity in such gross terms.

At critical points in disasters or at the height of mob action collective excitement approaches its peak. Attention becomes so concentrated upon a common object—the source of danger, the rhythmic movements of dancers, or a traitor who might escape punishment—that many participants lose their self-consciousness. They also become immediately and uncritically responsive to one another, and rumors develop instantaneously.

Case 15. THE EXPLOSION IN HALIFAX. During World War I, Halifax was the major Canadian terminal on the Atlantic, and by 1917 it had become the third largest port in the British Empire. For some time the possibility of the city's being shelled by Zeppelin raiders or by a German fleet had been discussed. All street lights had been darkened by military order, and the forts were fully manned.

Early in the morning of December 6, 1917, a French munition ship loaded with trinitrotoluol reached Halifax from New York and was proceeding toward anchorage. Suddenly an empty Belgian relief ship swept in her way. There was a confusion of signals, a few maneuvers, and then the vessels collided. In Halifax 2,000 people were killed, 6,000 injured, 10,000 left homeless, and $35,000,000 of property was destroyed. One of the greatest single explosions of the prenuclear age left 300 acres in smoking waste.

It was one sudden, devastating blast; the earth shook, and homes crumbled. This was followed by a shower of debris, oil, shrapnel, glass, and wood. Water rushed forward from the sea in a gigantic tidal wave that swept past the pier and embankment into the lower streets. Nearly 200 were drowned. Trees were torn from the ground; poles were snapped; pedestrians were thrown violently into the air. Then came fire. The air was full of vapors which suddenly burst into flame. Soon there was nothing to the north but a roaring furnace.

At first all was in confusion. Some ran into their cellars; others ran into the street. Some ran to their shops, and those in shops ran home. Rescuers turned northward. Then came word, attributed to soldiers whose barracks were in the heart of the danger area, for everyone to flee southward to the open spaces. There was danger of another explosion! The alarm spread almost instantaneously. People needed no additional warning. They turned and fled. Hammers, shovels, and bandages were thrown aside. Stores were left wide open with piles of currency on their counters. Homes were vacated, and children were dragged along. Many never looked back. Some were scantily clad; women fled in their nightdresses, and a few were stark naked, their bodies blackened by soot and grime.

The refugees were dominated by one idea—the expected Germans. Eyes were turned upward, and many insisted they had seen a Zeppelin. A man from Dartmouth Heights, overlooking the harbor, claimed that he had heard a German shell shriek over him. Many contended that immediately after the explosion they saw a German fleet maneuvering at a distance. Few doubted that shells had actually come, and some warned others not to run because "two shots never fall in the same place." By evening, as refugees huddled together in theaters, churches, stables, box cars, and basements, the accepted explanation was a German assault.

As each person becomes progressively more responsive to the demands imputed to others immediately around him, conventional barriers to social intercourse disappear, and new communication channels develop spontaneously. Strangers talk freely to one another, and everyone joins in a common spirit of camaraderie. Interpersonal relations are transformed, and personal identity becomes less important; in extreme cases the collectivity is changed into a gathering of anonymous individuals. With the relaxation of personal reserve men become more suggestible and respond more sympathetically to one another. In his study of news of the Kennedy assassination, for example, Banta (1964) reports that everyone was approachable; perfect strangers stopped and shared the latest information. This does not mean that auxiliary channels disappear altogether; especially in disasters victims try to remain close to their friends and relatives. Nonetheless, as Deutscher and New (1961) point out, long-standing enmities are weakened; antipathies are temporarily forgotten as people help each other do whatever is necessary. In such contexts information is accepted from sources that under other circumstances would be questioned. The study by Kerckhoff, Back, and Miller (1965) of a hysterical outbreak in a Southern factory is illuminating in this regard. During the summer of 1962, sixty-two persons suffered from purported insect bites; most of the victims fainted or complained of severe pains, nausea, or feelings of disorientation. When a physician and an entomologist visited the plant and could find no toxic element or poisonous insect, a sociometric study was made of the victims. It revealed that the attacks began with isolated individuals, spread through informal friendship ties, and finally broke out beyond the boundaries of cliques. Thus, when collective excitement was moderate, contacts were largely confined within friendship circles; as tension developed in intensity, however, contacts broke through the usual barriers.

This suggests that the mathematical diffusion models proposed by some students of informal communication might apply best in contexts in which tension is high. Several attempts have been made to construct mathematical formulae to describe message diffusion through a population, one of the most extensive being Project Revere, carried on at the University of Washington. The objective, as described by Dodd (1952), was to ascertain how far and how fast a message dropped in airborne leaflets would spread. An effort was made to record who was most likely to pick up a message, how many others would hear about it from them, how accurately it would be transmitted, and how long it would take to cover various distances. What Dodd called "rumors," however, were civil defense instructions printed on cards, announcing rewards for those who complied. The major findings have been reported by DeFleur and Larsen (1958), who found extensive dissemination in spite of evidence that auxiliary channels were operating. They suggest an explanation: most of the leaflets were picked up by children, among whom restrictions to social intercourse of the adult world do not hold (p. 191). In other attempts Rapoport and Rebhun (1952) developed a formula that fit

Dodd's data quite well; they note, however, that their formula rests upon the assumption that each individual tells each of the others independently. Landau and Rapoport (1953) developed an even more complex formula, but this too assumes the probability of contact of any pair to be the same. In spite of the sophistication of these scholars and the great care with which they worked, their results are disappointing. One possible reason is that the type of material and situation with which they worked is more likely to elicit deliberation in which auxiliary channels would still be operating. Rapoport (1953) was cognizant of this difficulty and tried to meet it, but with little success.

As milling continues, each participant experiences increasing tension, and his impulses become more difficult to control. A sense of urgency develops to do something—anything. Even bystanders are caught in this communicative process and begin to feel impatient; occasionally one is astonished to find himself calling for action. Records of religious revivals reveal, for example, how condescending observers who had merely wanted to watch the "trash" make spectacles of themselves suddenly found themselves unable to resist further and joining in the dancing and yelling. Somewhat like subjects in a hypnotic trance, persons in rapport become uncritically responsive. Rumors in such contexts are often from anonymous sources; no one can vouch for their accuracy. Yet, if the information is thought to be pertinent, it is not ignored. *Standards of plausibility* also change, and as Hamblin and Wiggins (1957) show, suggestions are accepted that in calmer moments would be challenged. Social interaction in such contexts may be contrasted with critical deliberation. Questions are not raised about sources; indeed, a person who asks for verification of a rumor thereby severs himself from the group. Men respond intuitively to one another; they speak freely, thereby releasing their pent-up feelings. In a discussion the participants make up their minds; in behavioral contagion they are often just swept along.

This suggests the hypothesis that *if collective excitement is intense, speed of rumor construction is limited only by accessibility of communication channels.* As Greenberg (1964) points out in his study of local reactions to the Kennedy assassination, all communication channels were operating so that the speed with which any given individual got the news depended entirely upon physical proximity to some source. Since little time is expended for critical evaluation, rumors develop very quickly—"like wildfire." LeBon speaks of an excited crowd as being in a state of expectant attention, which renders suggestion easy; and Sighele (1891, pp. 25–26) also notes that as excitement is heightened, suggestibility increases, and messages pass instantly through a crowd and lead rapidly to concerted action. When a public is large and geographically dispersed, the pattern of development is more complex, but rapidity is nonetheless impressive. In the period immediately following the bubonic plague epidemic in fourteenth-century Europe, for example, rumors that a conspiracy of Jews to poison wells was responsible for the desolation were first recorded in southern France in 1348; within two years they had spread over the entire continent (Case 11). Considering the state of communication facilities at that time, this is quite remarkable. More detailed records are available on the "Great Fear" of the French Revolution, which spread through most of the country in sixteen days.

Case 46. THE GREAT FEAR. French peasants became apprehensive of brigands long before the revolution. As economic conditions deteriorated, many of the poor became vagabonds; they formed bands and went through the countryside, forcing themselves on farmers by threatening to burn their crops. As the price of bread rose steadily, marketplaces became scenes of disturbances, and grain shipments were sometimes halted and plundered. Agitation was pronounced in rural areas, where tithes and manorial dues were driving the peasants to desperation. People were afraid of each other. In the spring of 1789 beggars were everywhere. As the fear of brigands intensified, local officials allowed villagers to arm themselves for protection.

Fear of an aristocratic conspiracy developed initially in Paris. As the crown made various concessions to the Third Estate, many became convinced that the nobility would not give up its privileges without a fight. Noblemen would outwit the well-intentioned king, dissolve the National Assembly, take up arms, enlist brigands, and wage civil war. Foreign monarchs would also be called upon to help. Various rumors emerged and created the impression of a plot not only to prevent the Third Estate from liberating itself but to punish it by pillage and massacre. One rumor was that the Comte d'Artois had left the country to seek aid in Sardinia, Spain, Italy, and Austria. Another was that an English squadron was lying in wait off Brest and that the nobles of Brittany were preparing to throw open a port for it. Brigands were said to be operating in the suburbs of Paris. Parisians believed their city to be surrounded by royal troops and brigands. Barricades arose; gunsmiths were cleaned out; and some people went to the Bastille to get more guns.

From Paris fear of an aristocratic plot spread to the provinces, and the distrust of noblemen became fused with the fear of brigands. Wheat was ripe in July, and marauders were a source of special concern. Paris and the larger towns were expelling vagabonds, who then had to wander about. Periodic grain riots heightened the tension. What has been called the "Great Fear" was not so much a panic as an alarm and a state of mind. Everywhere preparations were made to resist; armed units were formed, and villages arranged for warnings and mutual aid. Once the cry went up, "The brigands are coming," these extraordinary preparations were activated. For example, in Guéret the alarm came at 5 P.M. on July 29. People buried their money; women rushed out of town to hide in the woods; and thousands of men armed with spades and pickaxes assembled to support the militia. Couriers were sent to neighboring towns for aid, and the baker was ordered to work all night to provide food for the allies. An estimated 8,000 to 10,000 men gathered, and all of them had to be fed and entertained before being sent home.

From July 20 to August 6 brigands seemed to be everywhere. The cry was heard throughout France. Marketplaces were the main center for news about uprisings in various locales. The alarm was also disseminated by fugitives justifying their own fright, postal carriers, servants sent to warn friends, and village officials arranging for defense. The terror spread quickly, for there were no means of verification. Indeed, anyone who expressed skepticism was himself suspected of being involved in the conspiracy. Once the fear had developed, the smallest incident served as confirmation. Many travelers were attacked, and a number of local uprisings resulted. In Franche-Comté peasants set fire to several chateaux. Nor did the terror disappear when the brigands failed to materialize. Other rumors followed of large contingents of brigands gathering at various places. As late as 1791 and 1793 the alarm was again sounded in various parts of France.

What was extraordinary about the "Great Fear" was the rapid diffusion of the alarm over such a great distance, at a time when communication systems were not too efficient. When it finally became apparent that brigands would not appear, everyone agreed that such a widespread delusion could not have developed without deliberate plotting. The revolutionaries accused the aristocrats of deliberately sowing anarchy to paralyze the National Assembly, and the aristocrats accused the bourgeoisie of getting peasants to take up arms against them. Charges were made that the terror was disseminated by mysterious messengers and that it broke out everywhere at the same time—on the same day and almost at the same hour. In one of the most detailed studies ever made of communication channels, Lefebvre (1932) demonstrates that this was not true. After a careful examination of local records throughout France he shows that there were six waves of alarms, each traceable to a local incident. The fear did not break out everywhere at once, and several parts of the country were not affected at all; it did not, for example, touch any area that had recently witnessed an insurrection. On July 23, in Franche-Comté a National Guard unit going to a manor for a search was mistaken for brigands. This resulted in a local uprising and also sent alarms as far as the shores of the Mediterranean, more than 200 miles away. On July 24, in southern Champagne some people coming out of a forest were mistaken for brigands, and this alarm spread as far south as Ain. On July 26, a group of harvesters were frightened by strangers emerging from a forest in Beauvais; this alarm spread northward to Flanders and southward to the Marne Valley. On July 28, an alarm was set off at Angoulême and spread through southwestern France down to the Pyrenees, almost 180 miles away. On July 29, a rumor that dragoons were arriving touched off a disturbance in Nantes that spread to Poitou. The last alarm originated near Montmirail forest, and it alerted the northwestern region to Normandy. Lefebvre's painstaking research gives some indication of how a widely dispersed public mobilizes to meet a common threat and of the manner in which communication channels both facilitate and limit the efforts of men to cope with danger.

A contrast between deliberative and extemporaneous modes of development is provided by cases in which the public is divided. Part of those concerned with an event retain a high degree of critical ability and examine both the source and the plausibility of reports; the other part consists of persons who are too excited and relax their usual standards of conduct.

Case 23. THE RUSSIAN INVASION. Soon after the outbreak of World War I, German and Russian forces clashed in Tannenberg, East Prussia. For the most part the countryside was empty, for people had to flee from villages and farms to get out of the way. There had been no official word of the outcome of the battle, and on the morning of September 6, 1914, a number of rumors developed among the Germans living in the area. In Osterode it was contended that the Russians had won.

"Do you know that the Russians are in Neidenburg again?"

"No."

"Yes, a hotel operator from Neidenburg who is living with us learned of it. The prefect of whom he had asked permission to return refused because the area was being evacuated again."

Similar conversations corroborated this tale. Shreds of conversations could be heard wherever one went—all on the same theme. One could feel a nervous tension in the air. At the railroad station a number of people asked the stationmaster if they could go to Neidenburg; they were surprised when he replied that they could. One officer asked some soldiers on the steps whence they had come.

"From Neidenburg, sir."

"Are the Russians really there again?"

The soldiers laughed. "No, sir. We were watching there yesterday evening."

The officer smiled and nodded, but in the crowd behind him someone remarked, "Indeed! While such as you watch, they come." Even the strength of the advancing troops was estimated.

In Hohenstein no newspapers were yet out, but everyone knew of the affair at Neidenburg. Passengers on a train from Osterode were asked whether it was true; there were conflicting opinions, but no one actually knew for certain. When an officer declared that German troops had been withdrawn from Neidenburg on the previous day, some argued that this was further indication that the Russians were coming. Others felt that the withdrawal of German troops gave no indication of where the Russians were. One city official who was skeptical about the rumor argued that the Russians would not return to a place where such a fierce battle had just been fought, but his reasoning was not convincing. As tension slowly developed, everyone seemed to get caught in it.

As a railroad repairman approached, he was asked, "Do the Russians come again?"

"Many disagree," he nodded, "but the Russians are coming nonetheless. They all say so. Over there they are already pushing along." He pointed with his finger to the horizon where a highway came over a hill. Dark spots were moving—refugee carts. When the refugees were questioned, they indicated that they had come from beyond Neidenburg.

"Have you seen the Russians?"

"If I had seen them, I would not be here. But they all say they are coming."

That evening the railroad station of Hohenstein was full of people with bundles, sacks, and pillows. Many were women and children. One officer protested, "You have all become insane. There is no report of danger."

The people listened wearily. "When everyone goes, I do not want to remain here alone." They boarded the trains. The evening newspaper contained a passionate protest from the commanding officer of the area against false rumors. In spite of threats of punishment the discussions went on. People were still convinced that the Russians were on their way.

On the following morning newspapers announced a victory by German forces in Masuria. Suddenly everyone was gay and laughing. All the refugee wagons disappeared, as did the rumors.

Once intense collective excitement has developed, precipitous action often follows. Sometimes this impulsive deed solves the problem; if so, tension is dissipated, and the people are able to return to their old way of life. In many instances, however, crowd behavior turns out to be inexpedient. When tensions have been dissipated by movement, people return to their old perspectives and begin to reevaluate their acts from a conventional standpoint. Upon learning of what they had done, they are often shocked, embarrassed, or filled with remorse. Such reactions imply that there had been a temporary change of standards. A search may begin for "agitators" thought to be responsible. If information on which they had acted turns out to have been erroneous, it is labeled as "rumor," condemned, and a search may begin for "rumor-mongers." As the contrast between the frightened German civilians and the soldiers who scoffed at them shows, behavioral contagion is based upon ephemeral standards; as soon as rapport is broken, the participants cease supporting one another and revert to their conventional outlook and roles.

The Successive Alteration of Standards

Observers sometimes designate as "suggestible" anyone who accepts a report that the observers themselves regard as ridiculous. It must be emphasized, therefore, that suggestibility can be measured only in terms of what the subject takes for granted. Every universe of discourse has shared assumptions concerning the nature of various objects and their relationships, concerning what is possible and not possible; all observations and reports are normally checked against these standards. A man may be regarded as suggestible only to the extent that he accepts uncritically materials that are *inconsistent with his own standards.* Thus, acceptance of a given report may constitute suggestibility for persons from one cultural background but not for those from another. Suggestibility, then, is not to be identified in terms of content that is implausible to an outside observer, but in terms of the way in which some item of information is handled—without questioning something which under other circumstances would be challenged. This implies some kind of breakdown of self-control. Individuals vary considerably in suggestibility, but there are some circumstances under which most human beings relax their critical ability; involvement in intense collective excitement is one of them. In our 60 case studies 246 rumors developed in publics marked by extreme tension; of these 32 were inconsistent with the cultural norms of the public and became the object of more detailed scrutiny. We may begin our study of this type of rumor construction by examining a concrete case.

Case 14. BELGIAN FRANCS-TIREURS. When the German Army invaded Belgium in 1914, it anticipated no resistance. The soldiers had been instructed that they were merely seeking passage through Belgium, that there was no quarrel with the Belgian people, and that they were to pay for anything that they took. But the Belgians elected to resist. Because of their numerical inferiority the Belgian High Command decided to engage in guerrilla operations rather than open battle. Thus, German troops, anticipating either friendly reception or orthodox battle, were shocked by these unexpected tactics. The hidden enemy emerged suddenly for surprise ambushes. Vanguard units were attacked, but by the time the main body appeared the attackers had disappeared; only a few civilians remained. Isolated detachments were fired upon; then the assailants would vanish into the countryside. The German soldiers, most of them seeing action for the first time, harassed by an elusive enemy and unforeseen tactics, became filled with apprehension.

The attacks were immediately labeled as treachery. Many soldiers recalled what they had read in their military manuals of harassment of the German Army by French *francs-tireurs* in 1870. They had also read of such unfair fighting by civilian raiders in popular literature. Even the costumes of Walloon peasants suggested the uniforms of *francs-tireurs,* and the attacks quickly became an obsession.

A widespread belief soon developed that the Belgian people, instigated by the Catholic clergy, had intervened in the operations between organized armies. Rumors arose of surprise attacks on isolated outposts, of spying by civilians, of disclosing troop positions to the enemy, of signaling from church belfries. Other rumors were of atrocities against injured and defenseless German soldiers—of poisoning, mutilation, and murder. Women and children were said to have joined in cutting off fingers, noses, and ears. Tearing out eyes was regarded as a favorite practice, and in one sector it was claimed that someone had a pail filled with German eyeballs.

Priests were charged with exhorting the people into crimes from the pulpit, promising them rewards in heaven. They also incited the populace to murder by offering to pay 50 francs for each head of a German soldier. Machine guns were mounted in the belfries of churches, manned by priests.

Rumors that started in the ranks of the invading army quickly spread through Germany, in spite of denials by German officers. They reached Germany through wounded soldiers and through letters and were seized by a populace eager for news. They were reinforced by charges of atrocities by German civilians who had just been repatriated from Belgium. Newspapers published many of these accounts, along with descriptions of similar tactics used by French guerrillas in 1870. This resulted in widespread attacks on Catholics throughout Germany, which soon became so serious that they constituted a threat to internal order. At this point the German General Staff made a serious effort to suppress the rumors, but the belief had already become fixed.

Even those who are anti-Catholic do not as a rule look upon priests as warriors in disguise nor upon peasants as creatures who collect eyeballs in buckets. A number of observers, among them Claparède (1928, p. 103) and Dauzat (1919, pp. 58–59), have noted that in the heat of excitement people accept statements without customary restraints and that rumors are formed from pieces of information that would ordinarily be rejected, or at least questioned. Standards of judgment do change under intense excitement, but *they are not entirely displaced*. As Prasad (1935) and Sinha (1952) point out, victims of disasters from different cutural backgrounds fear different objects and make quite different accusations. Sighele (1891, pp. 74–94) agrees with LeBon that individuals do things in crowds that they would otherwise not do; he disagrees, however, with LeBon's contention that the improbable does not exist for highly excited men. No individual is susceptible, even under hypnosis, to suggestions that are repulsive to him. With many students of hypnotism, then, Sighele insists that there are definite limits to suggestibility. Thus, in the 60 case studies 214 of the 246 rumors in situations marked by extreme excitement remain consistent with group presuppositions. Even in such contexts, then, men are not completely gullible. They are not suggestible in *any* direction, for responsiveness is selective even when critical ability is relaxed. Those who are excited and in rapport are suggestible only along lines consistent with their emotional dispositions. No matter how excited they may be, men in lynching mobs are not likely to be persuaded that pixies and elves are really behind their difficulties.

Some notion of what is involved may be gleaned from a brief glance at emotional behavior. In popular thinking emotion is often regarded as a "state" which in some way affects human conduct; it is often opposed to rationality and viewed as a primitive condition to which men occasionally revert. Although psychologists are by no means agreed on the nature of emotion, one widely respected view is that of Cannon (1929), who sees it as an attribute of interrupted behavior. When an on-going line of activity is interrupted, automatic reactions occur within the body—acceleration of heartbeat, constriction of blood vessels, inhibition of stomach contraction, increased liberation of sugar from the liver, increased secretion of adrenalin; all of these transformations may be regarded as an emergency mobilization of the organism for extraordinary effort to overcome the obstacle. "Feeling" is what one experiences subjectively as these physiological changes are taking place. One does not "cause" the other; both are components of a common action system. If emotion is an attribute of adjustive activity that has been thwarted, all emotional behavior, with the possible exception of anxiety, is oriented toward some goal: to attack a frustrating object, to flee from danger, to appropriate a desired object. It would follow that the perception, cognition, verbalization, and motor set of anyone emotionally aroused would be constricted, i.e., pointed in a limited direction.

Since verbalizations are a part of adjustive behavior, the gestures of men who are emotionally aroused tend to be consistent with their affective inclinations. Freud points out that emotional dispositions tend to gain expression in verbalizations, sometimes in camouflaged forms, even in situations that are less critical. Men who are more severely upset become preoccupied with objects thought to be related to their discomfort, and their speech deals almost exclusively with them. For example, Hanna Reitsch, describing the last days of Adolf Hitler in a bunker in surrounded and doomed Berlin, reports that the dictator spoke of little other than General Wenck's success in breaking through to the city from the south. He talked of strategy to anyone who was willing to listen (Work, 1946). Similarly, in his discussion of interethnic tension Bogardus (1928, p. 234) notes that almost any person in a moment of fear—fear for his own status or that of his group—may impetuously give vent to startling remarks; if he wishes to secure a hearing, he exaggerates or speaks with greater force than the circumstances warrant. In moments of anger wild accusations are made. The organization of communicative acts is definitely related to the emotional atmosphere in which one is involved, for people are more likely to say things that they feel when others are responsive and appreciative. As tension mounts, speech becomes more spontaneous. Expressive movements play an increasingly conspicuous part in social interaction; symbolic communication continues, but all gestural interchanges become subject to less conventional control.

All perception is selective, but under conditions of frustration perceptual selectivity becomes more acute. As collective excitement is heightened, it tends to limit even more the range of response and increase the intensity of the impulses not inhibited. When excited people are in rapport, their perspectives become similarly constricted so that the range of alternatives from which choices might be made is narrowed. Angry persons are sensitized primarily to possibilities for aggressive action, while those who are frightened concentrate upon avenues of escape. There is a progressive restriction of the perceptual field, attention becoming increasingly focused upon a limited number of objects—in the case of a lynching mob upon the culprit, his crime, his victim, and what ought to be done about him. Participants not only lose consciousness of themselves, but they perceive only a very limited aspect of their environment, overlooking completely other items that are inconsistent with their dispositions.

Responsiveness to communication content is also limited by emotion. The speech and expressive movements of others are perceived from a constricted standpoint. Studies by Murray (1933) and by Feshback and Singer (1957) show, for example, that maliciousness is imputed to others more frequently by persons who are frightened; and Weingarten (1949) has shown that the manner in which other people's problems are rated by consulting psychologists is related to the latter's own personal difficulties. Since men are highly responsive to remarks that support their inclinations, a person who is already frightened may be more sensitive to a horrifying report that would socialize his feelings. In the construction of rumors under such circumstances only those items consistent with the prevailing mood are seriously entertained. Selection is increasingly in terms of aroused feelings, and with mounting tension some rumors may be more felt than believed. Turner (1964, p. 391) suggests that participants in a crowd seek justifications for a course of action that is already under way; rumors often provide the "facts" that sanction what they want to do anyway. Thus, in February 1917, when Russian workers first revolted against the Czar, many soldiers wanted to join the rebels but were deterred by the possibility of having to fight against regiments loyal to the government. They became highly sensitized to reports of defection in other units, and as soon as word of such uprisings came, they joined the revolution (Case 50).

Since exclusive attention to some things tends to inhibit response to others, there is a definite limitation to the range and character of news to which excited people are responsive; remarks that are inconsistent with the developing mood are either overlooked or denounced and do not gain currency. Once a common mood is established, even reports from institutional channels tend to be rejected if they are inconsistent. In situations of intense collective excitement, then, some definitions may emerge that are not plausible by conventional standards. Such rumors invariably provide vehicles for the expression of prevailing moods, and it is in such contexts that one can speak most justifiably of wish-fulfillment. Where rumors are primarily expressive, items that are logically inconsistent may be entertained simultaneously. In some crises, as in the situation following the assassination of President Kennedy, contradictions in alleged fact may stand unnoticed side by side. LeBon (1911, pp. 86–91) contends that affective logic is different from rational logic; images are juxtaposed and associated rather than logically connected.

Through accentuated selectivity in perception each individual's outlook is constricted, and through selective communication this new perspective is reaffirmed and reinforced. A collective definition of the situation is constructed by individuals who perceive only a limited part of their environment and project on to it much that outsiders are not able to imagine. In a lynching mob, for example, the suspect comes to be visualized as an arrogant, vicious, rapacious monster whose continued existence is a threat to the community. This collective image, upon which the lynchers act, is built up in communication and is not an accurate depiction of the man—who is cowering in jail, completely bewildered by the turn of events. The definition is more a product of the participants' reactions to one another than of their response to the situation. The fact that *most* rumors in such contexts are plausible, however, suggests that excited men do not actually accept any proposal; what is involved is a temporary transformation of standards. Suggestibility is a response to a definition from a constricted standpoint. Attention has become focused upon a limited number of objects, and what seems odd from the standpoint of an outsider actually appears quite sensible from the standpoint of the actors. *Suggestibility involves use of a different frame of reference.* Even in cases of rumors that are more felt than believed, considerations of plausibility are not entirely absent. As the tension level of a public rises, then, there is a successive modification of perspectives. Standards of judgment are *temporarily* transformed; they do not disappear.

Once attention has been focused upon an object, the slightest cues are sufficient to set off action patterns that have been mobilized. Thus, in his discussion of the German soldiers invading Belgium, Langenhove (1916, pp. 118–214) notes that the men became obsessed with *francs-tireurs,* and every unusual event was explained within this framework. The manner in which fortuitous events are interpreted from a constricted standpoint and become rumors is more clearly revealed in the following case.

Case 45. THE MIRACLE AT SABANA GRANDE. On May 25, 1953, more than 100,000 people jammed into an area of about ten acres in Sabana Grande, Puerto Rico, to witness the appearance of a Virgin Saint. They had been coming for days—not only from all parts of Puerto Rico, but from Haiti, Cuba, and even as far away as New

York. Travel to Sabana Grande was tortuously slow. The area was blocked off, and those who drove had to leave their cars and walk about three miles. Some stayed with relatives in the area; others camped in the fields. They had to stand in line for hours to get water; latrine facilities were inadequate; and there was not enough food. On the appointed day special buses and trains brought in more people, and guards were posted to maintain order.

About a month before seven children had reported to their teacher that the Virgin had appeared at a well during recess. For a time she reappeared daily. Although interviews revealed some inconsistencies in their accounts, the mass media took up the event with enthusiasm. The mayor of a nearby town had an altar built at the well and organized worshipers into processions. Parents urged the children on, encouraging them to continue their visits with the Virgin. The Catholic Church was almost alone in opposition, but absence of formal sanction did not dampen enthusiasm. News coverage increased, and by May 26 a substantial portion of the space in *El Mundo* was devoted to the miracle. Radio station WKAQ made daily broadcasts from the site; on May 25 there were seven broadcasts.

The pilgrims gathered around the well, which was surrounded on three sides by steep hills. From time to time one of the children would pray, and others followed in unison. The children had indicated that the Virgin would appear at 11 A.M., and as the hour approached, tension grew. At 10:45 it started to rain, but the umbrellas that went up were quickly lowered, when word spread that the children had said no umbrellas were to be opened. Various individuals reported seeing miracles: the Virgin appeared silhouetted in the clouds or in rings of color around the sun. People who had been sick for years suddenly felt well. Just after 11 o'clock a cry went up that the Virgin, dressed in black, was walking down the west hill toward the well. Some of the devout were overwhelmed. Investigation revealed that this was just an old woman dressed in black, but it took some time for the gathering to accept this disappointment. Then another cry went up that the Virgin, dressed in white, was walking up the east hillside. Investigation revealed that this was an old man in a white shirt. The crowd started to dwindle about noon, but many kept watching for hours. Those who were closer to the well followed the prayers of the children. By 5 P.M., people began departing in droves.

Afterwards considerable disagreement arose over what had happened. Some who themselves had not seen the Virgin believed that the children had; they argued that only the pure and untainted could be so honored. Many who had been doubtful left as believers; they felt that something supernatural must have happened. Even if they had not seen the Virgin, they had spoken to others who claimed they had. Some had come seeking relief from illness, and they felt better. They saw others who claimed to have been cured. Unusual celestial movements were also cited. Of course there were some skeptics whose disbelief was confirmed. In the years that followed a steady steam of people visited Sabana Grande—about 200 on each weekday and about 3,000 on Sundays. They poured water from the well on afflicted parts, filled bottles for others close to them, picked up loose artifacts to take home as blessed objects, and donated money for beautification of the altars that had been erected there after the miracle.

Crowd behavior, then, can be understood only in terms of the constricted outlook that develops as the participants reinforce one another's emotional dispositions; their definition of the situation rests upon temporarily transformed standards. Innocent men may be hanged; popular heroes may be crushed by their admirers; men may trample one another in panic; in religious revivals the pious may yell, growl, bark, dance, and have visions. All this suggests the possibility that the action taken may dissipate tension but may be quite unconnected with the difficulties that had upset the various participants to begin with; indeed different individuals, frustrated in unlike ways, may become participants in the same mob. Psychoanalysts in particular, among them Fraiberg (1947) and Eissler (1949), have suggested that participants in riots may be restless for highly idiosyncratic reasons and may take advantage of the situation as a way of giving vent to impulses that would otherwise remain blocked. It is possible, then, that the victim of an aggressive mob is always a "scapegoat."

The relationship between emotional atmosphere and rumor content can be shown more easily in those situations in which the dominant mood changes. As the prevailing mood changes, rumors tend to be displaced. Mood is transformed when orientation to action changes. When men are already responsive to each other, this transformation may occur very quickly. Perception and communication are focused in another direction. The fear that prevails in a disaster, for example, may be transformed suddenly into anger; those who are blamed are then pursued with vengeance. When an economic boom ends, limitless optimism is replaced by gloom, embarrassment, and hostility against the promoters. Rumors then emerge about the whereabouts of those deemed responsible.

This approach to behavioral contagion is consistent with some of the findings in studies of hypnosis and suggestibility. Several students of hypnotism—among them Hull (1933), Kubie and Margolin (1944), and Arnold (1946)—regard it as heightened suggestibility, in which voluntary control over one's activities is transferred to symbolic communication from without; subjects are no longer able to distinguish between their own thoughts and the hypnotist's words. As the subject's usual frame of reference is contracted, he thinks as the hypnotist wants him to think, and he translates his imagination, which is being manipulated symbolically, into overt movements. Apparent contradictions in the literature on the hypnotic inducement of antisocial behavior are of particular relevance here. Early students of hypnotism, like Moll (1890, pp. 171–72), had indicated that subjects in a hypnotic trance who are asked to do something contrary to their moral standards decline the suggestion, wake up, or break into a hysterical outburst. Subsequent studies have shown that this is not always true; yet men who are suggestible are not completely uncritical. Modification of perspective may be cumulative so that proposals that would be declined at one stage in a serial process are subsequently accepted. For example, in a series of experiments Erickson (1939), Wells (1941), and Brenman (1942) showed how initially declined suggestions will subsequently be accepted if the subject's perspective is transformed. In one study a hypnotized subject who had refused to steal someone else's money was persuaded to take a dollar from the experimenter's pocket—after it had been suggested that the coat and dollar actually belonged to him. Similarly, a woman was induced to examine the contents of a strange purse after first being persuaded that it was her own; she refused to touch the purse, however, as long as she believed it belonged to someone else. Thus, evidence shows that conduct that would otherwise be inhibited can be induced only after the subject's outlook has been altered so that the act is defined in an acceptable light. In a study of prestige suggestion Asch (1948) shows that previously rejected statements that are then attributed to authors with great prestige are seen in an entirely different light; their subsequent acceptance is not gullibility but action in a different frame of reference. This is not to suggest that excited individuals are hypnotized; these findings only give some indication of how perspectives may be transformed and how quite different definitions may result. It gives some indication of how individuals might take seriously reports that they would otherwise reject. This also suggests that many "distortions" arise not so much from faulty memory as from changing outlook.

The transitory character of the altered standards can be seen readily not only by noting the disillusionment and embarrassment that so often follow the dissipation of tension but also by examining what happens in split publics in which each faction develops a somewhat different mood. Those who are not in sympathy with the developing mood of a crowd refuse to participate actively and sometimes remain in the vicinity to scoff at those who are involved. They are part of the public, but they define the situation quite differently.

Case 41. THE COMING DAY OF JUDGMENT. Restlessness was prevalent in New England during the early part of the nineteenth century. People appeared to be straining for ideals that were seemingly unattainable; new religious sects were springing up everywhere, for many were dissatisfied with the established churches. In the midst of this confusion one voice stood out. It was the voice of William Miller, who went from village to village with the strident warning: "Behold, the end of all things is at hand!" Some shrugged their shoulders and laughed derisively, but others went home troubled and nervous. Word spread that Prophet Miller had not only forecast the Second Coming of the Savior but also the destruction by fire of the earth and all the wicked that were on it.

Miller stated that the Second Advent was coming sometime between 1843 and 1844. No sooner had the year opened than fanaticism, which had been held more or less in abeyance, became widespread. Before this, the impending cataclysm had seemed far away, but now the days were slipping by, and those who had accepted the doctrine began to feel themselves on edge. Even those who had scoffed felt the effect of the constant reiteration that the end of all things was at hand. Newspapers were full of it, and people talked of little else. The orthodox clergy was almost without influence, and wherever Miller and his co-workers held meetings, huge crowds gathered, including many from denominations opposing Miller. As the excitement increased, Miller was attacked from all sides by his opponents, and he was besieged by requests from his impatient followers to name the date on which the end was to come. The indefiniteness of his prophecy in giving it a year in which to fulfil itself made them restive.

The tension was too much for Miller, and he collapsed while lecturing near Saratoga Springs. When there was some danger of his dying before the appointed time, some of his followers began to waver. At this critical moment an unexpected event turned the tide. At noon, when the sun was shining brightly, a great rival light appeared in the sky. People ran out of their houses to look at it, and pedestrians standing in the streets gazed upward in amazement. Frightened people in cities, towns, and secluded hamlets stared at the celestial stranger. It was a comet—the great comet of 1843!

Its appearance created a sensation everywhere, but the exaltation of Miller's followers knew no bounds. Here, indeed, was a sign to justify their confidence in the approaching end of the world. Camp meetings began. The general view developed that the end would come in April. Miller had said nothing, but rumors were that it would come before the beginning of May. As the various days believed to be the last approached, believers made their preparations. Some packed all their valuables and strapped them on to themselves. Others contemptuously cast away all their worldly goods; businesses were sold or given away. A few could no longer stand the strain of hourly watching for the end and became insane. As the summer drew to a close without any sign of the end, there was again a fluttering of doubt and hesitation. Then, someone recalled that as far back as 1839 Miller had stated that he was not positive that the event would occur during the Christian year of

1843 and that he would claim the entire Jewish year—carrying the prophecy forward to March 21, 1844.

As the months passed, voices of the Millerites could be heard singing and shouting and exhorting one another to stand firm. Winter passed. At last, as the appointed day in March approached, the exaltation grew feverish. The last day came, and nothing happened! Hour after hour groups of men, women, and children stood gazing toward the clouds, looking for a sign of the coming end. Some were terror-stricken; others had worked themselves into a frenzy; some were too dazed to speak. But the dawn of March 22 came. Even among the faithful there were many who inwardly rejoiced. However, to many others realization of a cold fact was overwhelming. How could they face their neighbors?

Miller himself held to his faith, although he confessed publicly that he had made an error in calculation. Other leaders of the movement sought to place the blame for miscalculation elsewhere. The followers had to run a gauntlet of merciless ridicule. A few continued to hold fast to the belief that the day was not far off, but most of them fell out of the movement.

Rumors are both instruments and products in the evolution of emotional atmospheres. They are instrumental in that they constitute part of the communicative activity which makes possible the mutual reinforcement of excitement. They are products of the common mood in that the organization of component communicative acts is circumscribed by the developing atmosphere, and many of the items would not have been taken seriously were it not for the special sensitivities arising in the heat of excitement. Often the accuracy of rumors that are strongly felt is not challenged. Especially in rumors among highly excited men many of the component acts may be more cathartic than instrumental. What is important about these expressive remarks is that they contribute to the formation of an emotional atmosphere, even if they themselves are not very instructive. Verbalizations that are cathartic, then, are important in that they contribute to the transformation of perspectives, which makes possible subsequent suggestibility to other reports. Such rumors are themselves contagious transactions that play a vital part in the development of other forms of crowd behavior.

Personal Equation in the Rumor Process

Rumor is a collective transaction, which is made up of the interrelated activities of individuals who constitute a public. The contributions made by each participant, while segments of a larger unit, are at the same time episodes in the lives of separate human beings. Although the transaction as a whole cannot be explained adequately in terms of the motives and traits of the participants, there is little doubt that the course of development of each rumor is significantly affected by the distinctive qualities of some of them. As Ramnoux (1948) shows in his detailed protocols of a serially transmitted story, the inventive genius of a single strategically located individual can under some circumstances alter the course of development. A question may therefore be raised as to the conditions under which individuals can and cannot significantly intervene in the course of events, even though they are all subject to some kind of social control.

Degree of personal involvement in an event varies from individual to individual, and this results in differential participation in rumor construction. Some regard themselves only as observers; others conceive of themselves as active participants; still others are observers, whose interests are closely allied with those of an active participant. In the previously cited study of a rumor in a housing project of the Communist affiliation of a woman trying to organize a nursery school, Festinger and his associates (1948) found that those who felt their status threatened by the proposed school were more enthusiastic supporters of the rumor that disrupted the program. In his study of a rumor in a rural Canadian community that a stranger renting a cabin there was a German spy, Doob (1941) found that the four most active participants were a woman who had wanted to rent her cabin to the stranger and had been turned down, a man who had originally defended the stranger and had gotten into trouble for it, a man with a long-standing feud with the family supplying dairy products to the stranger, and a person reputed to be suspicious of everyone and locally labeled as "queer."

Agitators in lynching mobs are often persons, such as friends and relatives of the victim, who are especially concerned lest the alleged offender escape punishment. Those who would benefit by the adoption of some program of action—the election of an official, the declaration of war, the passage of an ordinance—tend to be more receptive to reports that support their contention. This does not mean, however, that deliberate manipulation is involved; in most cases participation is more a matter of selective attention. Sometimes interests are unconscious; persons who feel guilty or frightened are simply more responsive to reports that tend to justify their feeling. Thus, Allport and Lepkin (1945) show that the rumors of waste and special privilege that developed on the American home front during World War II were taken more seriously by those who felt the rationing program to be unfair or unnecessary and who had no close friends or relatives in the war zone.

There has been much speculation about personality traits that would affect participation in rumor construction. Since rumor is often condemned as pathological, it is not surprising that psychiatrists and psychologists have generally cited neurotic traits; the most commonly assigned are the various forms of compensation for a low level of self-esteem. Hart (1916, pp. 19–23) cites the desire of an insecure person to figure as one of distinction, to occupy the center of the stage, to have the admiration of his neighbors as a source of important news. Several others have pointed to the temporary prestige enjoyed by those having "inside information"; these include LaPiere (1938, pp. 177–78), Rose (1940), Knapp (1944), and Peterson and Gist (1951, p. 166). Indeed, these writers point out that the desire to be the center of attention may be so great that one may forget details that make a rumor dubious and emphasize those that make it seem more plausible. This point, of course, has been made by many others. Centuries before, Jean de la Bruyère wrote of the tendency on the part of vain persons to lie and exaggerate rather than to appear ignorant and to quote false authorities when their statements are challenged.

Other individuals are believed to be acting altruistically; when confronted with difficulties, they willingly share whatever they have, including news, with others suffering the same fate. Especially in disasters certain individuals devote considerable time and effort, sometimes at great personal cost, to assist others (Fritz and Williams,

1957; Deutscher and New, 1961). In their careful study of a rumor of a broken dam that threatened new perils to a recently flooded New York community, Danzig, Thayer, and Galanter (1958) indicate that a number of individuals took it upon themselves to broadcast warnings to anyone within range. In a spirit of mutual friendship such persons try to provide much needed information. It has also been suggested that persons who are overly helpful may be insecure, badly in need of the sense of appreciation that ostentatious service will bring.

Individuals differ considerably in critical ability. Some persons are able to withstand much emotional pressure before breaking, being able to retain self-control even in the face of acute danger or pain. Others lose their critical ability at the slightest provocation and are labeled by their acquaintances as "hysterical." The threshold apparently varies with certain personality traits. Janis (1954), for example, reports that compliant persons are generally more suggestible than others; conformists refrain from raising objections and sometimes acquiesce even when they are still in doubt. McDavid (1959) compared high school students who were "source-oriented" with those who were "message-oriented" in their habitual reaction to disagreement. In an experiment in which they were presented with beliefs that contradicted their own, he found that message-oriented subjects are less susceptible to influence and under pressure tended to compromise with an unacceptable position rather than agree with it. Some studies suggest that the threshold may depend upon special knowledge in the area and upon self-confidence. Studies of collective hysteria by Cantril (1940, pp. 112–19) and D. M. Johnson (1945) show that persons with low income and low education tend to be more suggestible. Education may become a crucial variable in some situations in that it provides a better basis for judgment. When confronted with reports of an invasion from Mars or of a phantom anesthetist, a better understanding of astronomy, chemistry, and popular psychiatry renders comprehensible things that remain strange to the uneducated. Kelman (1950) produced differential insecurity by telling one group of subjects that most of their judgments on a previous exercise were correct and another group that they were incorrect. Then he found that individuals who had succeeded were less influenced by a "planted" confederate in their judgments than those who had failed. The manner in which a given individual contributes to the formation of a rumor depends upon his threshold of critical ability, which rests both on his knowledge and his excitability.

Granted that individuals exist in all publics who because of interests or traits are easily attracted to rumor construction, the extent to which they can actually do as they wish is limited. Communication, after all, is subject to social control. Whether or not a person will express his personal views and whether or not he will be heard depends upon the context. In stable situations anyone who speaks out of line is not taken seriously; agitators are not effective, and if they persist, they may be punished. Thus, *the extent to which any individual can effectively intervene and alter the course of events is related inversely to the degree of formalization of the transaction.* The more highly structured the activity, the fewer opportunities for individual deviations. As conventional norms are relaxed, however, various individuals become more susceptible to influence, and greater opportunities arise for exercising some measure of leadership. When news is disseminated by formal channels, competing accounts will not be seriously entertained. When news is formed through auxiliary channels, certain persons who occupy key roles in established networks are in a position to affect content. When formalization is almost absent, when news is improvised in spontaneously formed channels, each individual has a much greater opportunity to contribute according to his personal interests.

In unstructured situations men are thrown more on their own resources, and opportunities arise for individuals to assert themselves. Since participants are no longer bound by customary obligations, the personal interests of each, including those normally inhibited, may be expressed more openly. Precisely because established procedures are inoperative, the special interests of a few persuasive individuals who happen to be present can exert a disproportionate influence over the course of events. In the heat of intense excitement, even persons who are generally dismissed as inconsequential may assume temporary positions of leadership. But opportunities for manipulation are not unlimited. Even an excited agitator is a product of the crowd. As Rossi (1902) emphasizes, many leaders of mobs do not even know that they are leaders; they become the focus of attention because they happen to articulate effectively the views shared by others. Thus, control of a crowd is circular; an individual who is stimulated by the others assumes leadership and in turn heightens their excitement.

When collective excitement is moderate, much depends upon the individuals who enact central *roles* in auxiliary channels. In critical deliberation, then, in addition to the conditions cited in Chapter 3, the extent to which wish-fulfillment becomes incorporated into rumor content depends upon *whose* critical ability is relaxed. Most important is the personality of the decision-maker. The aggressiveness of protagonists also makes a difference, as does the critical ability of messengers, interpreters, and skeptics. Auditors least affect the direction of a transaction, but they often provide brakes. Sometimes the mere presence of an easily excitable person at a crucial point of contact gives impetus to an interpretation that would not have developed without him. Conversely, the presence of a rigidly conventional person in that role may lead others to become ashamed of themselves and terminate any budding rumor. Those who are regarded as having special competence on the subject under consideration become central in deliberation, for they are continually consulted, and their personality traits assume disproportionate importance. If pivotal personnel in a communication network are unable to withstand tension, the entire public may be converted quickly into a crowd. As collective excitement is intensified, auxiliary channels break down, and roles become progressively less distinguishable. As rumor construction becomes more extemporaneous, the course of development depends increasingly upon the *proportion* of individuals who manage to retain some measure of self-control.

Consequences of Rumor-Consciousness

From the discussion thus far it becomes apparent that the manner in which rumors are constructed tends to vary with intensity of collective excitement. When tension is moderate, most participants tend to be critical of both source and content. As the tension level rises, an increasing proportion become less critical until standards are temporarily transformed. These observations suggest the hypothesis that degree of formalization of the communicative activities through which rumors are formed is inversely related to intensity of collective excitement in the public. Although this generalization holds in most cases, there are some notable exceptions. Intense excitement was generated in 36 of the 60 cases, but in several of these the participants on the whole did not become suggestible.

In disasters, when survival may depend upon accurate intelligence, most individuals struggle to retain their critical ability, even when many others around them are becoming hysterical. Since institutional channels have been impaired or destroyed, they must accept information from wherever it comes, but they evaluate it carefully. To the extent that it is possible, they check with those who are in a position to know. In the previously cited study of the rumor of a broken dam in Port Jervis, New York, Danzig, Thayer, and Galanter (1958, pp. 33–36) found that 85.9 per cent of those interviewed took the rumor seriously—61.5 per cent did not doubt its accuracy; yet 42.3 per cent made some attempt to check. In his study of the Orson Welles broadcast on Halloween night of 1938, Cantril (1940, pp. 111–24) found that the basic difference between those who fled the invaders from Mars and those who did not was that the latter checked with other sources or through internal evidence ascertained that the broadcast was just a play. The percentage of respondents who reported checking was comparable to that at Port Jervis.

In conflict situations it is foolhardy to underestimate one's opponents, and rumors affecting strategy are evaluated critically. Whenever there is opposition of interest, men are more likely to retain their critical ability. Especially when they realize that their opponent's success would mean severe loss to themselves, men on each side struggle to retain their self-control, even when collective excitement becomes intense. Students of military psychology have characterized the typical outlook of front-line troops as one of "defensive pessimism"; actually this is nothing more than the kind of realism that makes survival on a battlefield possible. Kelly and Rossman (1944) point out that American infantrymen in World War II were for the most part wary of rumors; they considered each one seriously, however, for they realized that their life might depend upon it. Thus, in the heat of combat soldiers make hostile, salacious, and derogatory remarks about their foes, but privately they retain a healthy respect for their adversaries. Reports of enemy activities tend to be evaluated carefully.

Whenever men become conscious of the possibility of being duped, they take special precautions to defend themselves against suggestibility. Explicit awareness of the importance of accuracy develops, for it is recognized that a mistake could be costly. Men in such contexts become acutely self-conscious. They warn one another of the danger of "rumors." Sometimes they become hypercritical, overly careful, examining each step they propose to take. Every effort is made to obtain the most reliable information, and when news is not available from institutional channels, they put off their decisions until the last possible moment, still hoping for some kind of confirmation.

The generalization must therefore be qualified. If a substantial portion of those who make up a public feels high ego-involvement in an event, attention becomes focused upon accuracy, and interaction is likely to remain critical even when collective excitement is intensified. Critical ability, of course, is an attribute of individual behavior, and in such situations each participant undergoes an internal struggle between his impulses and the dictates of his judgment. Whether or not a given instance of rumor formation remains deliberative depends upon the proportion of participants who refuse to relax their standards and upon the roles that they happen to enact. Along a similar vein Allport and Postman (1947, pp. 35–36) suggest that individuals who are "rumor wise," who have some understanding of the phenomenon, are less likely to participate. Chorus (1953) suggests a revision of their formula to read. $R \sim i \times a \times 1/c$, where c stands for critical ability. As critical ability becomes greater, the fraction gets smaller, and there is less rumor. Since these writers conceive of rumor as a process of distortion, presumably they are referring to uncritical participation.

Summary and Conclusion

Two polar types of rumor formation have been devised. If unsatisfied demand for news is moderate, auxiliary channels remain intact, and rumor construction is deliberate and subject to informal social control. Such rumors are plausible, consistent with cultural axioms. If unsatisfied demand for news is excessive, collective excitement becomes intense, and rumor construction occurs extemporaneously through spontaneously formed channels. Except where conscious awareness develops of the danger of being duped, participants become suggestible. The extent to which any given instance of rumor construction will approximate one of these poles depends upon the extent to which the participants retain their critical ability. When collective excitement is moderate, the degree to which informal social control is relaxed depends upon the critical ability of those performing essential roles in auxiliary channels. As tension reaches a higher level of intensity, these channels break down, and the extent to which rumor construction becomes subject to behavioral contagion depends upon the percentage of participants who relax their self-control.

It would appear, then, that LeBon's thesis needs qualification. Several of his critics—among them Miceli (1899), Blondel (1928, pp. 205–06), Lefebvre (1934), and Miotto (1937, pp. 24–25, 59–62)—have stressed that human beings are social products. Even in the heat of excitement they reflect with social tools, though perhaps from a standpoint somewhat different from that of persons who remain unmoved.

The record shows that most rumors are consistent with cultural axioms. Except under intense excitement, rumor content tends to be limited by considerations of plausibility. One implication of this is that social reconstruction is generally circumscribed by the culture of the group, even when ingenious individuals are present who might invent other solutions. Since implausible proposals arising in problematic situations are selectively eliminated, what can be seriously entertained is largely limited by the alternatives that appear sensible in terms of what is already taken for granted. As Toch (1955) points out, however, such perceptual defenses do not operate in severe crises, where drastic ideological reevaluations sometimes occur from an examination of ideas that would otherwise remain unnoticed. Lasting social changes have emerged among persons initially united in crowds; labor unions have developed from strike violence, and religious denominations have arisen from dancing manias. Situations marked by intense tension, then, are potential crucibles for the development of drastically different beliefs; in this sense collective excitement is one of the gateways to social change.

5
THE FORMATION OF POPULAR BELIEFS

Napoleon is said to have dismissed history as a "pack of lies agreed upon," and Fontenelle wrote of history as a "fable" on which there was accord. These views, of course, represent cynical extremes. But any professional historian knows that much of historical knowledge, though presumed to be accurate, is actually unverified. Even the new "scientific" history, based exclusively on written documents, contains much that is suspect; for as anyone who has participated in the preparation of official reports knows, the fact that a statement is written does not necessarily mean that it is true. The distant past is irretrievably gone, and in the absence of eyewitnesses to cross-examine or a device like H. G. Wells's time machine, there is no way of checking the accuracy of the best available documents that remain. Our conception of what happened in the past, then, is largely a matter of consensus—consensus among the experts. History is assumed to be true, when it is only the best estimate that is available.

The question of accuracy, both of history and of current testimony, is important because men act on the basis of their beliefs. The interest of scholars, of publicists, and of men of affairs in rumor is aroused primarily by their concern with the consequences of collective definitions. In studying this problem care must be taken to avoid the difficulties inherent in a mechanical treatment of "effects," which tends to oversimplify complex processes. The problem may be re-phrased: how do rumors enter into the attempts of men to cope with the problematic situations in which they emerge? How do they enter into the process of mobilizing for joint activity? There is also a question of further consequences. Some rumors persist and become incorporated into popular lore; others are dismissed as nonsense as soon as collective excitement is dissipated. What are the conditions under which rumors persist?

Termination of the Rumor Process

The concept of *public opinion* refers to that amorphous, ill-defined something that politicians and administrators must always take into account, for a miscalculation of it could result in serious repercussions. It refers to the prevailing frame of mind of those who constitute a public. German scholars in particular have distinguished between public opinion and openly expressed opinion, viewing the former as a deep, pervasive force. W. Bauer (1933) sees it as an articulation of judgments and desires, an integration and momentary crystallization of the sporadic sentiments and loyalties of a public. Prevailing stance implies that the view is not unanimous; indeed, that opinions exist at all means that there is some disagreement, that options are being entertained, that the question is not settled. Public opinion may be contrasted with culture, a set of beliefs so well established as to be taken for granted; it arises only when alternative views are possible, when something is not fixed in custom, and it exists only until a new set of beliefs is established through discussion. The event which becomes the focus of attention is symbolized and eventually defined within a cultural framework, but public opinion itself must be distinguished from culture (Lee, 1945). Public opinion may be regarded as one phase in the mobilization of a public for action. Once an issue is settled, procedure is established, and it becomes a part of culture and is no longer subject to discussion (Park, 1940).

In the classic literature on public opinion emphasis is placed upon the way in which it is shaped and reshaped in discussion. Bryce (1888, pp. 3–170) notes that whenever an unusual event is reported, it arouses expectations of things to follow; those who are concerned talk to their associates, and their views begin to crystallize in this interchange. Although each may think that his opinion is his own, he holds it because of his acquaintances. Tarde (1901, pp. 63–158) also stresses the importance of conversation. In the course of talking to each other vague dispositions crystallize into specific attitudes and acts. Although the media of mass communication are important sources of information, public opinion is always shaped in local discussions. Where persons who have somewhat different conceptions of what ought to be done compare their views in an effort to work out some kind of reasonable program for meeting the situation, sharp disagreements sometimes arise. Sometimes differences arise because some persons are not convinced; they simply require persuading (W. Bauer, 1914, pp. 157–89). Thus, the formation of public opinion is a phase of collective problem-solving, and rumors often play an important part in it.

Since rumor is an interpretive transaction made up of communicative acts, it is terminated when those in a public stop talking and thinking about the common object of attention. Since rumors emerge as part of the efforts of men to cope with a problematic situation, the activity ceases when something has been done about the problem; this does not necessarily mean, however, that the problem must be successfully resolved. Rumors may be terminated in several ways, but the problem of termination has attracted the attention of relatively few investigators. Data are more difficult to collect, for most observers turn to other matters during this phase of development.

As Dauzat (1919), Fechter (1934), Rose (1940), and Caplow (1947) point out, rumor construction may be terminated by verification or refutation from formal news channels. Where faith in institutional channels is high, people rely on rumors only because of insufficient news from more trusted sources. Especially where intense collective excitement has developed over some unusual event, tension drops suddenly when an acceptable explanation is provided in institutional channels. Conventional perspectives are quickly restored. In the previously mentioned windshield-pitting incident in Seattle, for example, publication of a scientific explanation—that cenospheres, formed by improper combustion of bituminous coal, were common in Seattle—made many realize that in their excitement they had looked *at* their windshields rather than *through* them and had noticed "pits" that had always been there. Interest suddenly dissolved (Medalia and Larsen, 1958). If a rumor is confirmed, it is regarded as a good guess; in some cases it is simply relabeled "news." If a rumor is contradicted, it is dismissed as a "rumor." If certain individuals had been prominent in its development, they may be subjected to criticism. Among the rumors already considered that were terminated in this manner are the belief that the Halifax explosion had resulted from a German attack (Case 15), the fear of German civilians that the Russian Army was invading East Prussia (Case 23), and the rumor in Port Jervis about the broken dam (Case 39). In such instances all subsequent activity is predicted upon the authoritative definition.

Where institutional channels are not completely trusted, however, rumors may persist even after formal denials, at least in part of the public. This is especially true when the rumors appear more plausible than the official announcement. When Crown Prince Rudolph of the Hapsburg monarchy and a young woman were found dead in a hunting lodge in Mayerling in 1889, for example, many rumors emerged of the details: Rudolph had been murdered by a jealous husband; he had killed his mistress by accident and then had turned upon himself in remorse; the woman had castrated Rudolph while he slept, and he had then strangled her and shot himself. The government issued an official explanation; since it was assumed that the monarchy would suppress information on such delicate matters, however, speculation continued—and indeed has still not ended (Case 3). Similarly, the previously mentioned rumors on the disaster at Pearl Harbor were not terminated by official denials.

Case 18. THE ATTACK ON PEARL HARBOR. On December 7, 1941, units of the Japanese Navy virtually destroyed the military and naval effectiveness of Pearl Harbor. In an air attack that lasted from 7:55 to 9:45 A.M. the U.S. Navy suffered one of its most disastrous losses, and almost 3,000 defenders were killed. At 11:42 A.M. the Governor read a Proclamation of Emergency over the radio, which was then silenced on military orders to prevent enemy planes from bearing in on the stations. Thus, in the midst of consternation and confusion throughout the islands no official news was available. Police and military authorities were besieged by telephone calls asking about hundreds of rumors.

Military personnel knew for certain only that they were under enemy attack. Some were cut off from their command posts and had to act on their own. Those who were in radio contact were almost as confused, for those sending the messages were also confronted with rumors: the Japanese were landing on Diamond Head; they were invading from the north; forty transports had been sighted off Barbers Point; sampans were landing enemy troops at the Navy Ammunition Depot; paratroopers were landing at Nanakuli Beach. Defenses had to be improvised, and sporadic shooting broke out at various points.

The attack had obviously been well planned. How had the enemy been able to plan so carefully, catching the entire area off guard? Where had he gotten the detailed information necessary to execute it with such precision? The finger pointed directly at Hawaii's 160,-000 residents of Japanese ancestry, and hundreds of rumors arose implicating them. Among the most widespread of these rumors were: a McKinley High School ring was found on the body of a Japanese flier shot down over Honolulu; the water supply had been poisoned by the local Japanese; Japanese plantation workers had cut arrows pointing to Pearl Harbor in the cane fields of Oahu; the local Japanese had been notified of the time of attack by an advertisement in a Honolulu newspaper on December 6; Nisei armed with machine guns drove up to the main gate at Pearl Harbor in trucks and as the side panels dropped off shot down marines; automobiles driven by local Japanese blocked the roads from Honolulu to Pearl Harbor; Japanese residents waved their kimonos at the pilots and signaled to them; some local men were dressed in Japanese Army uniforms during the attack.

Residents in the Japanese communities realized in the most acute way the seriousness of their situation. Those who were members of military or police units reported for duty; some were able to participate actively in defending the islands and in maintaining order, but others were met with suspicion. Rumors developed among the Japanese that the U.S. Army planned to kill everyone of Japanese ancestry in Hawaii. Many fully expected retaliation from outraged Americans and were immobilized with fear.

Rumors of the complicity of local Japanese were immediately denied by military and civilian officials, and the denials were apparently accepted by most Hawaiians. On the mainland, however, the tales persisted; they were disseminated in newspapers and magazines and even incorporated into motion pictures, such as *Air Force*. That many persons of Japanese ancestry had committed acts of treachery during the attack on Pearl Harbor became a widely accepted belief and figured prominently in demands for their evacuation from the Pacific Coast.

The rumors of treason at Pearl Harbor persisted even though they had been denied by the Chief of Police of Honolulu, by the Director of the F.B.I., and by the Secretary of War. This did not reflect lack of faith in the United States government. Many believed that the truth was being suppressed by wartime censorship; others did not notice the official denials, which did not receive the same publicity as the sensational charges. Similarly, many Americans have not accepted the findings of the Warren Commission on the Kennedy assassination.

Even when a denial from institutional channels is accepted, rumors may still persist. Because of their dramatic character many items that become rumors are remembered, often for many years. After some time has passed, however, the various accounts become somewhat blurred in memory. Men cannot always remember the sources of vaguely recalled items; they forget that some rumors had been disqualified, recalling only that they had "heard" something. The information may therefore enter into the definition of subsequent situations. In a succession of experiments on the "sleeper effect" Hovland and his associates (1949, 1953) have shown that with the passage of time people tend to dissociate communication content from their evaluation of sources. Acceptance of material from channels that had once been suspected rises with time, just as belief in reports from sources that had originally been rated high in credibility often decreases. Especially in the absence of any clear necessity of acting on the basis of accurate definitions, the distinction becomes hazy, details are blurred, and ambiguous impressions emerge. Other studies have shown that the precautionary phrase "it is rumored" is not a particularly effective warning. Kirkpatrick (1932) found that the expression tends to drop out in serial transmission. G. H. Smith (1947) confronted three groups of subjects with identical statements about Russia, one set labeled as "rumor," another as "fact," and the third without any label. He found that in general the "fact" label tended to swing subjects in the direction of greater belief; and the "rumor" label, toward somewhat less belief. Subjects who had definite attitudes for or against Russia, however, scored consistently in the direction of their inclinations, regardless of label. DeFleur (1962, p. 67) found that people often attributed a message dropped in airborne leaflets to a plausible source, claiming that they had learned of it from the radio, newspaper, or some other source in which it might have been expected. Thus, rumors that have been rejected may still leave a residue. Furthermore, emotional reactions to objects defined in rumors may persist even after the rumor itself has been forgotten; this may account for the origin of some prejudices.

When situations marked by intense collective excitement have run their course, tension is dissipated and rumors just disappear even when no official announcement is made. When conventional perspectives are restored, many rumors appear ridiculous to the participants themselves. During the first month of World War I, for example, rumors became current throughout England that Russian troops from Archangel were passing through the isles on their way to the Western front. In every part of the country people claimed that they had actually seen the Russians. They were riding in trains with the blinds down—to hide from German spies. They had been observed on station platforms, stamping the snow off their boots. At Carlisle and at Berwick-on-Tweed they were reported to have called hoarsely for vodka. In Durham they were said to have jammed the penny-in-the-slot machine with a ruble. The number of soldiers varied with each report, but hundreds of trains were said to be speeding night and day from northern Scotland, bringing the mighty Russian Army. The people looked hopefully toward an early termination of hostilities, as soon as such reinforcements landed in France. As the initial tension was dissipated and as they settled down to the new wartime routine, more and more people began to appreciate the absurdity of these rumors (Case 24). In the previously mentioned spy scare in a rural Canadian community the rumor disappeared when residents began to wonder why Hitler would pay a man to spend three months in a place where all vital information could be obtained in a few hours (Doob, 1941). As D. M. Johnson (1945) suggests, outbursts of collective hysteria tend to be self-limiting in that the bizarre details that capture public imagination during the height of the episode become rather ludicrous when examined with more leisure.

Where interest in an event is moderate, rumors disappear as the public is dissolved. People simply become preoccupied with other matters. In situations in which no immediate action is necessary, lengthy discussions may occur among those who are disagreed on appropriate lines of conduct. Issues may not be resolved in such speculation and comment, and different individuals merely form separate opinions. Then, concern over the event is displaced by new interests.

Case 55. RECEPTION OF ZUNI VETERANS. Unlike some other Indian tribes, the Zuni were not enthusiastic supporters of American participation in World War II, feeling that a fight among white men was none of their concern. They did their best to avoid military conscription, often seeking exemptions on religious grounds. Nonetheless, from February 1941 to March 1946, 213 Zuni men were drafted.

When they returned after the war, they were not welcomed home as conquering heroes. Instead, they were forced to undergo a cleansing ceremony before they could once again participate in community life. A rumor developed that terminal leave pay was another way of getting Zuni into debt to the U. S. Government, a debt that would have to be repaid by further military service. When one of the veterans tried to organize an American Legion post, a rumor arose that he was planning to use the dues collected for his personal ends. After a few meetings, indifferently attended, the project was dropped. For a time there was much drunkenness among discontented veterans, and the more "progressive" among them left the pueblo.

When a public is made up of factions with conflicting interests, cleavages may be intensified through communication, as each side comes to appreciate more fully how the purposes of the opposition encroach upon its interests. If some kind of compromise arrangement is not negotiated, the confusion that follows may be so great that the public is immobilized. If some kind of action is felt to be necessary, violence may ensue. The following case is an episode in a period of sustained tension that led eventually to the establishment of a military dictatorship.

Case. 57. THE BOGOTÁ RIOT. In the 1946 election the Liberal party, which had been in power in Colombia since 1930, was split by two candidates—Jorge Gaitán, champion of the masses who demanded radical reforms, and Gabriel Turbay, who was more moderate. As a result Mariona Ospina Pérez, the Conservative candidate, was able to win the presidency with only 42 per cent of the votes. The widespread discontent that had developed in Colombia in the postwar years was aggravated. Violence broke out in rural areas, where Liberal and Conservative partisans engaged in street fighting. At first the police were impartial, but eventually they became an arm of the Conservative party; bands of dispossessed Liberals gathered in the hills to fight back. Many hungry, homeless refugees gathered in Bogotá, but the government did nothing to help them; the dispossessed pinned their hopes on Gaitán. On February 7, 1948, an estimated 100,000 gathered at the main square in Bogotá for a protest demonstration at which Gaitán was the main speaker.

The real power in the Conservative party was Laureano Gomez, who had openly supported Fascism in the legislature and in his newspaper, El Siglo. Ospina Pérez had been his choice. In selecting delegates to the ninth Inter-American Conference, which was to meet in Bogotá in April 1948, the president passed over Gaitán. The snub led to much grumbling, for it was interpreted as a gesture of contempt; just before the Conference began a rumor developed that an attempt would be made on the life of George C. Marshall, the American Secretary of State. When the president appointed Gomez to preside over the Conference, many in the Liberal party were enraged.

On April 9, Gaitán was shot to death as he was having lunch in a downtown restaurant. The assassin was immediately beaten to death by infuriated bystanders. As word of the assassination spread through the city a rumor formed simultaneously that Gomez had ordered the killing. Mobs formed quickly; one attacked the office of *El Siglo,* and another went to the Gomez residence. Finding him gone, it burned down his house. With Gaitán's killer dead and Gomez beyond reach, the mob turned to looting and destruction. Crying "death to assassins," "Death to Gomez," "Down with the Conference," or "Viva revolution," the rioters raged through Bogotá, falling upon anything identified with the Conservative party. Buildings were razed; cars and streetcars were burned; windows were smashed and stores looted. Then another rumor shot through the crowd: priests were firing at the people from church belfries. The Catholic Church had long been associated with the Conservatives. The cathedral was attacked, other churches were desecrated, and the residences of the archbishop and of the papal nuncio were attacked. When the Bogotá garrison was ordered out, it refused to leave the barracks; many of the police joined the rioters. Late in the afternoon units of the Regular Army arrived, but there were not enough soldiers to restore order until two days later. The number of people killed in the *Bogotázo* has never been ascertained; estimates run from 2,000 upward, many of them killed by the Army in its attempt to restore order.

In the months that followed many rumors arose to explain what had happened. In Conservative circles it was rumored that Communists had taken advantage of the murder to provoke riots in a deliberate effort to wreck the Inter-American Conference. Some even charged the Communists with instigating the murder with this end in view. Another rumor was that the liberal government of Venezuela had planned Gaitán's murder as part of a plot to overthrow the Conservative party in Colombia. On the other hand, among Liberals the prevailing view was that the Conservatives had instigated the killing to remove the leading candidate from the 1950 election.

As order was restored in the capital, fighting spread to the rest of the country. Villages fought against villages, at first on political grounds and later for other reasons. Some 150,000 to 200,000 are estimated to have been killed in the disorders between 1946 and 1958. The government became increasingly more authoritarian, and in 1950 the demoralized Liberal party refused to put up a candidate. In 1953 a military coup led to the establishment of a dictatorship.

In some instances consensus is formed through rumors, and some form of concerted action follows. The most plausible and popular account becomes accepted in the public as the definition of the situation. It may never be tested in action; sometimes it is accepted by default from lack of a serious challenge. As Fechter (1934), LaPiere (1938), and Rose (1940) suggest, the rumor process is terminated in such contexts when everyone who is interested knows of it. If action is felt to be necessary, it is planned and executed in an orderly manner. A great many events are defined in this manner, and only later, perhaps when a historian discovers some contradictory evidence, are such accepted beliefs revised. When collective excitement is intense, some form of crowd behavior may develop. The ease with which consensus is established depends upon the extent to which a public is drawn from persons who share a common cultural background and upon the extent to which their interests are compatible. Further studies on the conditions under which the formation of consensus is facilitated include those of Guetzkow and Gyr (1954) and of Torrance (1957).

The process of *rumor construction is terminated when the situation in which it arose is no longer problematic.* The ambiguity may be resolved by a formal announcement that is accepted as true. As soon as those who are concerned are satisfied that they have arrived at an adequate comprehension of the situation, tension is dissipated, and their demand for news drops. Similarly, when tension drops in situations marked by intense collective excitement, demand for news drops. Some crises are never successfully resolved. In some instances people just become weary of talking about a topic; as interest wanes, so does the demand for news. Crisis situations are generally initiated by some dramatic event, but the incident that touches off emergency reactions may or may not constitute the root of the difficulty. In disasters, of course, the disruption itself is the precipitating event, and the problem can be resolved by meeting it. But in situations of social unrest, the striking event merely focusses attention upon certain objects; meeting the immediate situation may dissipate tension but may not eliminate the deeper roots of discontent. If so, other crises are likely to erupt periodically. When a situation is no longer ambiguous, then, indeterminacy is transformed into a feeling of certainty, and rumor as a collective transaction is terminated.

The Development of Consensus

Concerted action rests on *consensus*. Before collaboration can take place, the partners must reach minimum agreement upon essentials; they must develop mutual orientation to coordinate their respective contributions. Even when joint action is not contemplated, the socialization of one's outlook may become important. If others cannot understand what one is doing, they may ridicule his conduct or even interfere. Consensus is not static; it is situational and continually developing. The concept refers to the definition of the situation shared by participants in a transaction at a particular place and time. The environment is constantly changing, and it must be successively redefined. What is strange is interpreted in terms of what is already accepted, and as new definitions emerge, they are tried out in action. If conduct based on such beliefs is successful, they are at least partially confirmed; if confirmed, they are incorporated into the general body of popular knowledge. The reconstruction of perspectives occurs largely through institutional procedures, but in this study interest has centered on the manner in which it happens when some measure of improvisation is necessary.

Rumor construction rarely occurs in a unilinear chain; each individual hears the same account from several different persons and several times. Unless something happens to discredit a rumor, its currency tends to enhance credibility. Mere reiteration may lead some of the doubtful to reconsider, for hearing the same report from several sources tends to weaken skepticism. Unless one has built up special resistance, knowledge that others are taking an account seriously makes it difficult to dismiss. For example, commenting on the rumor in England about Russian troops passing through on their way to the Western Front, Oman (1918) writes that he had initially attached little credence to the accounts; then he received three letters from friends claiming knowledge of the visitors. One wrote from South Gloucestershire saying that there were Russians at Avonmouth, only a few miles away. A second wrote from the Isle of Wight that he had been watching steamers with Russians on board emerging from Southampton Water. A third wrote from Oxford that numerous troop trains, laden with Russians, had been passing through Oxford station on their way to Southampton. Then, the eminent historian confesses, his doubts began to waver, for all three of his correspondents were writing from a very short distance from places where the allies were supposed to have been. Furthermore, when a rumor is widely entertained, even a fortuitous event quite unconnected with it may serve as confirmation. The following incident provides an example of this:

Case 54. THE HARLEM RACE RIOT. Negroes began migrating to New York in large numbers during World War I, and by 1920 there were over 250,000 living in the city. Since there was no tradition of hiring Negroes even as unskilled laborers or domestic help, they became severely distressed during the depression; one estimate was that less than 15,000 had regular work, and 100,000 were on relief. Harlem's business was run without Negro participation; outsiders ran the markets and owned the land. Food prices were abnormally high, but the segregated Negroes could not trade elsewhere; rentals in Harlem ran from 15 to 20 per cent higher than similar quarters in other parts of the city. This forced families to share apartments, raising the population density to 222 persons per acre.

One day in March 1935, a sixteen-year-old Puerto Rican boy trying to steal a knife was caught by the floorwalker. There was some talk of beating him, and a scuffle followed. Soon excited Negro customers began upsetting counters and breaking things. Police were called, but it required them until twilight to clear everyone out of the debris-strewn store. By this time an organization called the Young Liberators was issuing mimeographed handbills charging that a child had been brutally beaten and was near death. Another rumor was that a Negro woman had been attacked by the police.

Believing that Negroes had been victims of an outrage, a throng gathered in front of the store. Orators shouted of the injustices of white storekeepers in Harlem who refused to employ Negroes. Police reinforcements were greeted by a barrage of rocks; they began using their nightsticks and were starting to make some arrests. At this critical moment a hearse drove up, destined for a house in the neighborhood. A woman shrieked, "They've come for the child's body!" For the rest of the night Harlem was the center of bloodshed and pillage. Young Negroes went about breaking windows and looting. Over 200 shop windows were smashed, and a passing bus was fired upon. Police opened fire and shot five persons, one fatally. One man who was severely beaten later died.

There are, of course, some persons who remain unconvinced even when most others have accepted a definition. Even the most skeptical tend to waver, however, when they see everyone else acting on the basis of a rumor. As they reexamine their views, the previously rejected interpretation appears at least as a possibility. Sometimes a cumulative change of perspectives occurs, and items that had initially appeared ludicrous may become increasingly more plausible. Since rumors sometimes emerge in situations in which one's life may be at stake, people sometimes act on the basis of reports of which they are doubtful. In his study of the great earthquake of 1934 in Bihar, India, Prasad (1935, p. 14) notes that the victims just took precautions and in some cases belief or disbelief did not enter the picture. Danzig, Thayer, and Galanter (1958, p. 40) also note that seeing others flee confirmed the expectations of the residents of Port Jervis.

Case. 21. CONSECUTIVE EARTHQUAKES IN LONDON. In 1761 residents of London were upset by two earthquakes and a prophecy of a third that would destroy the city altogether. The first shock was felt on February 8; several chimneys fell in the neighborhood of Limehouse and Poplar. The second occurred on March 8, and this was felt chiefly in the north end and toward Hampstead and Highgate. People could not help noting that the interval between the tremors was exactly one month, and a soldier in the Life Guards was so impressed with the notion that there would be a third shock in another month that he ran about the streets forecasting the complete destruction of London on April 5. Most people thought that April 1 would be the more appropriate day. Thousands took the prophecy seriously and made arrangements to transport themselves and their family from the scene of impending calamity. As the frightful day approached, excitement became more intense. Villages within a circuit of 20 miles were crowded with refugees, who paid exorbitant prices for accommodations as they awaited the doom of London. Those who could not afford to pay for lodgings remained in the city until two or three days before the appointed time and then camped in the surrounding fields. The fear became contagious. As they saw others leaving, hundreds who had laughed at the prophecy only a week before packed their goods and joined the exodus. The river was thought to be a place of great security, and all vessels in the port were filled. Most of the refugees returned home on April 6, but some decided that it would be more prudent to allow another week to elapse before trusting their limbs in the city.

With widespread acceptance variations tend to be eliminated. Peterson and Gist (1951, p. 160) note that in the beginning those who make up a public may have diverse attitudes, but this variation is reduced in the course of discussion. In time a standard version arises over which there is considerable consensus. Thus, in the course of development there is increasing conventionalization of rumor content; this gives rise to a unified definition of the situation that is widely accepted. As Caplow (1947, p. 301) points out, in the end a rumor tends to assume a standard, almost stereotyped, form. It is this summary statement providing the gist of hundreds of interchanges that is ordinarily cited as a "rumor."

When a given interpretation is generally accepted, decisions and overt acts are predicated upon it. As patterns of joint activity develop, those who disagree are out of step with the others. *Once a definition is accepted, group sanctions are brought to bear against those who remain skeptical.* Once a person has reconstructed his cognitive orientation, as Janis (1959) points out, he tends to ignore or avoid information that is negative or to misinterpret negative evidence. He also tries to alter the perspective of others so that they will cooperate or at least understand what he is doing. Dissenters are subjected to ridicule, and occasionally even to violence. Their motives are questioned, and they are treated as deviants. Overt acceptance of a rumor may even become a symbol of loyalty to the group. Only a few are able to withstand such pressure, and even those who privately remain unconvinced acquiesce in their overt conduct. Thus, once a trend develops, there is a tendency to end disagreement by imposing sanctions.

Studies of small group interaction reveal the manner in which pressures are placed upon those who deviate from group conceptions of reality. In a classic study of judgments in ambiguous situations, Schachter (1951) showed that pressures toward uniformity vary with degree of group cohesion. Subjects were divided into thirty-two "clubs" of five to seven members each, each unit including three paid confederates. One confederate posed as a deviant from group judgments; one agreed with the average group performance; and the third began as a deviant and then slid to the average position. All units were under pressure to establish and maintain some kind of uniformity. In the experiments deviants were placed under considerable pressure to alter their views; if they refused, they were rejected. Sliders were rejected less than those who remained deviants, and the rejection was greater in groups engaging in tasks of importance to the participants. Other studies have supported these findings. Festinger and Thibaut (1951) found that when a range of opinion exists, most communication is directed toward those who hold extreme views. The greater the pressure toward uniformity, the greater is the tendency to work on those with extreme views. Emerson (1954) successfully replicated Schachter's experiment; communication directed toward sliders decreased as their position approximated the group average.

An extensive body of evidence has been compiled showing how individual judgments tend to comply with collective judgments, especially in situations marked by some ambiguity. The earlier studies, such as those of Jenness (1932) and of Thorndike (1938), were made in the tradition of forensic psychology, and they revealed how the views of individuals changed as they participated in discussions. Raven (1959) divided 344 subjects into units of 10 to 14 persons each. Each subject read a case history of delinquency and was asked to give a private evaluation of it. A false report of the average estimate for his group was then handed each subject, giving him the impression that he deviated from the others; the problem was to see who would modify his position to conform. Those who were assured that their work would remain private did not change nearly as much as the subjects who believed that their estimates would be disclosed to the others. Thus, persons facing rejection are more likely to comply. Similar results have been reported by Festinger and his associates (1952), Lewin (1952), and many others; a summary of such studies can be found in Kelley and Thibaut (1954).

When collective excitement is intense, pressures toward conformity are even greater. In situations in which importance of accuracy is explicitly recognized, the few who retain their critical ability and protest against emotional outbursts face considerable suspicion and hostility. As excitement increases in intensity, there is greater impatience with sober counsel; dissenters eventually find that they must either suppress their views or withdraw from the scene. Should they persist in contradicting the developing views, they may even be subjected to violence. Crowd behavior, as LeBon (1896, pp. 61–63) points out, rests on homogeneity of emotional disposition, and counter-sentiments are not tolerated.

Individual variations in responsiveness to group pressure have been noted. A key experiment is that of Asch (1951) in which each subject was placed in a small group in which *all* other members were confederates of the experimenter. The task was simple: to match the length of a line with one of three other lines of unequal length and to announce the judgment openly. Fifty subjects made twelve trials each, and each subject found himself repeatedly a minority of one facing a unanimous majority. One-third of the errors in judgment either complied with the majority estimate or were in that direction, but 68 per cent of the judgments were correct. What Asch found, however, were extreme differences among individuals. About a fourth of the subjects remained completely independent of the others; about a third made compromising estimates in at least half of their trials; some persons conformed with the majority in eleven out of twelve attempts. Even glaring discrepancies of more than three inches did not always result in independent judgment. Although some of the independent subjects were self-confident, others were filled with doubts. Although they refused to compromise, they readily conceded that they might be mistaken. Asch also found that if even one of the confederates sided with the subject, majority power was lost, and the subject became independent.

In other experiments Festinger and his associates (1952) showed that subjects in groups that they find attractive are more likely to alter their views in order to conform than those in less attractive groups. Several studies—such as those of Hochbaum (1954), Dittes (1959), and Di Vesta (1959)—have revealed that responsiveness to pressure also depends upon an individual's level of self-esteem. Similarly, Menzel (1957) reports that doctors who were not well accepted tried to create an appearance of dispensing prescriptions that was more up-to-date than their actual record at drug stores.

Although much has been written on the typical "effects" of rumors, what happens as a consequence of a rumor depends upon the *content* of the particular definition that emerges in a given situation. A planned and orderly coordination of efforts may follow, or the reaction may be wild and riotous. In some instances each individual may act privately, although individual decisions may converge into some form of mass behavior. A situation may be defined as one in which action would be foolhardy; angered men retreat quietly when confronted by an adversary rumored to be too formidable. Or a situation may be defined as one in which nothing should be done, and men return to their routine duties. There is no particular type of activity that can be regarded as an inevitable, or even typical, consequence of rumor. Once consensus is attained, through rumor or any other form of communication, any line of action deemed desirable is attempted.

That rumors demoralize is such a widespread misconception that it deserves more attention. *Morale* refers to the *quality* of coordination and integration of the contributions of persons acting together in some kind of common endeavor, the degree of effectiveness with which recognized objectives of collective enterprises are pursued. Effective accomplishment of group goals requires wholehearted co-operation and absence of defection. Especially in the face of adversity a test of morale is the willingness of participants to go on even when this involves great personal sacrifice, in some instances the voluntary sacrifice of one's life. Morale depends upon the convictions that men share concerning the worthiness and the rectitude of their cause and upon their faith in one another. Such convictions emerge and are constantly reinforced in communication, including propaganda and rumor. Whether a rumor strengthens or weakens group solidarity depends upon its content. Toward the end of World War II, for example, many German soldiers believed that their country possessed a decisive secret weapon. Thus, even though they realized the strategic hopelessness of their daily operations, rumors of the secret weapon provided a plausible justification for continued resistance (Gurfein and Janowitz, 1946). A report of the U. S. Strategic Bombing Survey (1947) shows that German civilians also held on with similar hopes. When the convictions that men have about their goals, their leaders, and one another begin to break down, they become less willing to make sacrifices for the cause. In such contexts rumors of corruption raise doubts; once dissension begins, rumors about opposing factions tend to deepen suspicions. Under these conditions certain kinds of rumors may be fatal. It appears, then, that the belief that rumors necessarily affect morale adversely is based upon two false assumptions: that a group's cause is so just that truth will always favor it and that rumors are always untrue.

Sometimes a rumor that forecasts an event becomes a self-fulfilling prophecy in that it contributes to its own outcome. As Merton (1948) points out, a rumor that a bank is insolvent, if believed by enough depositors, can result in the actual insolvency of the bank. Similarly, rumors of shortages result in buying panics that do create shortages. During the French Revolution, as Lefebvre (1947) points out, rumors of an aristocratic plot aroused so much hostility against the nobility that it led to their appealing to foreign aristocrats for help. Such rumors become an integral part of the situation and affect subsequent developments. They may be false in the beginning, but by eliciting the anticipated behavior they become true.

Reality Testing as a Social Process

Rumor is an ephemeral transaction; it is terminated as soon as the tension generated in the ambiguous situation in which it developed is somehow dissipated, often through satisfactory definition. Most rumors are soon forgotten, but some of them leave a residue. Definitions that develop in this manner sometimes persist long after the crisis has passed, and they are eventually incorporated into popular lore. What are some of the conditions under which this happens?

The acid test for any definition is overt action based upon it, and such reality testing is a social process. Men can never be absolutely certain of the environmental conditions to which they adjust, although they sometimes act as if they were. All knowledge is tentative and hypothetical; symbolic representations are not exact replicas of what is "out there"; they are reconstructions of the real world, which is there and has a recalcitrant character. The ultimate criterion for the acceptance of any definition, regardless of the channel in which it developed, is pragmatic. The more accurate a report, the more likely it is that action based on it will succeed. Each act constitutes a trial of the adequacy of the assumptions with which one approaches his world. But the testing of ideas is not confined to isolated individuals, for men support one another in developing their respective orientations. When the results of a trial are ambiguous, what constitutes success or failure in reality testing becomes a matter of social consent. By comparing experiences men try to arrive at some agreement. When inaccurate definitions lead to abortive adjustments, further exploration and reconstitution of outlook become joint endeavors.

Rumors that forecast events are easy to test; the events either do or do not take place. Other rumors often have implications for the future. Whenever activity based upon a definition fails, it is labeled as "rumor" and is dismissed. For example, during the latter part of

World War I, when London was bombed with considerable regularity by the German Air Force, people became accustomed to the raids. Then, on December 16, 1917, the raids suddenly stopped. All kinds of rumors emerged of a new scientific invention that would make further attacks impossible. Many details of the invention, including some that were scientifically impossible, were elaborated. On January 28, 1918, the Germans returned, and all rumors of the wonderful inventions vanished (Oman, 1918). Those who stopped taking precautions may have been killed or at least thoroughly frightened, and such failures provide convincing proof that one's outlook is inadequate. When rumors fail, the public is confronted with another crisis, for the situation once again becomes ambiguous.

If failures are sufficiently serious, the sources prominently involved in the development of a rumor may be labeled as unreliable. If it had been formed through auxiliary channels, the network may be completely disrupted. If such a rumor is prominently identified with certain individuals, they may be attacked by outraged persons who feel that they had been victimized by the irresponsible. If any source, even an institutional channel, provides frequent misinformation, it is labeled as unreliable, and men begin to discount *any* information from it. Even when a report is plausible, they accept it only tentatively, waiting for confirmation from some other source that has proved more reliable in the past.

But reality testing is often difficult, for negative evidence is sometimes difficult to detect. As Burke (1935) once put it, a perspective, once formed, interferes with its own revision. Many attempts at testing end inconclusively. A way of seeing is also a way of not seeing; those with special skills for detecting some things also develop a trained incapacity for noting other things that are obvious to everyone else. Hence, they cannot always read the results of a test. People in privileged classes, for example, are unable to see evidence that the underprivileged may be deserving; they continue to explain away all negative evidence until they are shaken by an explosive uprising.

The manner in which preconceptions interfere with reality testing is revealed by the procedures used in the Inquisition. Lea (1888) points out that most inquisitors were not vicious men; they saw themselves as having a sacred mission—the salvation of wretched souls. They had to ascertain the secret thoughts of those on trial, and they tried conscientiously to do so. External acts and verbal professions were not enough, for only a few heretics confessed; therefore, they had to dispense with the usual judicial procedures. Ecclesiastical authorities were wary of confessions obtained under torture and tried to lay down rules of what constituted evidence of heresy; any confession under torture had to be reaffirmed outside the torture chamber. False witnesses, if detected, were treated severely. Yet, in spite of all these conscientious efforts and safeguards, the Inquisition failed, for the entire procedure was based upon a presumption of guilt. Because of selective responsiveness to evidence of guilt it was virtually impossible for anyone to prove his innocence.

Similarly, what is called "black magic" derives its power from absolute faith and selective perception. When the victim of a magical attack discovers that he has been chosen, he sometimes dies of fear. Fortuitous events are interpreted as evidence that the end has come. Since numerous unaccountable deaths are attributed to black magic, the faith is continually reaffirmed (Leakey, 1952, pp. 49–50). Numerous studies of interethnic tension—among them Cooper and Jahoda (1947) and Middleton (1960)—show that motion pictures attacking anti-Semitism do not affect those who are anti-Semitic; the appeals are blunted by their failure to perceive the theme. The extent to which presuppositions may blot out negative evidence is shown in the following case.

Case 34. JAPANESE EMIGRANTS AND THE WAR. Most persons reared in Japan prior to World War II believed their nation to be invincible. From childhood they had been taught that Japan had not lost a war in its 2,600-year history. While many did not take seriously the myths of their divine origin, facts of recent history provided sufficient evidence to sustain their belief in Japan's military prowess. Emigrants to other parts of the world in many instances retained this faith. Hence, once the shock of the attack on Pearl Harbor was over, many who had migrated to the United States could not see how their adopted land could possibly win the war.

From the time of the Manchurian incident of 1931 most Japanese immigrants had come to distrust all American newspapers as sources of propaganda. Although they consulted them for other news, reports on international affairs were treated with skepticism. For war news in particular they relied upon dispatches of the Domei News Agency, disseminated in the Japanese language press. When the Domei reports were cut off by the outbreak of war, many were left without a single source that they regarded as trustworthy.

During the uncertain days between December 7, 1941, and the time of their evacuation from the Pacific Coast there were frequent discussions concerning the progress of the war. Many of them were clandestine affairs, for most Nisei, their children born and educated in America, were known not to share their outlook. A few feared that some Nisei were working as spies for the F.B.I., but most were apprehensive of the scorn with which most Nisei greeted claims of Japanese victories that were not reported in the American press. Some of these reports were attributed to Japanese short-wave broadcasts; others developed from attempts to "read between the lines" in distrusted sources and to speculate about what "really" happened. In the spring of 1942, when Japanese victories were acknowledged, many thought the war was almost over, for it was assumed that enemy gains would be minimized. Perhaps the most widespread rumor at the time was that General MacArthur was dead. As evacuation became imminent, another rumor was that the U. S. Army was tightening its control over enemy aliens because Japanese planes had bombed Alaska; this rumor was current for months before the actual bombing took place. Other rumors were that evacuation was being rushed because an invasion of California was imminent, that Pearl Harbor had fallen, and that some Japanese soldiers were already on American soil. A few people even refused to make preparations for evacuation; they were firmly convinced that Japan would win before the appointed date, making the move unnecessary. Most Nisei regarded the rumors as ridiculous and joked about them. Most of the immigrants were confused; the reports seemed plausible enough to them, but their children openly laughed at them.

During their period of confinement many more rumors developed concerning the progress of the war. Although short-wave radios had been confiscated and declared contraband in the centers, a number of persons claimed Japanese broadcasts as the source of news; the identity of the listener could not be revealed, they insisted, because of the presence of Nisei spies who would report them to the F.B.I. At Manzanar the Japanese fleet was rumored to be only 500 miles from Los Angeles; at Heart Mountain Japanese forces were rumored to have bombed and captured Vladivostock; at Jerome Japanese forces were rumored to have invaded Calcutta; at Granada it was rumored that the U. S. Navy had been completely destroyed, that China was about to surrender, that India was ready to surrender, and that Saipan had not been captured as reported in the American press.

On August 15, 1945, when Japan's surrender was announced to the world, many Japanese emigrants refused to believe the news. Even if they were to lose, Japanese would fight to the bitter end; Japan certainly would not surrender. In Rohwer some persons refused to leave camp even when they were free to do so, saying that they wanted to delay their departure until they saw how the war was progressing. In the autumn of 1945 a number of rumors developed in Granada: Japanese forces had retaken Okinawa and all other major islands; Japan did not surrender, and the alleged Emperor's peace rescript was forged in Washington, D.C., by a traitor whose identity was known; photographs of General Tojo's suicide attempt were faked. In Heart Mountain it was contended that the pictures had obviously been made in Hollywood, for the man playing the part of the general was a Caucasian.

By 1946 it became obvious that the war was over, for servicemen were returning home in large numbers. Furthermore, many wartime restrictions were being lifted. Among the returning veterans were Nisei, and these included their own sons and those of neighbors whom they had known from childhood. Even when the termination of hostilities was acknowledged, however, some insisted that *Japan* had won the war! In Granada it was rumored that Japanese troops had landed in San Francisco and that some had already reached Salt Lake City; in Rohwer it was rumored that three Japanese destroyers and two battleships had docked in San Diego. Another widespread rumor was that all Nisei serving in the U. S. Army had been captured and were being used to transmit orders to the conquered Americans.

Nisei who had renounced their American citizenship and immigrants who had requested repatriation were among those most convinced of the Japanese victory. They were encouraged by a succession of rumors of the imminent arrival of Japanese troops; they rejoiced when they heard that General MacArthur, apparently revived from the dead, had arrived in Klamath Falls, Oregon, on his way to apologize to detainees at Tule Lake, a segregation center for those who had refused to affirm their loyalty to the United States. As repatriation got under way, many were still convinced that they were returning to their victorious homeland, even though their trains were guarded by American soldiers and their ships were operated by the U. S. Navy. They assumed that a victorious Japan was compelling Americans to transport them. Several repatriates subsequently confessed that they did not believe that Japan had lost until *after* their arrival in Japan, when they heard the news from the Japanese themselves.

In time an increasing number in the older generation began to doubt claims of Japan's victory, largely because of reports from Nisei soldiers serving in the Pacific theater. From them came letters and photographs describing the utter devastation of Japan; however, many found it difficult to believe accounts of Japanese begging in the streets, of women prostituting themselves for food, and of men fighting for discarded cigarette butts. It was not until the autumn of 1946, when international postal service to Japan was reopened, that all doubt was removed concerning the accuracy of what had appeared in American newspapers. Their own brothers and sisters wrote to them describing their plight. These were not forged letters, for they could recognize the handwriting. The Japanese in Japan, unlike those who had migrated, had no illusions about who had won the war. They confessed their feelings candidly and appealed for help. About this time the movement to send relief supplies gained momentum.

When the results of reality testing are clear and unambiguous, perspectives are revised. This is shown by Erasmus (1952) in his study of the introduction of modern medicine into rural areas in Latin America. In rural Equador diseases are attributed to lack of cleanliness, psychological states, changes in temperature, and supernatural agents. For the treatment of tuberculosis, appendicitis, and diphtheria even folk specialists recommend going to doctors. Modern techniques have been accepted on the basis of empirical experience; they have succeeded in healing where others have failed. Programs of preventive medicine, however, have not been accepted; their efficacy is difficult to demonstrate. A healing skill is appreciated, then, even when the theory underlying it is not. Each culture has its own way of explaining things, and unless there is decisive proof through spectacular demonstration, old explanations tend to be retained.

In many situations an opportunity for decisive testing does not arise at all. A rumor may appear so plausible in the light of what is already taken for granted that no test may be deemed necessary. The new definition comes to be accepted by default, and consensus arises and is reaffirmed simply because the interpretation is neither contested nor contradicted. A surprising number of situations are defined in this manner; men simply assume that something is so because it is commonly believed to have happened that way. Thus, some popular beliefs are survivals of rumors that were never tested in action. Many Christians to this day believe that Nero deliberately burned Rome in order to build a new city, and tales of Jack the Ripper are periodically reenacted in plays and motion pictures. In the absence of opportunities for reality testing ideas are accepted by common consent.

Scientific knowledge undoubtedly enjoys the prestige it does because of its utility, and in one area after another it is displacing all other forms of knowledge. One of the central characteristics of science, of course, is that chances of accuracy are maximized by a built-in testing procedure: experimentation. Although we are inclined to view the scientific attitude as a recent development, no primitive group is entirely lacking in this type of thinking. As Malinowski (1925) points out, no art or craft could have been invented or maintained, no organized form of hunting, tilling, or search for food could be carried out without the careful observation of natural processes and a firm belief in their regularity. If adjustments based upon a given definition are consistently satisfactory, it is assumed to be accurate and becomes a part of the culture of the group. *The more accurate a symbolic representation of the environment, the greater its efficacy in facilitating adjustment;* for this reason there tends to be a progressive approximation of reality through a continual modification of perspectives. Collective thinking arises out of specific needs and frustrations; when it is successful, it leads to an increasing measure of control over the environment. In every society men tend to develop together increasingly more effective modes of approaching their environment, and rumor construction may be viewed as one of the early phases in the natural history of human knowledge. Every society possesses a considerable stock of empirically valid knowledge.

Although scientific knowledge is often regarded as being fundamentally different from other forms of human endeavor, the history of science reveals a developmental process not unlike the formation of common-sense knowledge. Thus, even in a realm in which ideas are presumably accepted or rejected solely on the basis of evidence, well-established perspectives tend to resist revision. Innovators have been subjected to carping criticism; other scientists not only disagreed with their radical ideas but made personal attacks upon them, often with an air of contempt. One need only consider the fate of Darwin and Freud. Very few fundamentally new ideas have managed to by-pass the heresy stage. Among outstanding discoveries only procedures with immediate and obvious practical applications have been relatively immune to violent criticisms: streptomycin, sulfonamides, antihistamines, ACTH, and cortisone. But new concepts in biology —Darwin's theory of evolution, Pasteur's contention that infectious diseases were due to germs, Pirquet and Richet's theory of allergy— all were greeted by biting, hostile remarks in which, as Selye (1956, p. 193) puts it, men who lacked originality tried to compensate for it by displaying their wit. P. G. Frank (1961, pp. 13–26) contends that scientific theories have been accepted for reasons other than evidence —for simplicity, agreement with common sense, or suitability for justifying desirable human conduct. It would appear, then, that scientific method is a refinement and formalization of the kind of collective problem-solving that occurs in emergencies.

Legendary Accounts and Historiography

Many scholars refer to legends as conventionalized versions of accounts that were originally rumors. This misconception probably arises from vagueness of linguistic usage in which both phenomena are differentiated from other forms of knowledge in terms of oral transmission and presumed falsity. Popular beliefs are designated as "legends" when they are suspected of being erroneous. Furthermore, it is assumed that errors are introduced into legends by the inevitable distortions of oral discourse. Rivers (1912) and Bernheim (1920, pp. 97–108) are among those who see legends as rumors that have survived, and Bernheim, along with Feder (1924), tried to set forth some of the conditions under which such accounts might be useful to historians.

In any group that is not highly literate legends constitute a folk history and provide a basis for many current decisions. Legends are usually contrasted to history, which is thought to consist of accurate accounts of what happened in the past. But the distinction is not so clear-cut. Sometimes historians can produce documentary evidence to support their contention that certain legends are mistaken, but often the available evidence is inconclusive. Doubts are entertained about many legends primarily because they are inconsistent with other things that are assumed to be true. As Malinowski (1925) points out, these tales constitute a folk people's way of seeing their world. Furthermore, such views are not necessarily inaccurate. McHugh (1957, pp. 391–436), for example, indicates that legendary accounts of the great Irish famine of the nineteenth century, while containing a personal and local flavor, do not differ significantly from documentary records. Vansina (1965) has attempted to set up a special procedure, specifying conditions in which falsifications are most likely to occur and instituting safeguards, for the use of oral traditions in reconstructing the history of peoples without written records.

Studies of legends show that tales that serve widespread interests tend to be accepted. Thus, among oppressed peoples tales that are expressive of hopes that cannot be proclaimed openly become very popular. Haworth (1928) cites the legends about the exploits of Robin Hood collected by the conquered Saxons, and Field (1919) indicates that legends of sleeping heroes are ubiquitous among conquered peoples. Many refuse to believe that their heroes are dead; on some supreme day of national crisis the hero will once again rise to rally the people in the manner of Joan of Arc. In the antebellum South Negro slaves revived the ancient tales of Brer Rabbit, dealing with the triumphs of one of the most helpless animals over his more fortunate fellow creatures through ingenious hoaxing and humbug.

Wolfe (1949) points out that in these tales the weak is always victorious over the strong; the latter is made ridiculous and in the end dies a violent death. One frequent source of conflict is the communal meal; indeed, the tales resemble a catalog of Southern taboos. The brer rabbit gets the woman and humiliates the fox. According to Park (1923), Negro spirituals emerged spontaneously out of the communal excitement of religious meetings, but only those that reflected the more permanent moods and sentiments of the downtrodden slaves have survived. Brown (1930, pp. 324–39) suggests that the blues, which arose during a period of urbanization, are expressive of the disillusionments of city life and of the nostalgic yearning for the folk world Negro migrants had left behind. Studies of different versions of legends also show an affinity to collective interests. Guérard (1924) shows how legends about Napoleon varied with the class interests of those among whom they developed, and Lewis (1929) reports somewhat similar results in his study of Lincoln legends.

This suggests the hypothesis that *whenever a situation remains ambiguous, even after reality testing, men are responsive to ideas that tend to support their interests.* Whenever the results of reality testing are not clear-cut, where there is room for doubt, they are sensitive to ideas that are useful. The survival of given beliefs implies the continued existence of certain sensitivities. This does not necessarily involve deliberate invention, but a selective responsiveness to views that happen to justify their acts and other beliefs. Thus, systems of social stratification are often supported by sincere convictions on the part of those in privileged positions of the inferior, animal-like quality of ethnic minorities or of the inborn stupidity of peasants.

Although history is often contrasted to legends, professional historians are painfully aware that what is generally accepted as history is not necessarily accurate, nor are these accounts unrelated to interests. Prior to the institution of formal procedures for the examination of sources some flagrant attempts were made to manipulate conceptions of the past. In pre-Columbian South America, for example, the Inca attempted to erase all history other than their own version. The monarch Pachacuti centralized historical records and created an official Inca history; selecting from many local traditions, he eliminated those not concerned with the Inca. The result, if not the purpose, of this selective manipulation of history was to represent the Inca as the sole bearers of civilization, a view not supported by archaeological evidence (Osborne, 1942, pp. 30–33). Although the rewriting of history with each change of administration in the Soviet Union has become something of a joke, a critical examination of all national histories reveals that the Russians are not alone, although there may be some difference in degree. For example, the story of George Washington and the cherry tree is widely used in the moral instruction of the young. So far as can be ascertained, however, it initially appeared in 1806 in a biography of the first president in which it was attributed to "an aged lady" connected with the Washington household. The author of the book, Parson Weems, claimed to be the "Rector of Mount Vernon Parish," but all checks have shown that this was not true (Kellock, 1928). Furthermore, an examination of other documents on the American revolution reveals a picture quite different from the standard version given American schoolchildren in their textbooks. There was, for example, a large element loyal to England; the revolution was not a spontaneous uprising without dissident factions. Military blunders of the revolutionary leaders are glossed over, and the persecution and terrorizing of "Tories" are rarely mentioned (Fisher, 1912). As Kallich and MacLeish (1962) show, British views of the affair, even of those favoring the colonies, were quite different from the American treatment.

Of special interest to students of rumor is the discrepancy between British and Indian accounts of the uprising of 1857. Just prior to the insurrection new rifles had been issued which required the greasing of cartridges before they could be rammed into the barrel. Many British sources describing the Sepoy mutiny place emphasis upon a rumor among native troops that loading the new rifles would require biting into pig's grease, a violation of religious taboos (Chadwick, 1932, p. 30). This has been repeated so often that it has become the standard version in Europe, given even in the authoritative *Cambridge History of India* (Dodwell, 1932, vol. vi, pp. 173–74). Such an account creates the impression that the uprising was almost whimsical, wholly the result of a misunderstanding based upon a childish superstition that would be dismissed by civilized men. As Tinker

(1958) puts it, Englishmen tend to see the uprising as an aberration in a solid background of British achievement, a temporary setback in the process of building order. One implication would be that the people of India were still in need of further tutelage. On the other hand, Indians now see the rebellion of 1857 as the first expression of Indian nationalism, even though it was not a mass uprising and was suppressed with the aid of loyal Sepoy troops. Indian nationalists who have written of it—among them Mehta (1946), Savarkar (1947), and S. B. Chaudhuri (1955)—all emphasize injustices of colonial rule, blunders of administration, and smoldering resentment and unrest that finally burst into revolt. From their standpoint it was a glorious uprising that failed only because of the superior force of the enemy, and they view with pride the heroism of those who fought against such overwhelming odds. Most Indian historians do not even mention the rumor. In a history of the affair commissioned by the government of India, Sen (1957) does mention the rumor of greased cartridges but indicates that it was only the proverbial "last straw." Both sides agree that there was an insurrection and that it failed, but the incident is viewed from such diverse standpoints that a neutral observer has difficulty at times in seeing that these accounts deal with the same events.

No one can ever develop a full knowledge of the past, and approximations are necessarily selective. Man's knowledge of the past is limited by information that can be derived from the sources at his disposal. Original accounts of events are never complete; in brutal conflicts, for example, records are left only by the survivors. News that is not contradicted is often accepted as an accurate account, even though it might not have happened that way. Accounts of the same event from different standpoints are often contradictory, as for example the treatment of the "Mau Mau" uprising by Majdalany (1963), based largely upon the testimony and records of European settlers, and that of Kariuki (1964), a member of the revolutionary movement. Care exercised in the preparation of documents varies considerably, ranging from authoritative records kept by self-conscious specialists striving for accuracy and fullness to what is vaguely remembered by a few surviving elders. Furthermore, selections are made from what has been recorded, and here much depends upon current interests and beliefs. History is continually being rewritten, not so much because of the discovery of new documentary evidence, but because the perspectives of historians themselves change. What appears reasonable to one generation may seem fantastic to another. Thus, even the outlook of professional historians contains many unverified beliefs; to make his data intelligible he must construct explanatory hypotheses, and he sometimes has to fill in gaps in his material with conjectures. In some cases he may not even be aware of some of his biases, believing himself to be objective. Despite conscientious efforts of specialists to prepare accurate reconstructions the boundary between truth and error is not as clear as one might suppose.

Modern historians are acutely conscious of the possibilities of deception and take every possible precaution against it—much as in scientific research or in critical deliberation. In spite of these safeguards, however, questions of accuracy are often difficult to meet. Since scientists are generalizing about recurrent events, they can verify their findings experimentally. Since historians are describing what happened at a particular place and time, however, no comparable way exists for testing their conclusions. Even the construction and testing of sociological generalizations on the basis of historical data will not test the data themselves.

Popular beliefs and scholarly knowledge develop in separate communication channels but in quite similar ways; they differ mostly in the extent to which use of critical ability is institutionalized. The "common sense" view of the world develops in informal give and take; while there is some concern with evidence, even conventional standards are periodically relaxed. In contrast to this, scholarly knowledge develops among specialists who are self-conscious of the problem of accuracy and who subject one another's efforts to merciless criticism. Although scholarly knowledge has repeatedly demonstrated its greater utility, the fact that it is constantly being improved and displaced indicates that it is not necessarily accurate. Furthermore, it is conceivable that new scientific discoveries will show that some beliefs currently dismissed as superstitions may be accurate after all. That victims of arthritis could foretell the coming of a storm by aches in their joints had been dismissed as an "old wives' tale," but recent research shows that some arthritic symptoms do flare up when barometric pressure and humidity resemble those preceding a storm. Ephedrine, widely used in the treatment of asthma, was isolated from a Chinese herb that has been used in the treatment of respiratory disorders for the past 5,000 years.

Despite impressive differences, both popular and scholarly knowledge are refinements of the adjustive tendencies of human organisms. G. H. Mead once spoke of science as evolution grown self-conscious. He looked upon evolution as a continuous process of problem-solving, at first by trial and error and later by reflective intelligence. Critical deliberation enables men to solve problems, and scientific method is essentially the formalization of the most efficient procedures for doing so.

Summary and Conclusion

The development of human knowledge is a social process. Both popular outlook and scholarly knowledge are shaped through the successive testing of hypotheses and retention of the successful ones. Men approach their world with expectations; if the test fails, the hypothesis is rejected or revised. Where tests are difficult to apply or results are inconclusive, ideas that are serviceable tend to be retained and are incorporated into the general body of knowledge. The process of rumor construction is terminated with the construction of a definition over which there is some measure of consensus. Definitions on matters of continued concern are subjected to reality testing; if they succeed, they are incorporated into the body of popular knowledge to be used again in analogous situations in the future. Should a future situation become problematic, exploration and testing are initiated again. Thus, perspectives are continually coming into existence. Many transactions leave traces, which become part of the framework for meeting future crises.

In modern physics it is generally agreed that absolute truth cannot be attained; all that can be hoped for is a progressive approximation of reality. Yet many social scientists still operate with what some philosophers call the "naive realism of common sense." They regard whatever they themselves perceive and believe as "truth" and view any discrepancy between their own experiences and the testimony of others as "falsehood." As Viscount Haldane (1914) puts it in his perceptive discussion of the meaning of truth in history, men are able to speak so freely about "distortion" only because of their own naive conception of truth.

6
A SOCIOLOGICAL THEORY OF RUMOR

In social psychology theorists have not yet resolved satisfactorily the problem of reductionism, and attempts are still made to explain collective phenomena in individualistic terms. In the study of rumor the most commonly used explanatory schemes have been developed by psychologists, and most of them rest on a principle akin to the Gestalt law of *prägnanz*. Allport and Postman (1947, pp. 36–38) declare, for example, that a report enjoys dissemination if it permits a "good closure"—if it allows relief from tension, justifies emotions that are unacceptable, or makes the world more intelligible. A more formal statement can be found in the theory of cognitive dissonance by Festinger (1957). Rumors are viewed, then, as attempts by confused individuals to comprehend ambiguous situations by filling gaps in their knowledge. As Goethe once observed, man cannot be put into a more dangerous situation than facing a great change without being prepared for it in his way of feeling and thinking.

These theories provide plausible explanations of why individuals act as they do while participating in rumor construction, and as such they are valuable. From a sociological standpoint, however, they constitute only partial explanations. Principles that describe regularities in individual behavior can only account for what an individual contributes to a larger transaction. If rumor is a collective transaction, a satisfactory explanation of it would also require generalizations about *things that men do together in units*. Accounting for the course of development of a transaction as a whole requires a different set of principles. The explanatory scheme to be presented is one that has long been familiar to sociologists but is apparently unknown to all but a few investigators of rumor.

Some Generalizations about Rumor

Rumor is a collective transaction whose component parts consist of cognitive and communicative activity; it develops as men caught together in an ambiguous situation attempt to construct a meaningful interpretation of it by pooling their intellectual resources. What makes rumor different from other forms of discourse in such contexts is that component acts are characterized by a low degree of formalization. In general, the degree of formalization of these transactions is inversely related to intensity of collective excitement.

The first problem is to ascertain the conditions under which this phenomenon appears and disappears. If demand for news in a public exceeds the supply made available through institutional channels, rumor construction is likely to occur. When information essential for adjustment is not readily available, the situation becomes problematic. Demand for news is positively associated with intensity of collective excitement, and both depend upon the felt importance of an event to its public. The greater the unsatisfied demand for news, the more likely it is that rumors will develop. When the situation in which it arose is no longer problematic, when either demand for news drops or supply becomes adequate, rumor construction is terminated. When the balance of supply and demand is restored, rumors disappear.

Rumors vary considerably along temporal and spatial dimensions, and the second problem is to account for these variations. Each crisis situation gives rise to a public, consisting of people who regard themselves as likely to become involved in the consequences of some event and are sufficiently concerned to interest themselves in the possibility of control. Although a public is seldom an organized group, it does in most instances have an evolving structure, which depends largely upon the organization of communication channels. The spatial distribution of a rumor depends on the size and geographic distribution of those who make up the public, limited by availability of communication channels. Speed of rumor construction depends upon intensity of collective excitement and accessibility of channels. When tension is mild, rate of development tends to be moderate, for the usual barriers to social intercourse remain in effect; when tension is intensified, however, speed is limited only by physical barriers to effective contact.

The central problem in the study of rumor is content-formation. This question has been approached by constructing two ideal types. If unsatisfied demand for news is moderate, collective excitement is mild, and rumor construction takes place in auxiliary channels through critical deliberation. In this case rumor content is plausible, i.e., consistent with the cultural axioms shared by the public. If unsatisfied demand for news is excessive, collective excitement is intensified, and rumor construction takes place in spontaneously formed channels through suggestibility. Under these circumstances content tends to be more expressive of emotional dispositions shared by a substantial portion of the public. The greater the unsatisfied demand for news, the lower the degree of formalization of communicative acts through which rumors are constructed, and the greater are the opportunities for individual participants to intervene and alter the course of events. Thus, as collective excitement is intensified, there are greater opportunities for wish-fulfilment. In such contexts rumors may emerge that are inconsistent with cultural axioms.

What is apparently decisive is the extent to which those who make up a public are able to retain their critical ability. Where a serious attempt is being made to define a situation, men are as a rule not gullible. They are aware of the importance of accuracy and make every effort to arrive at a reasonable interpretation. Whenever ego-involvement is high, especially in the face of opposition or danger, critical ability is likely to be enhanced. Reports are examined for adequacy of sources and for plausibility, and chances for personal intervention with private views that are cathartic are held to a minimum. On the other hand, where ego-involvement is low, rumors may be passed on for amusement; in such communication expressive remarks are more acceptable. Indirect expression of emotional dispositions is also facilitated in situations in which nothing can be done. Where collective excitement is mild, the course of rumor formation depends upon the roles enacted by those who relax critical ability; when tension is high, however, role distinctions become blurred, and the manner in which a rumor is constructed depends upon the proportion of participants who become suggestible.

The final problem is to ascertain some of the consequences of rumor construction; this is difficult because there are so many possibilities. Newly formed definitions are often tested in action. If the test fails, that interpretation is rejected. If a test succeeds, it is believed to be true, provided there are not other reasons for doubt. If a situation remains ambiguous even after serious attempts at interpretation, possibilities arise for personal intervention; wish-fulfilment may then enter into rumor content. In such contexts one possibility is as plausible as another. If the results of reality testing are ambiguous, men tend to choose alternatives that are serviceable, and these may be highly expressive.

Since these generalizations have yet to be verified, placing them within a broader theoretical framework may seem premature. The effort is being made primarily because the current literature on rumor is so one-sided in its individualistic bias. Even writers who declare explicitly that rumor is a collective phenomenon resort to individualistic explanations.

Society as a Communicative Process

The mark of society, that which differentiates a social group from a mere aggregate of individuals, is the capacity of the participants to engage in concerted action. This always involves a division of labor; different persons do different things, and their respective contributions fit together to make up a larger transaction. Coordinated action requires that participants make reciprocating adjustments to one another. Such adjustments can be made effectively, however, only when each is able to anticipate what the others are likely to do. Without some appreciation of the intentions of others cooperation is difficult.

Separate and independently motivated individuals are able to collaborate because of consensus, because they share a common definition of the situation. Collective tasks of all kinds are accomplished through intersubjectivity. In his imagination each man can project himself and participate vicariously in the subjective lives of others; it is through role-taking that each is able to anticipate the probable responses of others, impute motives to them, and make necessary adjustments. The sharing of perspectives, then, is a crucial prerequisite for joint endeavor. Consensus is established through reciprocal role-taking. When there is consensus, men can anticipate things together; hence, it becomes possible to make allowances, to take into account special difficulties or advantages, to appreciate the way in which particular exigencies must appear to other persons. The various participants are thus oriented to one another's plans of action; with an appreciation of the direction in which others are moving, it becomes possible to make adjustments to them.

Consensus is not static. As a situation develops the common definition of it also changes; thus, consensus is something that is always evolving. Perspectives cannot remain unaltered, for the world is in a state of continuous flux. Although some societies may give a superficial appearance of stability, some kind of change is inevitable. New events are continually taking place, and nothing happens twice in exactly the same way. Each situation must successively be defined as action develops in it, for the activity itself modifies the situation. Each participant in a transaction modifies his orientation somewhat, minutely or drastically, and comes out seeing his world a bit differently. But change is not displacement; most components remain constant and serve as the fulcrum upon which developing judgments are evaluated. Although persons differ somewhat in relative rigidity of outlook and societies differ in rate and extent of change, complete fixity can but lead to disastrous consequences.

As Mead (1934, pp. 152–64) points out, concerted action is possible largely because each participant is able to control himself, and

self-control on the part of separate individuals can lead to coordination because each approaches his world from the standpoint of a
common definition of the situation. Since he defines various objects,
other people, and himself from the same perspective that he shares
with others, he can visualize his own proposed line of action from
this generalized standpoint, anticipate the reactions of others, inhibit
undesirable impulses, and guide his conduct accordingly. In clearly
defined situations improper needs and interests are generally suppressed, as each individual conducts himself in ways that he believes
are appropriate for someone like himself. Each socialized person,
then, is a society in miniature; he sets much the same standards of
conduct for himself as he sets for others, and he usually judges himself in terms of the same values. For the most part an individual's
behavior may best be viewed as a component part of a larger transaction in which he is participating; what he does is not understandable
apart from what his fellows do and what he believes they expect of
him. In this sense virtually all of the things that men do are subject
to some kind of social control.

Voluntary conduct is a cybernetic process; it consists of a succession
of self-correcting adjustments to a changing environment. The person responds to his own intended behavior from the imagined standpoint of others, responds to it in advance of overt conduct. Thus, he
can inhibit acts that are likely to result in a breakdown of joint
action. Because he can imagine himself performing what he intends
to do and can respond to that image prior to overt commitment, he is
able to inhibit any intended act that is likely to result in difficulties.
For Mead, as for Norbert Wiener, autonomy depends upon feedback;
without it one becomes a creature of impulse or is subject to drift or
external control. A crucial feature of feedback in self-control is that
the self-image is formed from a standpoint shared with other people.
Since most acts are components of larger transactions, actors are interdependent; the impulses of one person cannot be consummated
without the cooperation of his associates. Each participant therefore
becomes concerned over the possible reactions of others to himself,
for he cannot afford to do anything that will jeopardize their support. Each person forms a perceptual object of himself through role-
taking, by reviewing his intended conduct from the standpoint of

those with whom he is involved in a common venture. Self-control is part of the on-going social current; as each person adjusts in advance to the situation in which he is involved, he thereby facilitates cooperation. In this process self-consciousness provides the basis for corrective measures.

Successful cooperation requires some appreciation of one another's inner experiences. How is this achieved? Direct mind-reading is apparently impossible; the inner experiences of others are not accessible to direct observation. Hence, men must settle for the next best substitute—the reading of external gestures that are indicative of inner experiences. Men communicate by making inferences on the basis of gestures. When carrying on a conversation with someone we listen carefully to what he says; we also watch his face intently, for it is another source of valuable hints. Especially by the use of language we are able to reconstruct another person's experiences. Because men are able to organize their experiences in terms of linguistic symbols it becomes relatively easy for them to appreciate vicariously orientations that others relate to them through words. In spite of numerous possibilities of error, concerted action rests upon this type of interchange. Communication is the touchstone of society; those who can communicate can share one another's experiences, define situations similarly, and act together as a unit.

Since consensus is always developing, communication is a continuous process rather than a mechanical interchange. The commonsense way of looking at communication is mechanical; individual organisms are viewed as influencing each other through interstimulation. Ideas are thought to be transmitted from one mind to another as they are encoded into signals, emitted to strike the sense organs of a second party, then decoded and interpreted as a message. Much of the research on communication can be summarized in Lasswell's famous formula: who says what in which channel to whom with what effect? The utility of this conception has been demonstrated, but it has several weaknesses; for one, it ignores the time dimension and is therefore misleading. To be sure, such mechanical interchanges do take place, but each constitutes a small part of a series extended in time. Exchanges of all kinds take place among those who are engaging in any form of concerted action, and the various things that people do and say are not isolated entities but parts of larger units of activity. The product of communication is not merely the modification of the listener's attitude or behavior through stimulation, but the establishment of some measure of mutual understanding. Consensus is an ongoing process, a sharing that is built up, sustained, and further developed through a continuing interchange of gestures. The communicative process is rarely a single instance of stimulation and response, such as an instinctive reaction to a scream of terror. Consensus is rarely completed even for purposes of a simple enterprise; it is partial. There are invariably areas of uncertainty, and it is about these that most of the interchanges take place. With each gesture uncertainties are successively minimized or eliminated, enabling each person to contribute his share and to enjoy greater confidence in the responses of others. In most situations, then, men who are cooperating maintain mutual orientations to facilitate continued coordination, and the interplay of gestures continues until the task is accomplished.

This suggests that consensus not only arises in communication but is sustained and creatively reaffirmed from moment to moment in a succession of communicative acts. We are able to experience a sense of certitude about our conception of the world because of the continual reassurances that we receive from one another. Participants in common transactions reinforce one another's perspectives, each by responding in expected ways. Nor is such mutual support necessarily confined to harmonious interactions; a man who insults another trying to provoke a fight is temporarily immobilized if he is met with a friendly smile. In all their activities, then, men are unintentionally perpetuating the fabric of group life; each person, by carrying out the expectations of others, gives confirmation to the developing social structure of the group. As Sumner (1906) notes, each person is an agent of the folkways to the extent that he gives his nod of approval when there is conformity and his frown of disapproval to each violation. Human society might best be regarded as a process, a becoming rather than a being—a succession of adjustments and readjustments among associated individuals.

This suggests that what is called "reality" is a social process; it is an orientation that is continuously supported by others. How does one differentiate between a hallucination and reality? A hallucination is a genuine sensory experience, but it is questioned precisely because it lacks social confirmation. One who sees an apparition or a flying saucer turns to his companions expecting a reaction of amazement; his faith in his own senses is badly shaken if the others act as if nothing had happened. In this sense all knowledge is social. Men approach their world in terms of hypotheses; participants in common transactions watch one another for reassurances that they are doing the right and expected thing. Each man's orientation toward his world is reinforced daily through the constant support he receives from others. The meanings of various objects are supported in the regularized reactions of others; social norms are reaffirmed through their conformity; and each man's conception of himself is similarly sustained in the consistent treatment he receives from others. Whenever his expectations are confirmed, one has a sense of assurance and can continue acting with confidence. Each person's conception of his world, then, is constantly being buttressed through communication.

Since effectiveness of communication depends upon the capacity of participants in concerted action to assume one another's roles, there is considerable variation in the degree of consensus that can be achieved. It can be established far more easily among those who share a common culture. The manner in which each person consistently defines a succession of situations depends upon his organized perspective. A culture may be regarded as an ordered view of one's world, what is taken for granted about the attributes of various objects, sequences of events, and traits of human nature. It is an organized conception of what is possible and what is plausible; it constitutes the matrix through which one perceives his environment. The fact that men have such ordered perspectives enables them to anticipate regularities and to conceive of their ever-changing world as being relatively stable, orderly, and predictable. As Riezler (1951) puts it, one's perspective is an outline scheme which, running ahead of experience, defines and guides it. Each man has a working conception of the nature of the world in which he lives, and what he perceives depends almost as much upon his assumptions as upon his sensory experiences.

Crisis and Collective Adjustment

Although in common parlance the word "crisis" refers to catastrophes of considerable severity, sociologists have used the concept to designate any break in the established routine of life. A crisis is any situation in which the previously established social machinery breaks down, a point at which some kind of readjustment is required. Crises are often provoked by environmental changes. They may also arise from incapacity to cope with the exigencies of a situation; what needs to be done may prove too arduous for the facilities at hand. Inability to act may also arise from the perplexity of those who are caught in a dilemma, where the alternatives with which they are confronted are equally attractive or distasteful. Often they arise from ambiguity. A crisis is a crisis precisely because men cannot act effectively together. When previously accepted norms prove inadequate as guides for conduct, a situation becomes problematic, and some kind of emergency action is required. Since activity is temporarily blocked, a sense of frustration arises; if the crisis persists, tension mounts, and an increasing sense of urgency for doing something develops. There are many kinds of crises. Some are trivial, like the excitement aroused by a child's temper tantrum; others are catastrophic. Some, like the illness of a friend, involve but a small segment of a community; others, like war or depression, involve almost everyone. Some crises are quickly resolved; others may drag on for some time; still others may be cumulative, interest gradually building up to a feverish climax. Thus, crises vary in temporal span, scope, complexity, and dramatic quality.

Though confronted with modified life conditions, somehow men must keep going. As Sumner (1906, pp. 2–3) puts it, the first task of life is to live; with a change in life conditions new needs arise, and new modes of adjustment must be developed. Often initial efforts at satisfying new needs are clumsy and blundering. The procedure is one of trial and error, which often produces pain, loss, and disappointment; nevertheless, it is a method of rude and unconscious experimentation and selection. Activity is groping and exploratory.

Some efforts, whether by accident or by intelligent design, work better than others and are pursued further. Trials are usually performed by many persons, and activity is guided by the results of these trials. Tentative changes occur in perspectives and are tested in action; abortive attempts affect developing perspectives by their failure. New openings occur that could not have been anticipated; possibilities that had almost been overlooked rise in stature and render others obsolete. The direction of approved action gradually arises from a series of selections from successful experiments (Cooley, 1918). Throughout this exploratory process accurate information is of crucial importance.

If collective adjustments are to succeed, the participants must develop a definition of the situation that is both adequate and shared. To enable effective moves to be made the definition must be sufficiently accurate. It must also become shared; otherwise, each would move off in a different direction, and the various persons would not be able to mount a common enterprise.

It is precisely in such contexts that rumors emerge, and some psychologists have attempted to explain rumor in terms of the psychological condition of men caught in such situations. Ketchum (1965, p. 59) declares that man's primary need is to live in an organized mental world, one where his present and future are known and predictable. Lacking such a world he is driven to construct one, using the two kinds of materials available to him: his own wishes, fears, and guesses, and the suggestions he gathers from others. Festinger (1957) has attempted a more formal statement in his theory of cognitive dissonance: the existence of inconsistency is uncomfortable, and a person will (a) try to reduce it and (b) actively avoid situations and information that are likely to increase it. Such theories account for sensitivity to news by individuals and their participation in rumor construction; it must be emphasized once again, however, that they do not explain the course of development of a collective transaction.

If an adequate definition is provided by institutional channels, consensus arises at once. Even if disagreements occur over what ought to be done, at least there is agreement concerning the facts of the situation. Furthermore, the interpretation is shared by all those who accept the channel as authoritative. If such information is not forth-coming from formal news channels, demand for news remains. Men still have to meet the situation; unless they can put together some kind of definition, they cannot act. In such contexts they are likely to pool their intellectual resources and to improvise an interpretation.

If men require one another's support in routine situations, they need it even more in crisis situations; their interdependence is heightened. In routine activities objects are defined from the cultural standpoint; each person reaches a conclusion similar to that of his fellows, and only minor adjustments are necessary through communi-cation. But when something unusual happens, participants must consult one another to be sure that their respective definitions are sufficiently alike to enable them to continue cooperating. The impor-tance of mutual support becomes especially apparent in severe crises. When changes in life conditions disrupt established social relation-ships, a transitional period ensues during which people are not cer-tain of just what to expect. Under such circumstances they become highly sensitized to one another. They ask questions; they compare experiences; they make suggestions but do not insist upon their being carried out. They are hesitant, reluctant to commit themselves, and watch to see what others will do. Transactions proceed in a halting, tentative manner. Those who act do so with caution, proceeding in a trial-and-error manner. They watch one another carefully for any hint of new patterns of adjustment. Thus, men in crises continually reinforce one another as they build up together a working orienta-tion toward their changed environment. Being unsure of themselves, they seem to crave some kind of reassurance from other human beings. Describing an infantry unit in combat, Marshall (1947, pp. 129–30) notes that when troops under enemy fire cannot see one another, all organizational unity temporarily vanishes; what had been a unified force becomes a scattering of individuals. Thus, as men actively seek each other's support, perspectives that are develop-ing are tested in communicative acts. As new definitions emerge and become shared, they are reinforced in reciprocating action. Those who undergo a derangement of their way of life together make ad-justments together, and they construct new schemes of coordination through communication.

Institutions and social structure of all kinds, then, are *products* of collective action. Earthquakes and fires, conflicts with enemies, difficulties in controlling rebels—any of the exigencies of living together that call for some kind of action—set up social patterns that repetition fixes in habit and that finally become institutionalized (Park, 1927). This is another way of saying that every institutional form has a history. However drastic the changes in environmental conditions, life must go on. Of necessity men act, and the effect of action is the creation of an action pattern. Some action patterns, as in the case of mobs, are ephemeral and exist only temporarily without any clearly defined organization. However, more permanent patterns may arise with the emergence of social structure, with its division of labor and specialization of roles. When in time the roles of participating individuals become fixed in habit, and especially when their special tasks have come to be accepted as customary, the emerging structure gains new stability. New orientations become fixed through social confirmation, as people act and support one another on the basis of changed beliefs. Most collective patterns arise from a series of trial-and-error experiments, at first unorganized, but gradually attaining clarity and coherence of purpose. Through repetition mutual expectations become fixed, and a new cultural pattern emerges. Thus, every custom and every social institution may be regarded as an organization of group behavior that grows up and facilitates the continuation of collective activity that originally took place quite spontaneously. Although joint action is facilitated by social structure, it is not entirely dependent upon it. People can and do act together in the absence of adequate definitions, but in the course of their cooperation new structures emerge.

Collective adjustments to crises are not just responses to events; they are also shaped in the *reactions of men to one another*. Although there may at first be confusion, in time men redefine the situation and develop action patterns better suited to the new life conditions. All those who are involved in the situation alter their perspectives in consultation with one another. It is through communication that new experiences and modes of action become shared. The adjustment of a group to a crisis is an organizing process; it brings about a system of coordinated activities better suited to the new circumstances. New social structures arise as by-products of efforts of men to live and to adjust to the exigencies of situations in which they find themselves.

Men tend to live in routine and customary ways until something out of the ordinary occurs to necessitate some modification of their habitual modes of action. It is only when the "cake of custom" has been broken, as Bagehot puts it, that men become susceptible to unfamiliar ideas. Crisis situations, then, are significant objects of sociological inquiry in that they constitute crucibles out of which innovations develop.

Development through Natural Selection

When needed information is not available from authoritative channels, definitions must be improvised, and the central problem is to describe regularities in the manner in which this is done. A wide variety of initial reactions arise in most inadequately defined situations, but these are generally reduced to a few plausible alternatives which can serve as the basis for common endeavor. How is the direction of development to be explained? Why one alternative rather than another? Attempts have been made to account for direction in terms of the dominant attitudes of participants or the motives of leaders. Even casual observation reveals, however, that in all but the most intense crises a wide variety of motives and attitudes are represented, and the problem of how they converge still remains. Economic, demographic, and even ethnic factors have been cited, and some students of social change have felt that there might even be some over-all principle, such as progress, that might account for the line of development. The general hypothesis advanced in this study is that *whenever men are thrown on their own resources, new definitions develop through a process of natural selection.*

In many crisis situations *variations* in interpretation arise through differential reactions on the part of the individuals involved. It is not strange that a given event elicits a diversity of reactions, for the manner in which an individual responds to something depends upon the manner in which he happens to be oriented toward it; each man's reaction depends upon his personality and his perspective, both of which are unique. Each has a somewhat different background of experience. Crisis situations are more likely to evoke diversity of response than routine ones; with the suspension of many conventional norms opportunities are presented for more individualism. If members of a public are drawn from different social worlds, cultural diversity is also reflected.

Because men are interdependent and must act together, they must arrive at minimum accord before taking action. Hence, there is *competition* among various definitions of the situation. Each proposed definition contains or implies some line of action, each more or less linked with the interests of its proponents. The character of the competition varies considerably, depending upon importance of the decision and strength of the interests represented. Out of the welter of reports, comments, and speculations that surround any unusual event certain items are tentatively accepted while others are rejected. Rumor construction at least in the beginning is a trial-and-error process, a form of collective experimentation. In varying degrees each party seeks acceptance of its particular interpretation, and some who feel very strongly may even utilize special tactics to assure ascendancy of their views over alternative proposals. Each person does his best to understand what is happening, but each person sees things from his own distinctive standpoint.

Selection occurs as ideas are picked out and tested in use. Men involved in crisis situations discuss many things, but relatively few of these items come to enjoy priority in communication. Of the mass of verbalizations that occur a few items stand out as being sufficiently deserving of serious consideration. Thus, a rumor is not something imposed from the outside, as in experiments on serial transmission, but what is selected spontaneouly from the mass of communicative acts that constitute the hub of group life. Choice is usually unconscious, and when the developmental cycle runs its course, a standard version gains general acceptance. Since rumor is a collaborative process, selection is necessarily *collective;* an adequate basis for joint action exists only when a substantial portion of the public has agreed on a provisional interpretation. What is of interest to only a few is rejected by the others and soon forgotten. Only when a multitude of persons are sufficiently aroused by the same possibility does a rumor develop. Unless sensitivities are shared, people will not even talk for long about the same thing. Furthermore, what is finally accepted is what appears reasonable from the standpoint of most of the public. The common definition that eventually arises takes shape through the adoption of some views, the elimination of others, and the gradual integration of those items that have *survived*. The result is a collective product to which each participant has contributed in some way.

Variations in the manner in which crisis situations are defined suggest that there may be more than one basis for selection. A further hypothesis may be advanced: *the basis of collective selection varies with the type of social control that prevails in the public.* The extent to which communicative activities remain subject to conventional regulation—degree of formalization—becomes a key variable in the study of rumor. In different kinds of crises social control changes in different ways; therefore, the pattern of rumor development also varies.

When communicative activity is subject to informal social control, collective selection takes place on the basis of plausibility. When collective excitement is moderate, participants depend almost exclusively on auxiliary channels, and build up their orientations through a careful examination of the best available evidence. New definitions are consistent with previously accepted beliefs; indeed, new events are merely interpreted in terms of already established presuppositions. As long as informal controls are maintained, men retain their critical ability and tend to regard strange views with suspicion. Interpretations incompatible with their beliefs are rejected as unlikely, and the existing perspective is thereby reinforced. The unquestioned assumptions shared within a universe of discourse become the key selective factor in the formation of rumor content.

Several empirical generalizations, verifiable through observation, may be derived from the hypothesis that plausibility is the central selective factor when collective excitement is moderate: (a) All rumors developing in such contexts are compatible with the premises shared within the public, even if they seem strange to outside observers. (b) When persons drawn from different social worlds participate in the same public, different rumors emerge, each in accord with the expectations shared in that segment. (c) Reports that are implausible are rejected, or viewed with suspicion, even if they happen to be accurate. (d) Transformations in rumor content are always in the direction of greater harmony with shared assumptions. More drastic changes occur only when perspectives are successively altered so that what was initially questionable begins in time to appear increasingly more reasonable. (e) Reports that are contrary to widespread desire are accepted as the basis for action if they are in line with group premises. (f) Rumors that are implausible and seemingly projections of known predilections of their sponsors are not regarded by the participants themselves as serious attempts to define situations. They become the butt of jokes and sometimes of hostility.

As collective excitement is intensified, men become subject to another type of social control—behavioral contagion. The display of excitement tends to compel attention, and excited people become sensitized to one another. The more they become preoccupied with each other, the more likely they are to fall into a relationship of rapport. This increases the likelihood of suggestibility, response without critical reflection. Behavioral contagion is a form of social control that provides direction to joint activity among those who are no longer restrained by conventional norms. It might be regarded as a means whereby a number of human beings can act together quickly even when they have little else in common. Often participants in crowds feel as if they are being controlled from the outside; they are surprised to find themselves doing things without a sense of conscious, voluntary direction.

When communicative activities become involved in behavioral contagion, prevailing mood replaces plausibility as the basis for selection. In the heat of collective excitement men are responsive only to those proposals that are consistent with their aroused dispositions. Those who are upset are selectively sensitized to items relevant to their discomfort, and their verbalizations are expressive of their adjustive tendencies. Because their sensitivities are directed, they are receptive to some remarks and not to others; inappropriate statements are either unnoticed or condemned. Thus, reports that give fitting expression to the prevailing mood tend to gain priority in communication. As men become more and more excited, their outlook becomes constricted, and a successive modification of perspectives takes place. Standards of judgment are then temporarily transformed. When conventional norms are no longer operating, it becomes possible to consider seriously proposals that are alien to established beliefs. The formation of esoteric definitions implies that men are accepting and acting on the basis of reports that violate their customary standards of credibility.

Several empirical generalizations, verifiable through observation, may be derived from the hypothesis that prevailing mood is the key selective factor when collective excitement is intense: (a) Reports that are incompatible with cultural standards are sometimes accepted in such contexts if they are consistent with the prevailing mood. (b) Even announcements from institutional channels are rejected if the items are incongruent with the prevailing atmosphere. (c) Since crowds consist of men with homogeneous orientations, the affective components of all rumors in such contexts are mutually sustaining, even when some of the alleged facts reported contradict each other. (d) If a public is divided into factions in which different moods emerge, the definitions arising in each segment will be consistent with its own mood. (e) In fluid situations, as the dominant mood changes, a succession of rumors emerge, each in turn providing justification for prevailing dispositions.

The manner in which rumor construction occurs depends upon the extent to which certain participants are able to retain self-control. Suggestibility implies a relaxation of self-control. Since voluntary conduct is a cybernetic process, one cannot correct and regulate his own conduct without feedback, without forming self-images. Self-consciousness thus provides protection against impulsive behavior by making one more aware of his obligations to others. When self-consciousness is impaired or lost—as in shock, intoxication, or intense excitement—persons lose their sense of individuality; anonymous men, being socially detached, are in many cases no longer burdened with a sense of responsibility. In collective excitement attention is focused on some common object and upon the excitement of one's fellows; hence, members of crowds lose self-consciousness. As self-control in terms of conventional norms is relaxed, a person becomes more responsive to appeals that he would otherwise reject or at least examine with greater care. Therefore, anything that enhances self-consciousness facilitates retention of self-control. In a conventional setting each must exercise care in what he says lest he acquire a reputation of being a fool. When momentous decisions are in the offing, men struggle to inhibit impetuous moves. Similarly, in conflict a premium is placed upon critical ability.

The self-consciousness of individuals tends to vary with intensity of excitement. As Stratton (1928a, 1928b) points out, mild excitement tends to make one more alert. Receptive systems become more sensitive; selectivity in perception becomes greater than usual, and attention is narrowed along lines of adaptive action. Furthermore, there is more vigor and ease of movement as motor coordination is facilitated. Thinking is also facilitated in mild excitement, for irrelevant images are suppressed; this makes possible greater concentration and alertness, and critical ability is enhanced. Acute emotional upset, however, is a disintegrating process. With excessive visceral activity and innervation motor processes are jammed. In extreme emotion behavior often becomes ineffective and even harmful, as in an enraged boxer who "loses his head" or in a man who becomes paralyzed with fright. Perception is disorganized, and motor coordination is disturbed. Reflective thought becomes more difficult. Critical ability apparently rests on the smooth operation of perceptual and motor processes, and any impairment reduces capacity for self-control. Under severe pressure men lose self-consciousness and critical ability; hence they become suggestible and even subject to hysterical outbursts. If rumors occasionally prove inaccurate and implausible, this is more likely to be the result of a temporary suspension of critical ability than of defects of oral transmission.

There is always an aleatory factor in rumor construction, as in the development of any event in a particular historical context. Especially in periods of dislocation and readjustment activities tend to be more capricious. To the extent that clear-cut expectations break down, fortuitous events, such as the reluctance of a policeman to make an arrest, may take on disproportionate significance. The course of development in such fluid situations, then, often becomes subject to the vicissitude of events. Furthermore, behavior under such circumstances is marked by considerable spontaneity; as role obligations are minimized, inhibitions are relaxed, and suppressed dispositions become more conspicuous. Those caught in a crisis may choose from a wider range of alternatives, including behavior patterns that are ordinarily prohibited. Much depends upon who happens to be at a certain place at a particular time and upon the threshold of his critical ability.

Human society is a communicative process in which coordinated activities can go on as long as men support one another's perspectives. The social order is always changing, sometimes in minute increments and sometimes in cataclysmic upheavals; all these changes require modifications in the orientations of the participants. Collective adjustments, both to relatively stable and to changing life conditions, take place through natural selection. Ideas are perpetuated as long as they continue to be selected; as long as men act on the basis of certain definitions, the views persist. The survival of any idea depends upon its continued utility. The implication is that in the long run popular beliefs will be those that facilitate coping with extant life conditions.

Summary and Conclusion

Societies, no matter how stable they may appear, are on-going things. The world is in a state of continuous flux, and as life conditions change, knowledge must keep pace. Crisis situations arise whenever new events are incomprehensible in terms of established assumptions. Existing expectations are violated; new sensitivities arise; and new ideas emerge to be tested. In order that they may continue to act in association with one another men must alter their orientations together. Thus, the emergence of new hypotheses and their acceptance as part of a modified outlook is a social process. As long as there is a possibility of communication among those caught in a crisis, social reconstruction will to some extent depend upon the reactions of the victims to one another as well as upon their reactions to the events. It is by consulting each other and comparing their experiences that they alter their ways of acting. Rumor is an important part of this process of transformation. As such, it is not a pathological phenomenon, but an integral part of the processes whereby men develop more adequate ways of coping with new circumstances. Since it is very unlikely that every new event will be defined satisfactorily through authoritative channels, it seems that rumors will always play some part in the efforts of men to come to terms with their ever-changing world.

It has been found that the general principles used by Darwin to account for the origin of species serve admirably to explain the origin of ideas in crisis situations. This may occasion some surprise, for there are only infrequent references to natural selection in current sociological literature. Because of the excesses of social philosophers of the nineteenth century in their uncritical applications of organic analogies a strong reaction has formed against anything reminiscent of evolutionary doctrines. But the principle of natural selection need not be confined to biology; evolution is the continual development of new procedures better suited to new conditions. Indeed, as Dewey (1898) points out, the difference between man and other living creatures is not that selection ceases, but that conscious foresight introduces additional alternatives from which choices might be made. To deny the operation of natural selection in human society because of past abuses constitutes "throwing out the baby with the bath."

7
THE POLITICAL MANIPULATION OF RUMOR

On August 14, 1945, the ruling oligarchy of Japan—made up of representatives of the Army, the Navy, the civilian government, and the Imperial Household—decided to sue for peace. At that time the mainland had not yet been invaded; 2,500,000 combat-equipped troops were ready for action; 9,000 *kamikaze* planes were available for use; and civilian morale was still high. One explanation that has been given for the surrender is a rumor among high officials that Tokyo would soon be the target of an atomic attack. Since considerable controversy arose over whether use of nuclear weapons actually hastened the termination of hostilities, the U. S. Strategic Bombing Survey (1946) interviewed most of the men involved in the decision to surrender. The study reveals that there had indeed been such a rumor, attributed to a captured B-29 pilot. Most of the leaders were already in favor of surrendering, however, and apparently the rumor only intensified already existing pressures to end the war. In this case evidence is not conclusive, but it is conceivable that such momentous decisions could be influenced by rumors. It is not surprising, then, that those involved in politics would develop an interest in possibilities of manipulation and control.

Many attempts have been made to manipulate rumors for political purposes, and some publicists have even claimed to have mastered reliable techniques for doing so. No doubt some successful "whispering campaigns" have been conducted, but there is some question of whether the accomplishment was by accident or design. This chapter deals with various procedures that have been utilized in attempts to control rumors to see which have been successful and which have failed. Effective manipulation of any phenomenon implies adequate knowledge, systematic or intuitive, of the processes involved. Propaganda may be regarded as the introduction of artificial selection into the construction of beliefs; as in the breeding of desired characteristics in species, successful control can come only from knowing and utilizing the laws of natural selection. Thus, records of success and failure should provide a crude test for generalizations; if the hypotheses presented are valid, all attempts that violate them should result in failure.

Informational Strategy in Politics

Ordinarily we think of politics in a restricted sense. On the international scene we think of competition among nations for resources and markets, of diplomatic maneuvers, and of wars; on the national scene we think of pressure groups, mobilization of popular support for legislation, and contests between political parties. It is important to remember, however, that the same processes occur in many other social contexts. In modern industrial societies labor and management, while bound in a common enterprise, often have divergent interests; strikes, lockouts, collective bargaining, and arbitration are means whereby some of these differences are successively resolved. Many voluntary associations are split into factions, and competition, however subtle it may be, arises for control of the organization. Cliques of deacons in a church, of leaders in a P.T.A., of professors on a university faculty—all use political tactics in pursuing their interests, and in common parlance such maneuvers are called "peanut politics." Even within a family sibling rivalries occur. A child trying to retain his favored position in relation to his brothers and sisters resorts to similar tactics—fighting, informing, negotiating, forming conspiracies. Political activities, then, can be found in any situation in which values are in short supply and where different parties find it necessary to compete for them.

The study of politics, as Lasswell (1935) puts it, is the study of who gets what, when, and how. The "who" may consist of a party, a nation, a social class, an ethnic group, a clique, or an individual. The "what" may consist of deference, income, safety, or merely reassurance. The "how" involves the manipulation of events, particularly the behavior of other human beings, in the pursuit of what one regards to be his interests, especially in the face of real or anticipated opposition. There are many commonly used techniques: forming conspiratory groups, pressing chance advantages that arise, building a solid basis of operations through expedient alliances, fighting, arguing according to fixed rules, using persuasion to broaden support for one's program, negotiating and bargaining with opposition that cannot be intimidated, changing rules of procedure by force. Conflicts vary in intensity, and the kind of tactics permitted depends upon severity of opposition and importance of stakes.

Although they do not always realize it, opponents in conflict are interdependent. Taking a political public as a collective unit, the direction in which a given transaction develops arises in the successive give and take between the opposing parties. Each must orient its action to the actual or anticipated reactions of its adversary. Each tactical maneuver is predicated upon expected countermeasures, and much of politics consists of trying to anticipate the moves of opponents and getting into position for effective reply. Such interaction is almost always critical and self-conscious. Each maneuver must be deliberately planned and its consequences carefully weighed. The use of fixed procedures in such situations places one at a disadvantage, for competitors can easily anticipate and take countermeasures well in advance. To be successful tactics must be flexible, and politicians must be able to adjust to exigencies of the situations in which they find themselves. A premium is placed on alertness, ingenuity, and a command of facts. In general, politics tends to be rational and calculating, and the successful practitioner is one who can maintain self-control even under tension. Although it is rarely regarded in this light, conflict is one way of resolving a crisis situation.

Active participants utilize political tactics to gain whatever advantages they can. Limitations to the naked pursuit of power are set, however, by custom and law; hence, in some cases circumvention of the law, an attack on custom, or an attempt to influence or control governmental agencies may become tactical objectives. Equally effective limitations are set by public opinion. Since public support facilitates the pursuit of one's program and hinders the opposition, mobilization of such backing becomes one of the most important aspects of politics. As vague and amorphous as it may be, public opinion is of crucial importance, and leaders of interest groups continually seek the support or at least the acquiescence of their audiences. Should some inept move misfire, interested spectators may become enraged, and their anger may result in the mobilization of collective protest. A public may at times be converted into a mob that demands immediate action. Even dictators are sensitive to possibilities of public protest and are careful not to arouse the populace against them. Passive members of a public set the conditions under which the active may perform, and politicians must not only concern themselves with opponents but with the public as well.

Since men act on the basis of definitions, attempts are made to get the public to interpret events in desired ways. Various promotional techniques are used, and *propaganda* refers to persuasive tactics devised to seek public support by manipulating symbolic representations (Lasswell, 1933b). Because of the size and geographical dispersion of publics in mass societies, efforts of present-day propagandists center largely upon manipulating the content of the media of mass communication. Among the commonly used techniques are misrepresentation of facts, censorship of items tending to favor the opposition, exploitation of popular beliefs and values, and arousing antagonism against scapegoats to divert attention from embarrassing issues. Such propaganda is effective especially when competing channels are not readily available and when people have confidence in the mass media. Some politicians, however, are not content with manipulating communication content; they try to modify perspectives by altering the conditions under which people act—by manipulating events. Special sensitivities are cultivated through the staging of events— distribution of food to starving people, mass slaughter of innocent men to create an atmosphere of fear, public trials and executions to create an impression of ubiquitous spies, starting wars or plotting assassinations to divert attention from domestic problems. Subsequently the gratitude of hungry people or the anxiety of a terrorized populace may be exploited for other purposes. Such promotional devices are used not only to attack opponents and to seek public support, but also to gain and hold membership in one's own party. Thus, some promotional campaigns ostensibly directed outward may actually be intended for bolstering morale within the group.

Whenever possible propagandists tell the truth, but the slanting of news is an old and widespread practice. Informational campaigns are total efforts to persuade men, directly or indirectly, to define situations in a desired manner. It is often assumed that all propaganda is false and that all propagandists are liars. But any publicist would prefer to use accurate reports. In political publics opponents stand prepared to expose errors and weaknesses in one's argument, and a premium is placed upon facts because they will stand even under critical examination. Furthermore, reports resulting in inexpedient action may result in the discrediting of channels so that they become useless for subsequent promotional efforts. Whenever possible, persuasion is based upon facts, and reports are fabricated only when absolutely necessary. That falsehood must be cleverly disguised is an indication that men in conflict situations are generally not gullible.

Although publicists face difficulties enough when trying to persuade their supporters, they are confronted with even greater obstacles when trying to influence opponents. Special difficulties arise as opposition intensifies into open conflict; opponents become further isolated from each other, and communication between them becomes almost impossible. Group boundaries become more sharply drawn, as a progressive bipolarization of the arena takes place. Intense and unreasonable fear and hatred of enemies is based upon contrast conceptions (Copeland, 1939). Men interact not so much in terms of what they are but in terms of the conceptions they form of each other. Concepts are not duplications of reality; they are constructed through selective perception and communication. In viewing enemies, men become especially sensitized to their unfavorable characteristics, overlooking or explaining away the favorable. The concept of the enemy is often constructed by projecting onto it all the attributes most hated or despised in one's own group; the enemy thus becomes the exact opposite of oneself. One's own side is viewed in idealistic terms; it is endowed with all the noble virtues, fighting selflessly for a worthy cause. Motives imputed to the enemy, however, are almost invariably vile, and the enemy becomes the living embodiment of everything condemned. In all severe conflicts—strikes, wars, interethnic tension, or revolutions—opponents are strangely alike: immoral, vicious, and incapable of appreciating human sentiments. In the heat of struggle participants act on the basis of a sincere belief in the depravity of the opposition, and this makes possible the bestial conduct so often found in conflict. With increasing distrust in communication channels controlled by opponents each party by default becomes more restricted to its own resources; therefore, chances of testing contrast conceptions and making corrections are minimized.

If the enemy is such a monster, obviously any information coming from his camp is immediately discredited. It is necessary to guard against being duped into a foolish move, and every effort is made to close ranks against outsiders. Opposition of interest is an important condition for retention of critical ability. Fostering of rumor-consciousness in a populace is often part of a deliberate effort to enhance critical ability.

The major problem in addressing propaganda to a hostile audience, then, is the establishment of a channel that is above suspicion. It is precisely in such situations that "black" propaganda is attempted. "White" propaganda is promotion in which the source is openly acknowledged, as in most advertising. Propaganda is "black" when the source is concealed or disguised so that the target group is led to believe that the information is coming from within its own ranks (Becker, 1949). Some publicists have advocated the use of rumors to gain access to target groups that would otherwise be inaccessible; the major advantage claimed for rumors is anonymity. General Ludendorff is quoted as saying, for example, that rumor is the most dangerous means of propaganda precisely because beliefs are planted from sources that cannot be traced (Bartlett, 1940, p. 90).

When the impression is created that information originated within the group being propagandized, victims feel that the reports come from parties with whom their own interests are identified, and they are less cautious. Thus, the deliberate use of rumors in politics involves the exploitation of many persons who believe they are sharing news.

In considering procedures for manipulating rumors, we must remember that combatants are quick to charge their opponents with spreading false rumors. Indeed, much of what has been written on this subject consists of indignant accusations against foes. Especially in time of war, when many are concerned with the preservation of morale, countless polemics arise against the enemy and his diabolical propaganda schemes. But the very parties denouncing enemy falsehoods are often not too careful about the accuracy of their own charges, and many of these accusations are themselves propagandistic. The charge of an outraged party that an opponent had taken unfair advantage of him through calumny is not per se evidence of successful control of rumors; this is a political accusation. We must distinguish carefully between evidence that someone has successfully manipulated informal communication and charges made by politicians.

The Deliberate Propagation of Rumors

The manipulation of informal communication has always been a part of politics. Rumors of secret treaties, partial mobilizations, troop concentrations; and conspiracies have long played parts in international relations. In heated election campaigns character assassination is often accomplished through rumors; charges that cannot be published with impunity are whispered. Rumors about the perverse tendencies of various candidates have been prominent in several American presidential elections. Thomas Jefferson was charged with being an atheist, with fathering several Negro children, and with debauching the daughter of a well-known Virginian. Martin van Buren was said to be the illegitimate son of Aaron Burr, and his running mate was reported to be a Negro. Grover Cleveland was described as a drunkard who constantly abused his wife (Adams, 1932). Rumors have sometimes been used to contradict what has to be announced publicly. In the bitter struggle in 1945 for the mayor-alty of Detroit, labor leader Frankensteen was the victim of many rumors. Although he was an Episcopalian, he was rumored to be Jewish, and among Jews it was charged that he was anti-Semitic. His opponents circulated cards, ostensibly coming from Frankensteen headquarters, urging Negroes to vote for him in order to eliminate residential segregation; the cards, however, were circulated in white areas in support of rumors that Negroes had been promised some-thing "special" for their votes (Smith and Sarasohn, 1946). In these instances political interests were well served by rumors that devel-oped at convenient times, although evidence that they were delib-erately initiated by those who profited from them is not available.

In time of war some leaders have attempted to impair the determi-nation of enemy troops and to sap their will to fight by "leaking" false information on their own strength. This is an old trick. Genghis Khan, who conquered most of Asia and a large part of Europe, did not have enough manpower to win by force alone. He used mobile forces and relied heavily on intelligence and propaganda. Before attacking, he had agents plant reports exaggerating the number, stupidity, and ferocity of his men in order to frighten his enemies. His "numberless hordes" were actually small, highly mobile cavalry units (Linebarger, 1948, pp. 14–16). General Smedley Butler (1931) of the U. S. Marines relates an incident in 1912 in which 375 Ameri-cans were ordered to open a railroad between Managua and Granada in the midst of a Nicaraguan revolution. Butler claims that he ar-ranged a "leak" to native channels that the Marines were 1,500 strong and equipped with heavy artillery. He then placed extra cam-paign hats on poles and covered with canvas small cannons elongated with dummy barrels. The guerrillas apparently had no desire to attack 1,500 well-equipped troops, and the railroad was opened with-out further difficulties. Reports of current guerrilla activities in Guatemala indicate that the rebels are now using similar tactics. Whenever government troops come to a village, peasants relate to them the latest word on the guerrillas. One widespread rumor was that Sosa, the guerrilla leader, had been on Havana radio with Fidel

Castro and had promised to be back with more arms. Rumors of increasing guerrilla strength tend to demoralize the soldiers, who are only peasants in uniform who for the time being are subject to military discipline (Gilly, 1965, pp. 25–30).

In a capitalistic society, where so many are preoccupied with accumulating wealth, it is not surprising that attempts would be made to manipulate market prices through rumors. Oman (1918) reports an incident in 1814, when a group of speculators in London who had gambled on the early collapse of Napoleon's defensive fight in Champagne worked out a detailed imposture. They sent a bogus Russian officer to land at Dover with news that the emperor had been defeated and slain. While the semaphores carried this message, a group of supposed French officers drove through London with the same report. The speculators were able to sell out. When official news arrived later, they were easily detected, for they were the only ones who had sold out, at once and without hesitation, and had profited.

Informal communication channels have also been used in advertising campaigns. In 1934 sales of Chesterfield cigarettes were affected by a rumor that a leper had been found working in the factory in Richmond, Virginia. This report was apparently introduced into informal channels by two-man teams; they would enter a crowded subway car at opposite ends, move toward each other, and then carry on a conversation about the leper while others were still standing between them. They attributed the information to newspapers. Liggett and Myers offered a reward of $25,000 to anyone who furnished evidence identifying the party responsible; in 1938 the company even posted signs in stores repeating its offer, but no takers have appeared (Jacobson, 1948, pp. 159–86). Paid agents who mingle with potential customers in public places to extol the virtues of certain goods have been used to advertise many other products. Several public relations firms have used these methods, and some even advertise such services openly (Cole, 1936; Littell and McCarthy, 1936; Grant, 1946). Unlike open advertising, such remarks are not labeled as paid publicity and discounted; furthermore, such agents can make claims for a product that an advertiser would not dare make in print. Although allegations of this kind have been made periodically, as Liggett and Myers discovered, they are difficult to prove.

In modern mass societies both political activity and warfare are often carried on by large organizations that are highly bureaucratized. In many places informal promotion is planned and executed by departments specializing in such work. In his study of public opinion in the Soviet Union Inkeles (1950, pp. 67–131) reports that the Communist party places great emphasis upon face-to-face contacts between party representatives and the masses. Party members and reliable sympathizers are recruited for "oral agitation" duties; their task is to meet periodically with fellow workers in factories, collective farms, and other establishments to bring the "correct" interpretation of various events to the people. According to Alexander Orlov (1963, pp. 20–23), a Russian intelligence officer who defected to the West, one of the eight lines of activity pursued by the K.G.B., the Soviet intelligence apparatus, is devoted to misinforming and misleading foreign governments. Once high-level decisions have been made on the impression to be created abroad, this bureau arranges "leaks" to officials of the governments involved. Nor are the Russians alone in such activity. In an N.B.C. telecast on May 4, 1965, a former operations chief in the C.I.A. admitted sending a psychologist to Guatemala to start a rumor campaign against the Arbenz government, which was subsequently overthrown.

In modern warfare crucial decisions are made by a relatively small number of men who make up the high commands. Since these decision-makers must work on the basis of their estimates of the situation, psychological warfare operations have been aimed at them, and these sometimes include the use of rumors. One operation in World War II, designed to discourage a German invasion of the British Isles, has been described by J. B. White (1955, pp. 1–10), a former intelligence officer. British defenses in 1940 were inadequate, and the plan was to create the impression that Britain intended to defend the homeland by setting fire to the sea. After chemical warfare experts had confirmed its possibility, the report was fed to pipelines in Stockholm, Lisbon, Madrid, Cairo, Istanbul, and New York. That the rumor was being entertained by German soldiers was confirmed in interrogations of Luftwaffe pilots shot down over England. Then three incidents provided apparent substantiation. An R.A.F. unit on an incendiary bombing mission happened to catch a German battalion in invasion practice at Calais and dropped its load. Since hospital facilities there were limited, Germans who were badly burned had to be sent back to Paris, where a rumor developed that these men had been wounded in an abortive invasion attempt. The British Navy captured a German trawler, guarded by soldiers drawn from several different army units. Radio broadcasts were made in German that these men, identified by name and organization, had been "rescued from the sea." Each unit could identify its own man on temporary duty elsewhere, and the impression apparently developed that the other divisions named, whose actual whereabouts were cloaked in military secrecy, had been involved in an invasion attempt. Then the German command began some experiments on fireproofing invasion barges with asbestos. When they sent troops into a pool of burning gasoline in Normandy, the experiment failed, and the men were badly burned. Word of their wounds leaked out. By mid-September of 1940 many German soldiers facing the British channel were convinced that their comrades had been burned in an invasion attempt, and morale is reported to have dropped. Of course, the decision of the German High Command against invading England in 1940 was based upon many considerations, including the failure of the Luftwaffe to destroy the R.A.F. This is more a record of what was attempted than of what was actually accomplished.

As Dauzat (1919, p. 21) points out, encouragement and exploitation of rumors that are already developing is much easier than planting new ones. To take advantage of conditions after they arise is one thing; to create them for the sake of advantage is another. Sometimes astute politicians have taken advantage of spontaneous communication simply by maintaining official silence. In March 1939, André Philippe disclosed the following incident to the French Chamber of Deputies. Arabs in Tunisia were skeptical of French newspapers, and it was difficult to neutralize Italian appeals for their support. Accordingly, when the Italians in neighboring Libya adopted a colonial policy inimical to the Arabs—bringing in settlers from Italy to dispossess natives of their land—the French newspapers printed nothing about it. Instead news was permitted to drift in by marketplace discussions. Arabs heard of the new policy from trusted sources. As a result, when Tunisia was threatened by the Italians in early 1939, they united solidly behind the French in spite of their nationalistic aspirations (Rose, 1940).

Although some publicists have made extravagant claims of successful campaigns they have organized, such professions are difficult to assess in the absence of independently collected evidence. Boasts of professional propagandists are to be discounted, for records of such attainments are obviously to their advantage, adding to their professional stature. Similarly, charges that opponents have sown inconvenient rumors must also be viewed with caution. During World War II many American officials were convinced that German agents were using rumor campaigns, but careful studies have failed to produce concrete evidence. In a study for the Office of Naval Research Kishler and his associates (1960) checked confessions and diaries of German propagandists, logs of short-wave broadcasts, and records of the O.W.I. and other agencies with listening posts. They note many parallels between Axis radio broadcasts and current rumors; during one seven-month period there were as many as 79 items. Bruner and Sayre (1941) found that prior to United States entry into the war many Italians in Boston listened to short-wave broadcasts and then disseminated the information to others. Ruch and Young (1942) interviewed 400 people each in New York and Boston and found that almost 20 per cent of their sample had heard at least one of four items monitored at a C.B.S. short-wave listening post. That persons with pro-Axis sympathies would listen to short-wave broadcasts is not surprising, nor is it unusual that members of the German Embassy would make statements favorable to German policy. If some of these reports were seriously entertained by other Americans, this is not proof that a systematic whispering campaign had been launched. It would mean only that many Americans found these accounts more plausible than what they saw in their newspapers. The Kishler report concludes that effectiveness of rumor campaigns cannot be evaluated on such insufficient data.

Some enthusiastic publicists suggest that whispering campaigns are easy to organize, that desired results may be obtained merely by planting reports in informal channels. Of course, arrangements can easily be made to plant reports within most groups. The major difficulty, however, is controlling rumor content after the transaction gets under way. Like mobs, rumors are difficult to keep in check. They form spontaneously, and the line of development depends upon fortuitous events, momentary emotional reactions of those who happen to be on the scene, and the particular interests of those who make up the public. Within certain limits agents may be able to direct and redirect conversations, but the extent of their effective intervention appears circumscribed. Regardless of the skill of an agitator, proposals are not accepted unless they reflect the developing mood. Especially in situations marked by intense excitement an agitator can succeed only if he gives fitting expression to what is already "in the air." Overly solicitous concern shown by those whose interests are served by a rumor often arouses suspicions and enhances skepticism. The ultimate product is a definition that is plausible from the standpoint of the target group. When its morale is high, a planted rumor may well boomerang against its initiators. Thus, many experienced propagandists are inclined to discount the effectiveness of rumors. For example, when Dr. von Strempel (1946), who had been First Secretary of the German Embassy in Washington, D.C., was questioned after the war about promotional techniques used by German agents in the United States, he admitted that some of his colleagues had indulged in "whispering campaigns" in 1940 and 1941. They had encouraged reports that Germany would win the European war, had contradicted atrocity stories, and had supported anti-Semitic tales. When asked for his personal estimate of such operations, the propagandist dismissed them as "nonsense."

Several attempts have been made in studies of small group interaction to generate rumors experimentally, and a careful examination of these cases reveals that all the successfully manufactured rumors were items that would have developed spontaneously in these contexts anyway. The already cited study of Schachter and Burdick (1955) was the most successful. When girls in a small school were removed from their classrooms without explanation, rumors were very likely to develop, and the experimenters provided a plausible reason. Sinha (1952) experimented with ten subjects soon after a landslide in Darjeeling, and the experimental rumors developed just as the others. Their contents, however, were indistinguishable from the spontaneous rumors he had collected on the scene. The study by

Festinger, Schachter, and Back (1950) also developed as expected; information concerning national publicity for the housing project reached only those who were thought to be interested. Back and his associates (1950) were also successful, but they too used the kinds of news items that would be of concern to employees in the organization they studied. On the other hand, Schall, Levy and Tresselt (1950) worked with material that was not plausible to the subjects; their study failed.

The manipulation of events for promotional purposes has on occasion been quite successful, and rumors have sometimes figured prominently in these schemes. Cromwell's conquest of Ireland during the Puritan revolution is a case to the point. In 1649 Cromwell found himself in a difficult position. Since a war with Scotland had already begun, he wanted to pacify Ireland without fighting; he wanted to save his troops. In his letters to Parliament Cromwell indicated his intention to crush resistance in Ireland through terror. After making dreadful threats against all who dared to oppose him, he ordered massacres in two towns—Drogheda and Wexford. These were carried out in a spectacular manner; although more than 4,000 were slain, care was taken that a number would escape in the midst of the carnage. As expected, the refugees fled to all parts of Ireland, giving extravagant accounts of the number killed and of frightful atrocities. Opposition collapsed; many Irish units dissolved when a Puritan army approached, and the area was subdued in less than nine months (Case 12). Edwards (1927, pp. 156–85) indicates that the purpose of terrorism is not destruction but the creation of an atmosphere of fear in order to faciliate political control. An attempt is made to create the impression that everyone is being watched and that any hostile move will bring instant retaliation. Rumors of the omniscience and vengefulness of those in power are encouraged, and from time to time such views are substantiated by dramatic public executions (Kohn-Bramstedt, 1945).

In three of the cases of the successful manipulation of rumors—the London financiers speculating on Napoleon's defeat, Schachter and Burdick's experiment, and Cromwell's massacres—it was the event rather than the report that was manufactured. Reports that reached the target groups were quite genuine, though somewhat exaggerated. Politically significant events were staged, and the situations were defined spontaneoulsy in the desired manner. The plans, of course, were based upon an intuitive recognition of the kinds of rumors likely to emerge. Thus, events may be manipulated to develop special sensitivities, which make men receptive to certain kinds of reports. Then the desired definitions may be planted, or they may arise spontaneously. For the cunning and unscrupulous this is a most effective form of promotion, and it is effective precisely because it is not identified as propaganda. People are suspicious of reports from anyone who stands to profit from them, but when events are staged, they are reported by eyewitnesses or others whose integrity and motives cannot be questioned. Not only is credibility of source unchallenged, the reports may even be checked, for they are accurate.

Although evidence is far from clear, it appears that a rumor may be successfully manufactured only under the same conditions under which it would develop spontaneously. There must be demand for news on that topic; it must come from a source that is trusted in the target group; and content must be plausible and consistent with the prevailing mood. This suggests that much of the success of propagandists may have been accidental and that they are not mentioning their many failures. Establishment of a successful information program requires much more knowledge. The initial step in organizing an information campaign is establishment of respect and receptivity for the channel to be used. Thus, Dr. von Strempel indicated that he made a special effort to stay away from American fascists so that he himself would not be discredited. Even with confidence in the source it is still necessary to ascertain the interests and beliefs shared in the target group. Mere presentation of messages is of little consequence, for men are selectively sensitized only to items relevant to their concerns. Furthermore, no matter how accurate a message, it will fall upon deaf ears unless it is consistent with what is taken for granted. Thus, Voice of America programs that are pleasing to Americans may be incomprehensible to outsiders. Formulation of messages requires special ingenuity; they must fall within the limits of plausibility and also reflect the current mood. In the long run, exaggerations and falsehoods are self-defeating. Falsehoods are exposed through inexpedient action, and such discovery leads to rejection of not only the message but the source as well.

The Suppression of Inconvenient Rumors

In the heat of conflict all kinds of proposals are made for the control of rumors. Even scholars occasionally lend support to plans which, when examined dispassionately, are amazing for their impracticality. Some officials apparently set as their objective the suppression of all rumors, but it is not clear whether they mean by this the elimination of (a) false beliefs, (b) beliefs that are inconvenient for the regime in power, or (c) a particular mode of communication. The elimination of all discourse other than discussions restricted to verified propositions is obviously an unrealistic goal—even for scientists discussing scientific data. Because many combatants believe that only their adversaries are liars they feel safe in advocating elimination of all false intelligence, but astute politicians know better; some even recognize privately that their own beliefs may also be biased. Although few people who advocate the suppression of inconvenient rumors realize it, rumor control, if taken seriously, constitutes an attempt at thought control. Because rumors are commonly identified with false reports most persons readily consent to their suppression, but rumors are not necessarily false. The suppression of rumors is actually a form of propaganda; it involves the manipulation of communication content so that desired perspectives will be formed.

The usual reaction of anyone who feels maligned is to issue a denial. Sometimes, if a rumor in retrospect seems absurd or if people are inclined to have doubts anyway, a denial from a trusted source is effective. Thus, in 1948, when rumors developed that the initials "JS" on the new Roosevelt dimes stood for "Josef Stalin," the director of the mint issued an indignant denial, and the matter was apparently settled. Usually, however, the denial of rumors is ineffective. People sometimes confuse the denial with the charge. Those who had not heard the charge may hear the denial and may find the latter unconvincing. Furthermore, mere refutation leaves initiative with the opponent. As Senator McCarthy amply demonstrated, spectacular accusations attract widespread attention, but only a few notice sober replies. Some students of propaganda have insisted that the only really effective defense against propaganda is promotion favoring some alternative program (Lasswell, 1933b, p. 526). Although antagonists are quick to accuse their foes of spreading malicious reports about them, they often fail to realize that rumors do not become current unless they are plausible to the public. The mere fact that someone makes a charge does not mean that others will take it seriously; men are responsive only to suggestions that are consistent with their beliefs and inclinations. Exaggeration on trivial matters leads only to amused skepticism, as in the size of canned olives, and implausible contentions on serious matters lead to rejection of report and channel. That embarrassing rumors are seriously entertained, then, is an indication that many people are already disposed to believe them. Rumors about an exaggerated number of pregnant women emerge, for example, whenever there are social upheavals that disturb traditional relations between the sexes. That young people who are uprooted will seek amorous adventures is an expectation that is widely shared, and such reports, though grossly exaggerated, are plausible. Only chauvinists who view their own women in idealistic terms find them slanderous.

Censorship has frequently been attempted, but it tends to aggravate the problem once its existence becomes known or suspected. The denial of reports people believe or the punishment of free speech makes official channels suspect. A feeling develops that officials are trying to hide something, even when they are not, and often what is suspected of being hidden turns out to be far more sinister than the facts. Once censorship is suspected, other items from official sources are also distrusted; rumors develop even when all known facts have been disclosed. Gilly (1965) reports that Guatemalan troops tend to believe peasant rumors of guerrilla successes. Even exaggerated accounts of the number of government casualties are accepted. Official news releases recount only victories and never mention army casualties; the soldiers know that these accounts cannot possibly be accurate, for they themselves have participated in engagements in which some of their comrades have fallen. Hence, they have formed an exaggerated respect for the prowess of guerrilla fighters. Commenting on the concern of civil defense officials with people's feelings of insecurity over atomic attacks, Janis (1951, pp. 224–25) reflects the considered opinion of authorities in the field when he advises that pessimism cannot be prevented by suppressing information. Once official channels are regarded as unreliable, people are no longer reassured by denials, and many rumors will develop.

Efforts have also been made to control spontaneous communication through law. In stock markets control of news has always been a problem, and the Security and Exchange Act of 1933 makes the deliberate use of rumors to manipulate stock prices illegal. Local exchanges also have rules against the practice, and officials are continually on guard against "tips," but such rules are difficult to enforce (Rose, 1951). Especially in time of war attempts are made to combat subversive rumors by fixing legal responsibility and punishing the guilty (Simon, 1915). During World War II the Germans attempted to control inimical rumors in conquered areas through stringent decrees; people were fined or imprisoned for making statements likely to jeopardize a successful occupation (Lemkin, 1944). In England a defense regulation made the spreading of alarm or despondency illegal; defendants had the burden of proving that they had reasonable cause to believe a rumor was true and that their intentions were not malicious (Rolph, 1944). In 1955, as tensions between Europeans and Africans intensified, the government of Southern Rhodesia passed a similar law, but its oppenents pointed to the danger that it might be used to suppress any political movement in disfavor with the government. Laws against slander and false witness are old, but they have always been difficult to enforce, and the legal regulation of rumor has generally proved ineffective.

One of the most common procedures for controlling rumors in times of calamity consists of appeals from respected leaders. In 1938 President Roosevelt made public his famous "letter to an unnamed citizen," lashing out against critics of his administration by pointing to its actual achievements and contrasting them to whispered charges. During World War II the Massachusetts Committee on Public Safety was dedicated largely to the prevention and control of rumors through publicity. Reports were collected at listening posts, refuted by authorities or experts, and published in the *Boston Herald*. Reprints of these articles were then sent to interested parties in other parts of the country. Although such campaigns are aimed against "rumors," what is actually being attacked is any verbalization that does not support the war effort. These appeals tend to enhance rumor-consciousness and put many people on guard. Since rumors develop spontaneously among men who sincerely believe what they are saying, however, such appeals are often ineffective. Even a man who agrees in principle that rumors should be discouraged will discuss a report he believes to be true, obviously because he does not label it a "rumor."

One procedure that has been recommended by virtually all who have investigated rumors seriously is providing adequate information through institutional channels. Uris (1954) and Hershey (1956), industrial consultants relying heavily on Allport and Postman, recommend that management supply information clearly and unambiguously to head off rumors, give personnel advance notice of contemplated changes, keep them informed of progress being made, and encourage their bringing questions to supervisors. This technique has sometimes been applied in ingenious ways with considerable success. In the autumn of 1953, for example, when the Pentagon announced a budget cut, rumors of closing or of curtailing production developed in various war plants throughout the country. Employees were naturally concerned with possibilities of staff and salary cuts. When such rumors disrupted morale at the Serv-Air Aviation Corporation in Kinston, North Carolina, the president of the firm ordered a white outhouse labeled "Rumor Factory" to be brought to the grounds and asked all employees to examine the two bulletin boards within. One was labeled "rumor," and anyone could jot down his favorite; the other was labeled "fact," and there the president answered all questions. During the next two months more than 100 questions were answered; in November, when ten days went by without a single new rumor being recorded, the building was draped in black crepe and hauled away. Tension had dropped, and morale was visibly improved (*Time*, 1953). Similar results are reported in the following case.

Case 9. THE LEPER WOMAN IN BLACK. Early in June 1957, elementary school children in San Diego were upset by rumors of a leper woman dressed in black who was begging pennies. Older children tried to frighten younger ones by exaggerated accounts of the danger, and the general impression developed that anyone touched by a leper would disintegrate. In one school the principal sent the school nurse to each classroom to discuss leprosy and to answer all questions students might have. No further excitement developed there.

In a second school the principal left the refutation up to individual teachers. In spite of their efforts several rumors developed. One was that the woman in black had already killed 100 people. Another was that the woman in black was lying dead in the girls' washroom. Late in the afternoon a boy with a window seat, seeing a woman living nearby pass the schoolground dressed in black, yelled, "There she goes!" Five girls became hysterical. Just before school closed, word spread that the woman in black had taken refuge in an apartment in the alley near the playground. After the bell students gathered in the alley and began to mill about. Some claimed that they saw the woman peering at them through a window. A rock hit the window, and boys talked excitedly of breaking down the door. The principal, several teachers, and a policeman arrived just in time to disperse the children.

On the following day a riot almost ensued at another school, when a mother who wanted to complain of the effect of the rumor on her children arrived in a black dress.

One counter-propaganda measure that has proved quite effective in rumor control is charging that the enemy has an impressive propaganda machine against which constant vigilance is necessary. As Lasswell (1927) indicates, the claim that the enemy conducts a lying propaganda is extremely useful, for any embarrassing report can be dismissed as another effort by the opposition to sow disunity. Adverse reports about the shortcomings of allies, unfortunate conditions on the battlefield, and inefficiencies in bureaucracies at home are bound to develop. A psychological barrier can be interposed between such dangerous information and the public by planting the suspicion that all unfavorable news is likely to be a specimen of cunning enemy propaganda. Once this supposition is firmly planted, a mighty weapon is forged against internal cleavages and defeatism. Thus, during World War I numerous articles appeared in American periodicals condemning reports undermining national unity as having been inspired by German agents and questioning the loyalty of those who repeated them; the Committee on Public Information distributed a pamphlet entitled *The German Whisper*, listing and refuting a number of rumors and inconvenient charges against government officials, allies, and various segments of the population. During the height of the depression, when banks were failing throughout the country, some businessmen accused Communists of spreading pessimistic rumors that touched off bank runs. By imputing vile motives to anyone who believed that banks might fail, an effort was made to discourage all such conversations (*Literary Digest,* 1931). During World War II this technique was used on both sides. Schöne (1936, p. 14) charged that techniques of calumny had been developed systematically by Germany's enemies. In 1941 Propaganda Minister Göbbels attempted to suppress grumblers in Germany through ridicule, by creating two characters with the comic names of Herr Bransig and Frau Knöterich, who listened to B.B.C. broadcasts. Later a campaign was launched against "black listeners," those who repeated what they heard on the broadcasts (Kris and Speier, 1944).

In the United States, Nazi propagandists were credited with having perfected systematic techniques for demoralizing opponents through rumors. Many officials were convinced that the Nazis had established an efficient organization of specialists in psychological warfare who were working on scientific means of controlling human thought (Farago, 1942). The part played by rumors in the "war of nerves" was frequently mentioned in popular literature. Some feared that they would become powerless puppets in the hands of clever madmen, and frantic calls were made for adequate defense. Social scientists, eager to show the part their skills could contribute to the war effort, made diligent efforts to analyze the phenomenon and to devise procedures for control. As the suppression of rumors became a key defensive measure, the populace was constantly cautioned against "loose talk," as if each American possessed vital secrets. Although this proved to be a fairly effective promotional device, there is evidence that it was developed inadvertently, for many American officials apparently *believed* their own charges. In some quarters fear of German rumors assumed almost hysterical proportions. The following case is indicative of the sincerity of high-level officials.

Case 30. REPATRIATION OF PREGNANT WACS. The Women's Army Corps was first organized in 1942, and during World War II almost 100,000 served. This was the first time that American women had been in the armed forces, and many questions arose. Since so few women were assigned to each post, most enlisted men found them beyond reach and resentfully labeled them as "officer's bait." In their constant talk of erotic matters many unsavory rumors about these women emerged: that a large percentage of WAC's had once been prostitutes, that volunteers found to be virgins were rejected, that any soldier seen dating a WAC would be seized by military police for medical examination and possible treatment for venereal disease. One widespread rumor was that the women were issued free contraceptives when going on leave. Since millions of male soldiers in the U.S. Army had been issued free prophylactics as a precautionary measure against venereal diseases, this appeared to be a reasonable policy for women as well.

During the spring of 1943 civic leaders were disturbed by rumors that large numbers of pregnant WAC's were being returned from North Africa. In Boston a campaign was waged against the slander; an eminent psychologist declared in the *Boston Herald* that anyone who took such accounts seriously was not only unpatriotic but immoral, and perhaps in need of psychiatric care. Official reaction was even more serious. Since women were being recruited to release men for combat duty, Nazi agents were suspected of attempting to discredit the Women's Army Corps to weaken American striking power. In June 1943, therefore, an extensive investigation was launched by the F.B.I. and the Military Intelligence Service to see what part had been played by enemy agents in the propagation of these rumors. The inquiry revealed that no German operatives were involved.

Subsequent investigations have revealed that German efforts in psychological warfare, especially their "scientific" character, had been greatly overestimated. Not long after the termination of hostilities

British Intelligence units discovered that the psychological sections of the German Army had been dissolved by order of the High Command on December 15, 1941, only a week after the United States had declared war. Military psychology had developed as part of the Nazi rearmament program and had hit its peak of influence in 1937–38; by the outbreak of the war, however, its prestige was declining. Although the Propaganda Ministry continued its operations, army psychologists were released, and some were subsequently drafted for other military duties (D. R. Davis, 1946). American officials knew only of the build-up and had no way of knowing the fate of the organization until after the war. Although it was apparently not planned intentionally, the belief that the Germans had succeeded in perfecting "whispering campaign" techniques appears to have been an exaggeration that served admirably the purposes of Allied psychological warfare. It was not until a decade after the war that many popular beliefs about German "fifth column" techniques were also exposed as having been grossly inaccurate (Jong, 1956).

Since men are responsive to rumors only if there is a demand for news, some have advocated lessening demand either by reducing anxieties or by keeping them too busy to think about news. Loewenberg (1943, p. 142) declares that the way to control rumor is to desensitize people and to reduce their internal anxieties as far as possible. He also recommends that individual "panic carriers" be isolated before they could influence others with their anxieties. Schöne (1936, pp. 9, 25–26) and Brinkmann (1943, p. 209) point out that rumors are related to disturbances in the routine of life; as long as the disturbances remain, it is useless to deny or contradict rumors. The only way to control rumors is to prevent disturbances or to restore order quickly. During World War II many psychologists advised military officials to keep their men busy. Knapp (1944, pp. 36–37) and Boring (1945, p. 442) advised against idleness and monotony. Anyone who has ever served in military units knows, however, that being required to perform unnecessary tasks usually leads to resentment and to rumors that the officer in charge is "bucking for promotion." What is called "idle gossip" can be minimized by work, provided it is productive and contributes to a goal toward which men are committed; mere "busy work" will definitely not discourage rumors.

Although there are cases in which rumors have been successfully refuted, as in Kinston, North Carolina, as a rule claims of successful suppression are difficult to assess. If no rumors develop over a given period, it is quite possible that nothing would have happened even if no precautions had been taken. Furthermore, a rumor believed to have been "nipped in the bud" might not have developed anyway. Nonetheless, there are indications that some procedures have been more effective than others, and these involve manipulation of demand for news and of the evaluation of sources.

Most serious students of politics seem to agree that retaining faith in the reliability of institutional channels is of decisive importance. But faith in communication channels cannot be established merely by advertising them as truthful. It is by demonstrating efficiency that channels attain their reputation; trusted sources are those that have in the past consistently provided adequate information. Several practical difficulties arise. Sometimes accurate news is embarrassing; it may favor the opponent. Sometimes, especially in war, accurate news may aid the enemy, and this poses a dilemma. Dedicated politicians differing in ideological commitments as widely as Sir Winston Churchill and Che Guevara have favored honest revelation of embarrassing news on the ground that a reputation of being unreliable is in the long run far more damaging than disclosing a few unpleasant facts. They argue that candid disclosure of uncomfortable news, which would probably come out anyway, earns a trust for the source that no amount of clever propaganda could possibly win. The recent handling of news by high officials suggests that this policy is *not* being followed by the United States government. The problem should perhaps be reformulated: it is not so much how to keep people from entertaining inconvenient beliefs, but how to provide reliable information to those in distress.

Limitations of Institutional Control

Although tyranny is not new, thoughtful men in recent years have become increasingly alarmed over awesome prospects arising from the development of effective techniques of political subjugation and con-

trol, especially through the manipulation of beliefs. In the last analysis political power rests on the consent or acquiescence of the governed, but if the views of men can be manipulated, is there any
safeguard to limit the power of those who control the channels of
communication? Informational strategy takes on far greater significance in modern mass societies, for the stakes for which interest
groups compete are higher. Systematically ordered procedures have
replaced the more informal means of persuasion that served smaller
societies, and efforts are constantly being made to develop even
greater proficiency. To what extent can men in mass societies be
duped into acting against their own interests, serving inadvertently
the purposes of a selfish few? Can they be permanently misled to
support a system of life which leaves them and their progeny in
disadvantageous positions? In the past slaves, downtrodden serfs, and
inferior castes have supported regimes that offered them little beyond
a vegetative existence. Can this be done on an even larger scale in the
modern world? Assuming that some madman would find it worthwhile to try, could the degree of political control depicted in George
Orwell's imaginative fiction be accomplished?

In a democratic society public policy is formed through deliberation; people are able to exercise some measure of control of their own
fate by participating in the formation of consensus. In modern mass
societies, however, transactions that most significantly affect the citi-
zenry—control of nuclear energy, fiscal policy, foreign affairs, civil
rights—are so complex that only specialists can understand them.
Furthermore, key decisions are made by a handful of men strategically located in vast bureaucracies. To be sure, decision-makers are
answerable to the public in that failure will eventually lead to their
downfall. But can any measure of popular control over public policy
be retained if those in positions of power are able to "manage"
news?

In mass societies men are not likely to learn about events that
occur beyond the confines of their local community unless they are
reported in the media of mass communication. Thus, news agency
personnel and those who control them are in a position to exercise
disproportionate influence over the definition of crisis situations.
Powerful interests can and often do influence the formation of collec-

tive definitions, but it should be emphasized that such parties cannot dictate belief. Perception being selective, men do not respond to all the material to which they are exposed; each notices only what concerns him. What men do perceive they interpret within the frame of reference of their own social world, and in each social world somewhat different standards of plausibility exist. Furthermore, men rarely perceive and decide in isolation. They discuss mass media content with others around them and form their judgments as a result of this discussion (Katz, 1957). It is precisely because men do not accept everything at face value that so many rumors arise.

Whenever men have interests that are not adequately covered in institutional channels, they get together among themselves to talk. If what they have to say is prohibited, they will speak only in private with their intimate friends and members of their family. Men act in terms of what they believe to be true, not what they are told by those in positions of authority. If custom or law requires that they avow a belief that they regard as untrue, people may pay "lip service" to what they are supposed to think, but they snicker when no one in authority is looking. They lose respect for those who take falsehoods seriously, and in a crisis they are not likely to act on the basis of beliefs they do not actually hold.

Totalitarian states have long been plagued with dictator jokes. Even with stringent laws and ubiquitous political police uncomplimentary jokes about dictators and other high officials cannot be stamped out. Every new policy seems to produce illicit, off-color jokes that mock the foibles of those in power. Social criticism that is suppressed finds an outlet in anecdotes told at risk of imprisonment. As the Nazis rose to power, for example, Germans quipped that an ideal Aryan was blond like Hitler, slender like Göring, tall like Göbbels, and virile like Schleicher (Lyons, 1935). During the latter part of the Fascist regime in Italy the people scoffed at their own newspapers. Their attitude was one of indifference or of contempt. Those who could read French or German consulted Swiss newspapers, and the Vatican press was popular until it too was brought under government control (S. R. Davis, 1941). That more recently instituted techniques of political control are no more effective is shown by the already cited study of Bauer and Gleicher (1953), showing that the better informed in the Soviet Union rely heavily on rumors. Communist regimes are also plagued by jokes that ridicule various regulations; there is boredom and exasperation with official ideology. In 1958 Boris Pasternak was forced to decline the Nobel Prize, and *Dr. Zhivago* has still not been published in the Soviet Union. It is unlikely, however, that there are many Russian intellectuals who are not aware of what happened; the uproar has apparently stimulated curiosity about the novel, and foreign observers indicate that many show familiarity with the contents of the book. Actual conditions in the Soviet Union reveal that external conformity with the law does not mean that men actually believe everything they are told. External conformity can be coerced, but what men actually believe cannot be controlled.

Accounts of the 1953 anti-Communist uprising in East Germany reveal how popular beliefs emerge in person-to-person interaction. Although the state controlled all the formal media of communication, it was unable to control auxiliary and spontaneous channels. As soon as people heard of the strike on Stalin Allee in East Berlin, protests exploded almost simultaneously throughout East Germany. Even after the uprising had been suppressed by the Red Army, strikes continued in many localities until most of the arrested men had been released. Then, a program of passive resistance began. Men urged each other to "work slower," and production figures dropped. Government charges of "fascist and imperialist agents" were openly mocked. Throughout the uprising and its aftermath the rebels had no access to institutional channels. Radio station RIAS in West Berlin could broadcast news, but plans for strikes and passive resistance could be transmitted only through personal contacts. The regime charged that "provocateurs" were responsible, but it is obvious that the uprising was unplanned and unled. No systematic attack was made on key targets, such as power stations, post offices, bridges, railways, and trunk roads. It was a spontaneous mass protest of people who had had all they could take (Case 59). That this could happen in East Germany is in itself evidence of the limitations of institutional control.

Even with increased education and improved techniques of news dissemination the incidence of rumors does not appear to have diminished. This suggests that unless rulers respect the interests of the ruled there will always be some discrepancy between officially sanctioned views and the actual beliefs of the people. As long as men feel that the news they have been given is incomplete or inaccurate, they will be curious about what they might be missing, and among their intimate friends some are bound to wonder aloud. Therefore, orientations that emerge in primary groups are always to some extent independent of views generally accepted by officials or even by scientists. Even where authoritarian controls are imposed, there are times when spontaneous and auxiliary channels supersede institutional sources. The development of rumors, though sometimes embarrassing and at times even disastrous, is an indication of independent judgment and of the unwillingness of men to accept passively formally approved definitions.

Summary and Conclusion

Although there is apparently a widespread conviction that procedures, based upon scientific knowledge, exist for the manipulation and control of rumors, evidence to support this conviction is not impressive. On the contrary, the record indicates that rumors are extremely difficult to control. Successful manipulation, when it occurs, rests upon a recognition, often intuitive, of the principles of natural selection. Definitions arise through spontaneous communication as people piece together items that are plausible or consistent with their emotional dispositions, and all promotional efforts that ignore this fact are doomed to failure. Certain observations on the relative efficiency of various promotional techniques support this view: (a) Politicians often exploit already current rumors, but they have difficulty in manufacturing other reports that may be more convenient for their purposes. The already current rumors are plausible. (b) When communication channels are suspected, announcements are of little avail. Enemy sources are discounted as soon as they are identified. Similarly, denials of plausible rumors are usually ineffective. Even legal prosecution and appeals to patriotism do not work in counteracting embarrassing items that are believed. (c) The most effective offensive use of rumors involves the staging of events; situations rather than communication content are manipulated, and definitions develop spontaneously. This rests on a shrewd utilization of natural selection. (d) The most effective defense against inconvenient rumors is the charge that the enemy is a clever propagandist. This is consistent with the contrast conception formed of him and at the same time arouses sufficient critical ability so that unfavorable reports are subjected to deliberation. Many of the efforts to control rumors are ineffectual precisely because these considerations are not taken into account. Thus, the record of those who have attempted to control rumors underscores Francis Bacon's contention that those who would control nature must first learn to obey nature's laws.

Various elite groups may seize institutional channels and persuade others to accept ideas that legitimize their ascendancy, but such advantages are generally temporary. Regardless of their formal philosophies most men are pragmatic in their actual orientation toward their world; a premium is placed upon accurate knowledge, for the simple reason that errors in the long run lead to painful consequences. Thus, successful politicians may gain temporary ascendancy through devious maneuvers, but before long their victims become suspicious and their colleagues cynical. So long as there is some disparity of interests between those who control institutional channels and others, some situations are bound to be interpreted through rumors. Of course, this does not justify complacency in the presence of liars, for as John Maynard Keynes is quoted as saying, "in the long run we are all dead." As long as shared beliefs emerge through natural selection, however, perspectives are succesively reconstituted to become increasingly more efficient instruments of adjustment.

APPENDIX

To facilitate comparisons, the diverse materials making up the sixty case studies were coded—to the extent that available information permitted. Since categories, such as intensity of collective excitement and the extent to which rumor content is congruent with cultural axioms, have not been formally defined in terms of specific sets of indicators, the scores in each instance are only subjective judgments on the part of the investigator. Before systematic verification becomes possible such concepts obviously will have to be translated into more precisely specified operations.

LOCATION AND SOURCES	PUBLIC	DEGREE OF TENSION	NUMBER OF RUMORS	INCONGRUENT RUMORS	PAGE
1. Lady Hasting's condition England, 1889 Martin (1962)	Court circles Newspaper readers	Mild Moderate	4 same		—*
2. Jack the Ripper England, 1888 Barnard (1953)	Residents of London	Intense	8	1	60
3. Suicide at Mayerling Austria, 1889 Crankshaw (1963); Payne (1964)	Mass audience in Europe	Moderate	4		132
4. Kidnap scare in Oaxaca Mexico, ca. 1930 E. C. Parsons (1936)	Residents of Mitla	Intense	3	3	—
5. Discovery of ambergris California, 1934 Time (1934)	Residents of Bolinas	Intense	1		—

* Not mentioned.

LOCATION AND SOURCES	PUBLIC	DEGREE OF TENSION	NUMBER OF RUMORS	INCONGRUENT RUMORS	PAGE
6. Negro Troops in Oahu Hawaii, *ca.* 1943 Kubo (1945)	Residents of Kahuku	Mild	2		—
7. Baby-sitter's murderer Missouri, *ca.* 1950 Peterson & Gist (1951)	Residents of a Missouri town	Moderate	35		84, 143
8. Discovery of a corpse Los Angeles, *ca.* 1955 Turner & Killian (1957)	Casual crowd on the scene	Moderate	2		35–36
9. The Leper woman in black San Diego, 1957 Padfield & Gorham (1957)	Elementary school children	Intense	3	2	204
10. President Kennedy's Assassination United States, 1963	Residents of Dallas	Intense	21	3	1–2, 14, 25, 100, 102–103
U.S. President's Commission 1964	Mass audience	Intense	22	1	

	Group	Intensity			
11. Aftermath of the plague Central Europe, 1848–50 Hecker (1859); Nohl (1960)	Gentile survivors	Intense	2		103
12. Cromwell's massacres Ireland, 1649 Bagwell (1963); Edwards (1927)	Irish soldiers and English royalists	Moderate	3		198
13. The siege at Peking China, 1900 Butler (1931); Fleming (1959); Purcell (1963)	Legation personnel Chinese rulers Relief force Home governments	Intense Moderate Intense Moderate	8 1 7 1		—
14. Belgian *francs-tireurs* Belgium, 1914 Langenhove (1916)	German soldiers German civilians	Intense Moderate	9 same	4	109–110, 114
15. Explosion at Halifax Canada, 1917 Prince (1920)	Victims	Intense	2		99–100, 132

217

LOCATION AND SOURCES	PUBLIC	DEGREE OF TENSION	NUMBER OF RUMORS	INCONGRUENT RUMORS	PAGE
16. The Paris gun France, 1918 McGinnis (1942); H. W. Miller (1930)	Residents of Paris	Intense	4	1	—
17. The Bihar earthquake India, 1934 Prasad (1935)	Victims	Intense	14		142
18. Attack on Pearl Harbor Hawaii, 1941 Kimura (1947); Lind (1946); Lord (1957)	Soldiers in Hawaii Civilians in Hawaii Japanese in Hawaii Mainland Americans	Intense Intense Intense Moderate	19 8 1 6	2 1	76, 132–134
19. The Bombing of Hiroshima Japan, 1945 Hersey (1946)	Victims	Intense	5	1	82–34, 82
20. Landslide in Darjeeling Nepal, 1950 Sinha (1952)	Victims	Intense	7		84, 197

218

Event	Group	Intensity			Pages
21. Consecutive earthquakes in London England, 1761 Mackay (1932)	Residents of London	Intense	1	1	142–143
22. Execution of Pugachev Russia, 1776 Bysow (1928); Kaus (1935); G. S. Thompson (1950)	Court circles	Moderate	1		81–82
	Nobles opposing Czarina	Moderate	2		
	Cossacks serving Czarina	Moderate	1		
	Pugachev's followers	Intense	1		
23. The Russian invasion Germany, 1914 Fechter (1934)	German civilians	Intense	1		106–107, 132
	German soldiers	Mild	same		
24. Russians from Archangel England, 1914 Chadwick (1982); Hart (1916); Oman (1918); Pollard (1915); Ponsonby (1928)	English civilians	Moderate	3		135–136, 141
25. Opening of Ruhleben Germany, 1914 Ketchum (1965)	English prisoners	Moderate	25	4	89, 91

LOCATION AND SOURCES	PUBLIC	DEGREE OF TENSION	NUMBER OF RUMORS	INCONGRUENT RUMORS	PAGE
26. The Mons retreat England, 1915	British soldiers	Intense	1		89–90
Oman (1918)	British civilians	Moderate	2	2	
27. President Roosevelt's condition United States, *ca.* 1935 *Time* (1935a); Childs (1936)	Rich Americans	Mild	6	6	90
28. Spy scare Canada, 1940 Doob (1941)	Farmers and fishermen	Moderate	5		121, 136
29. From Pearl Harbor to evacuation San Francisco, 1941–42 Shibutani (1944)	Japanese community	Moderate	34		65–68
30. Repatriation of pregnant WAC's United States, 1942–43 Treadwell (1954); Field notes	American soldiers	Mild	4		206
	American civilians	Mild	1		

220

	Audience	Intensity			Page
31. Waste and special privileges United States, 1942-43 Allport & Lepkin (1945)	American civilians	Mild	12		122
32. The enemy at Munda Solomon Islands, 1943 Wright & Mitchell (1943)	American combat men	Intense	5	3	—
33. Truncated training cycle Georgia, 1944 Field notes	Trainees	Moderate	7		10–13, 25
34. Japanese emigrants and the war Western hemisphere, 1945–46 Field notes; Kimura (1947); Lind (1946); Sady (1947)	Japanese in Tule Lake	Intense	3		150–153
	Relocation centers	Moderate	6		
	Japanese in Hawaii	Moderate	3		
	Japanese in Brazil	Moderate	2		
	Nisei soldiers	Mild	same	reject	
35. Execution of General Yamashita Japan, 1946 Field notes	Japanese mass audience	Moderate	2		—

221

LOCATION AND SOURCES	PUBLIC	DEGREE OF TENSION	NUMBER OF RUMORS	INCONGRUENT RUMORS	PAGE
36. General MacArthur's ancestry Japan, 1946	Underprivileged Japanese	Mild	6		77–80
Field notes	Educated Japanese	Mild	same	reject	
37. Marshal Göring's Suicide Germany, 1946	Prison guards	Moderate	1		82–83
Time (1946)	Newsmen in waiting room	Moderate	same	reject	
38. Famine in Tikopia Solomon Islands, 1952–53	Tikopians at home	Intense	2		47–49. 85
Spillius (1957)	Tikopians abroad	Mild	1		
39. The broken dam New York, 1955	Residents of Port Jervis	Intense	1		123, 126, 132, 142
Danzig, Thayer, & Galanter (1958)					
40. Operation Water Moccasin United States, 1963	Ultraconservative Americans	Moderate	2		80
Bowser (1964); Columbia Broadcasting System (1963)					

41. Coming Day of Judgment New England, 1843–44 Sears (1924)	Millerites	Intense	3		118–120
	Outsiders	Mild	same	reject	
42. Treatment of schistosomiasis South Pacific, 1944–45 J. D. Frank (1946)	Patients in military hospital	Moderate	3		50
43. Coming military occupation Japan, 1945 Field notes	Japanese civilians	Intense	4	2	—
	Japanese prostitutes	Intense	1	1	
44. Republican Convention Philadelphia, 1948 Time (1948)	Delegates	Moderate	5		50–52
45. Miracle at Sabana Grande Puerto Rico, 1953 Tumin & Feldman (1955)	Believers	Intense	3		114–116
	Curious bystanders	Moderate	same	reject	
46. The Great Fear France, 1789 Hampson (1963); Lefebvre (1932, 1947); Stephens (1902)	Residents of Paris	Moderate	5		103–105, 147
	Rural communities in provinces	Intense	4		

LOCATION AND SOURCES	PUBLIC	DEGREE OF TENSION	NUMBER OF RUMORS	INCONGRUENT RUMORS	PAGE
47. The Black Line Tasmania, 1830 Bonwick (1870); Turnbull (1948)	Settlers in Hobart	Moderate	7		—
48. Kishinev Massacre Russia, 1903 Dahlke (1952); Dubnow (1920)	Gentiles Jews	Intense Intense	3 1		—
49. John Chilembwe's uprising Nyasaland, 1915 Shepperson & Price (1958)	European settlers Africans	Intense Moderate	11 8	1	—
50. February Revolution Russia, 1917 Trotsky (1936)	Civilian demonstrators Soldiers	Intense Intense	9 1		113
51. Lenin's loyalty Russia, 1917 Trotsky (1936)	Victorious revolutionaries	Moderate	1		—

Case	Group	Intensity			Page
52. Mutiny in the German Navy Germany, 1918	German sailors	Intense	4	1	—
Schubert & Gibson (1932)	Kiel dockworkers	Intense	2		
53. Chicago race riot Chicago, 1919	Negroes	Intense	2		—
	White residents	Intense	1		
Chicago Com. on Race Relations (1922)					
54. Harlem race riot New York, 1935	Negroes	Intense	1		141–142
Time (1935b); Shapiro & Sullivan (1964)					
55. Reception of Zuni veterans New Mexico, 1945–46	Residents of Zuni pueblo	Mild	2		136–137
Adair & Vogt (1949)					
56. The sacking of Kashmir India, 1947	Moslem residents	Intense	4		—
	Hindu residents	Intense	3		
Alexander (1952); Birdwood (1956); Brecher (1953); Korbel (1954)					

LOCATION AND SOURCES	PUBLIC	DEGREE OF TENSION	NUMBER OF RUMORS	INCONGRUENT RUMORS	PAGE
57. The Bogotá riot Colombia, 1948	Underprivileged	Intense	3	2	137–139
Fluharty (1957); Holt (1964); Martz (1962)	Middle class	Moderate	5		
58. The "Mau Mau" emergency Kenya, 1952–55	European settlers	Intense	17	2	52–55, 159
Kariuki (1964); Leakey (1952); Majdalany (1963)	Kikuyu	Intense	5		
59. Anti-Communist uprising East Germany, 1953	Strikers at Leuna Works	Intense	4		211
Brant (1957); Wechsberg (1953)	Residents of Leuna	Intense	1		
60. Overthrow of Menderez Turkey, 1960 Weiker (1963)	Urban populace	Moderate	5		59

BIBLIOGRAPHY

ADAIR, JOHN, and EVON VOGT, 1949. Navaho and Zuni veterans: a study of contrasting modes of culture change. *American Anthropologist* 51 : 547–61.

ADAMS, JAMES T., 1932. Our whispering campaigns. *Harper's Magazine* 165 : 444–50.

ADBEL RAHMAN, AHMAD S., 1949. Rumor (in Arabic). *Egyptian Journal of Psychology* 5 : 2–18. (*Psychological Abstracts*, 27 : 5108).

ALEXANDER, HORACE, 1952. *Kashmir.* London: Friends Peace Committee.

ALLEN, FREDERICK L., 1922. Newspapers and the truth. *Atlantic Monthly* 129 : 44–54.

ALLPORT, FLOYD H., and MILTON LEPKIN, 1945. Wartime rumors of waste and special privilege. *Journal of abnormal and social Psychology* 40 : 3–36.

ALLPORT, GORDON W., and LEO J. POSTMAN, 1945. The basic psychology of rumor. *Transactions of the New York Academy of Science* 8 : 61–81.

———, 1946. An analysis of rumor. *Public Opinion Quarterly* 10 : 501–17.

———, 1947. *The psychology of rumor.* New York: Henry Holt.

ARNHEIM, RUDOLF, 1949. The Gestalt theory of expression. *Psychological Review* 56 : 156–71.

ARNOLD, MAGDA B., 1946. On the mechanism of suggestion and hypnosis. *Journal of abnormal and social Psychology* 41 : 107–28.

ARONSON, ELLIOT, JUDITH A. TURNER, and J. MERRILL CARLSMITH, 1963. Communicator credibility and communication discrepancy as determinants of opinion change. *Ibid.* 67 : 31–36.

ASCH, SOLOMON E., 1948. The doctrine of suggestion, prestige, and imitation in social psychology. *Psychological Review* 55 : 250–76.

———, 1951. Effects of group pressure upon the modification and distortion of judgments. In H. S. Guetzkow, ed., *Groups, leadership, and men.* Pittsburgh: Carnegie Press. Pp. 177–90.

AVIGDOR, ROSETTE, 1951. The psychology of rumor. *Psychological Newsletter* 34 : 6–10.

BACK, KURT, LEON FESTINGER, BERNARD HYMOVITCH, HAROLD KELLEY, STANLEY SCHACHTER, and JOHN THIBAUT, 1950. The methodology of studying rumor transmission. *Human Relations* 3 : 307–12.

BAGWELL, RICHARD, 1963. *Ireland under the Stuarts and during the interregnum.* Vol. II. London: Holland Press.

BAKER, GEORGE W., and DWIGHT W. CHAPMAN, eds., 1962. *Man and society in disaster.* New York: Basic Books.

BALES, ROBERT F., and FRED L. STRODTBECK, 1951. Phases in group problem solving. *Journal of abnormal and social Psychology* 46 : 485–95.

BANTA, THOMAS J., 1964. The Kennedy assassination: early thoughts and emotions. *Public Opinion Quarterly* 28 : 216–24.

BARNARD, ALLAN, ed., 1953. *The harlot killer.* New York: Dodd, Mead.

BARTLETT, FREDERICK C., 1920. Psychology in relation to the popular story. *Folk-lore* 31 : 264–93.

———, 1932. *Remembering.* London: Cambridge University Press.

———, 1940. *Political propaganda.* London: Cambridge University Press.

BASTIDE, ROGER, 1949. Transmission de légendes et groupes sociaux. *Psyché: revue internationale de psychoanalyse et des sciences de l'homme* 34 : 746–56.

BAUER, RAYMOND A., 1958. The communicator and the audience. *Journal of Conflict Resolution* 2 : 67–77.

———, 1961. Risk handling in drug adoption. *Public Opinion Quarterly* 25 : 546–59.

——— and DAVID B. GLEICHER, 1953. Word-of-mouth communication in the Soviet Union. *Ibid.* 17 : 297–310.

BAUER, WILHELM, 1914. *Die öffentliche Meinung und ihre geschichtlichen Grundlagen.* Tübingen: J. C. B. Mohr.

———, 1933. Public opinion. *Encyclopedia of the social sciences.* Vol. XII. New York: Macmillan. Pp. 669–74.

BECKER, HOWARD, 1949. The nature and consequences of black propaganda. *American sociological Review* 14 : 221–35.

BELGION, MONTGOMERY, 1939. The vogue of rumour. *Quarterly Review* 273 (July) : 1–18.

BERNHEIM, ERNST, 1903–04. Das Verhältnis der historischen Methodik zur Zeugenaussage. *Beiträge zur Psychologie der Aussage* 1 : 110–16.

——, 1920. *Einleitung in der Geschichtswissenschaft.* Berlin: Walter de Gruyter.

BINET, ALFRED, 1900. *La suggestibilité.* Paris: Schleicher Frères.

BIRDWHISTELL, RAY L., 1954. Kinesics and communication. In *Explorations: studies in culture and communication.* Toronto: University of Toronto Press. Pp. 31–41.

BIRDWOOD, CHRISTOPHER B., 1956. *Two nations and Kashmir.* London: Robert Hale.

BLONDEL, CHARLES A. A., 1928. *Introduction à la psychologie collective.* Paris: Armand Colin.

BLUM, JOHN M., 1949. Tumulty and Leavenworth: a case study of rumor. *Journal of abnormal and social Psychology* 44 : 411–13.

BLUMENTHAL, ALBERT, 1932. *Small-town stuff.* Chicago: University of Chicago Press.

——, 1937. The nature of gossip. *Sociology and social Research* 22 : 31–37.

BLUMER, HERBERT, 1936. Social attitudes and non-symbolic interaction. *Journal of educational Sociology* 9 : 515–23.

——, 1948. Public opinion and public opinion polling. *American sociological Review* 13 : 542–54.

——, 1951. Collective behavior. In A. M. LEE, ed., *The principles of sociology.* New York: Barnes & Noble. Pp. 167–222.

BOAS, FRANZ, 1916. The development of folk-tales and myths. *Scientific Monthly* 3 : 335–43.

BOAS, GEORGE, 1937. The complete scandalmonger. *Harper's Magazine* 175 : 270–74.

BOGARDUS, EMORY S., 1928. *Immigration and race attitudes.* Boston: D. C. Heath.

BOGART, LEO, 1950. Spread of news on a local event: a case history. *Public Opinion Quarterly* 14 : 769–72.

BOISEN, ANTON T., 1951. The development and validation of religious faith. *Psychiatry* 14 : 455–62.

BONAPARTE, MARIE, 1947. *Myths of war.* JOHN RODKER, trans. London: Imago.

BONNER, MIRIAM R., 1943. Changes in the speech pattern under emotional tension. *American Journal of Psychology* 56 : 262–73.

BONWICK, JAMES, 1870. *The last of the Tasmanians.* London: Sampson Low, Son & Marston.

BORING, EDWIN G., ed., 1945. *Psychology for the armed services.* Washington, D. C.: Infantry Journal Press.

BORST, MARIE, 1904. Recherches expérimentales sur l'éducabilité et la fidélité du témoignage. *Archives de psychologie* 3 : 233–314.

BOWSER, HALLOWELL, 1964. The wings of madness. *Saturday Review* 47 (October 24) : 26.

BRANT, STEFAN (pseud. for KLAUS HARPPRECHT), 1957. *The East German rising.* CHARLES WHEELER, trans. London: Thames & Hudson.

BRECHER, MICHAEL, 1953. *The struggle for Kashmir.* New York: Oxford University Press.

BREED, WARREN, 1955. Social control in the newsroom. *Social Forces* 33 : 326–35.

BRENMAN, MARGARET, 1942. Experiments in the hypnotic production of anti-social and self-injurious behavior. *Psychiatry* 5 : 49–61.

BRINKMANN, DONALD, 1943–44. Das Gerücht als massenpsychologisches Phänomen. *Schweizerische Zeitschrift für Psychologie und ihre Anwendungen* 2 : 200–12, 272–83.

BRISSEY, F. L., 1961. The factor of relevance in the serial reproduction of information. *Journal of Communication* 11 : 211–19.

BRITT, GEORGE, 1942. *Rumors (made in Germany).* New York: Council for Democracy.

BROCKHAUSEN, CARL, 1915. Wie Gerüchte entstehen. *Internationale Rundschau* 1 : 34–36.

BROWN, STERLING A., 1930. The blues as folk poetry. In B. A. BOTKIN, ed., *Folk say: a regional miscellany.* Norman: University of Oklahoma Press. Pp. 324–39.

BRUNER, JEROME S., JACQUELINE J. GOODNOW, and GEORGE A. AUSTIN, 1956. *A study of thinking.* New York: John Wiley.

BRUNER, JEROME S., and LEO POSTMAN, 1947. Emotional selectivity in perception and reaction. *Journal of Personality* 16 : 69–77.

——, 1949. On the perception of incongruity: a paradigm. *Ibid.* 18 : 206–23.

BRUNER, JEROME S., and J. SAYRE, 1941. Shortwave listening in an Italian community. *Public Opinion Quarterly* 5 : 640–56.

BRYCE, JAMES, 1888. *The American commonwealth.* Vol. III. London: Macmillan.

BUCHER, RUE, 1957. Blame and hostility in disaster. *American Journal of Sociology* 62 : 467–75.

BUCKNER, H. TAYLOR, 1965. A theory of rumor transmission. *Public Opinion Quarterly* 29 : 54–70.

BULL, NINA, 1951. *The attitude theory of emotion.* New York: Nervous and Mental Disease Monographs.

BURKE, KENNETH, 1935. *Permanence and Change.* New York: New Republic.

BURTT, HAROLD E., 1931. *Legal psychology.* New York: Prentice-Hall.

BUTLER, SMEDLEY D., 1931. Dame rumor: the biggest liar in the world. *American Magazine* 111 (June) : 24–26, 155–56.

BYSOW, L. A., 1928. Gerüchte. NATA VON WIESE, trans., *Kölner Vierteljahrshefte für Soziologie* 7 : 301–08, 416–26.

CAMPBELL, DONALD T., 1958. Systematic error on the part of human links in communication systems. *Information and Control* 1 : 334–69.

CANNON, WALTER B., 1929. *Bodily changes in pain, hunger, fear, and rage.* New York: D. Appleton-Century.

CANTRIL, HADLEY, 1938. The prediction of social events. *Journal of abnormal and social Psychology* 33 : 364–89.

——, 1940. *The invasion from Mars.* Princeton: Princeton University Press.

CAPLOW, THEODORE, 1947. Rumors in war. *Social Forces* 25 : 298–302.

CARRARD, ALFRED, 1953. *Psychologie de l'homme au travail.* Neuchatel: Delachaux & Niestlé.

CARROLL, JOSEPH C., 1938. *Slave insurrections in the United States, 1800–1865.* Boston: Chapman & Grimes.

CHADWICK, THOMAS, 1932. *The influence of rumour on human thought and action.* Manchester: Sherratt & Hughes.

CHAKOTIN, SERGE, 1940. *The rape of the masses.* London: Routledge.

CHAPLIN, JAMES P., 1959. *Rumor, fear, and the madness of crowds.* New York: Ballantine Books.

CHAUDHURI, PURNIMA, 1953. A synopsis of an experimental attempt on the study of psychology of rumor. *Indian Journal of Psychology* 28 : 79–86.

CHAUDHURI, SASHI B., 1955. *Civil disturbances during the British rule of India.* Calcutta: World Press.

CHEN, HSIEN-PING, 1939. *Yao-yen ti Tsin Li.* Changsha: Commercial Press *(Psychological Abstracts,* 15 : 365) .

CHICAGO COMMISSION ON RACE RELATIONS, 1922. *The Negro in Chicago.* Chicago: University of Chicago Press.

CHILDS, MARQUIS W., 1936. They hate Roosevelt. *Harper's Magazine* 172 : 634–42.

CHORUS, A., 1953. The basic law of rumor. *Journal of abnormal and social Psychology* 48 : 313–14.

CHURCH, GEORGE F., 1938. Socio-psychological nature of news. *Social Forces* 17 : 190–95.

CLAPARÈDE, E., 1906. Expériences collectives sur le témoignage. *Archives de psychologie* 5 : 344–87.

——, 1928. Le témoignage. *La psychologie et la vie* 2 : 103–05.

CLARK, CARROLL D., 1933. The concept of the public. *Southwestern social science Quarterly* 13 : 313–20.

COHEN, MORRIS R., 1933. Fictions. *Encyclopedia of the social sciences.* Vol. VI. New York: Macmillan. Pp. 225–28.

COLE, PERCY T., 1936. Whispers limited. *Canadian Magazine* 85 : 13, 34.

COLEMAN, JAMES S., 1957. *Community conflict.* Glencoe: Free Press.

——, ELIHU KATZ, and HERBERT MENZEL, 1957. The diffusion of an innovation among physicians. *Sociometry* 20 : 253–70.

COLOMBO, EDUARDO R., and FIDEL MOCCIO, 1961. El vampiro: estudio de un rumor. *Acta neuropsiquiátrica argentina* 7 : 12–19 (*Psychological Abstracts*, 36 : 3GE12C).

COLUMBIA BROADCASTING SYSTEM, 1963. *CBS reports: case history of a rumor.* Telecast on November 13.

COOLEY, CHARLES H., 1918. *Social process.* New York: Charles Scribner's Sons.

——, 1926. The roots of social knowledge. *American Journal of Sociology* 32 : 59–79.

COOPER, EUNICE, and MARIE JAHODA, 1947. Evasion of propaganda: how prejudiced people respond to anti-prejudice propaganda. *Journal of Psychology* 23 : 15–25.

COPELAND, LEWIS C., 1939. The Negro as a contrast conception. In E. T. THOMPSON, ed., *Race relations and the race problem.* Durham: Duke University Press. Pp. 152–79.

CORNETZ, V., 1919. De l'utilité du faux bruit. *Mercure de France* 131 : 605–18.

CRANKSHAW, EDWARD, 1963. *The fall of the house of Habsburg.* New York: Viking Press.

CREEL, GEORGE, 1941. The plight of the last censor. *Collier's* 107 (May 24) : 13, 34–36.

DAHLKE, H. OTTO, 1952. Race and minority riots: a study in the typology of violence. *Social Forces* 30 : 419–25.

DANZIG, ELLIOTT R., PAUL W. THAYER, and LILA R. GALANTER, 1958. *The effects of a threatening rumor on a disaster-stricken community.* Washington, D. C.: National Research Council.

DATTA, DHIRENDON M., 1927. Testimony as a method of knowledge. *Mind* 36 : 354–58.

DAUZAT, ALBERT, 1918. Les faux bruits et les légendes de la guerre. *Mercure de France* 128 : 241–62.

——, 1919. *Légendes, prophéties et superstitions de la guerre.* Paris: La Renaissance du Livre.

DAVIS, D. RUSSELL, 1946. *German applied psychology.* London: British Intelligence Objectives Sub-Committee. Final Report 970.

——, and DURGANAND SINHA, 1950a. The effect of one experience upon the recall of another. *Quarterly Journal of experimental Psychology* 2 : 43–52.

——, 1950b. The influence of an interpolated experience upon recognition. *Ibid.* 2 : 132–37.

DAVIS, SAVILLE R., 1941. Morale in fascist Italy in wartime. *American Journal of Sociology* 47 : 434–38.

DeFLEUR, MELVIN L., 1962. Mass communication and the study of rumor. *Sociological Inquiry* 32 : 51–70.

——, and OTTO N. LARSEN, 1958. *The flow of information.* New York: Harper & Bros.

——, and EDITH D. RAINBOTH, 1952. Testing message diffusion in four communities. *American sociological Review* 17 : 734–37.

DÉKANY, E., 1936. Une forme élementaire de la vie sociale: le public. *Revue internationale de sociologie* 44 : 263–78.

DEUTSCHER, IRWIN, and PETER KONG-MING NEW, 1961. A functional analysis of collective behavior in a disaster. *Sociological Quarterly* 2 : 21–36.

DEWEY, JOHN, 1898. Evolution and ethics. *Monist* 8 : 321–41.

——, 1910a. *How we think.* New York: D. C. Heath.

——, 1910b. *The influence of Darwin on philosophy.* New York: Henry Holt.

——, 1926. *Experience and nature.* Chicago: Open Court.

——, 1927. *The public and its problems.* New York: Henry Holt.

——, 1938. *Logic: the theory of inquiry.* New York: Henry Holt.

DI VESTA, FRANCIS J., 1959. Effects of confidence and motivation on susceptibility to informational social influence. *Journal of abnormal and social Psychology* 59 : 204–09.

DIECK, ALFRED, 1950. Der Weltuntergang am 17 März 1949 in Südhannover: ein Beitrag zur Erforschung von Gerüchten. *Neues Archiv für Niedersachsen* 20 : 704–20.

DIGGORY, JAMES C., 1956. Some consequences of proximity to a disease threat. *Sociometry* 19 : 47–53.

DITTES, JAMES E., 1959. Attractiveness of group as function of self-esteem and acceptance by group. *Journal of abnormal and social Psychology* 59 : 77–82.

DODD, STUART C., 1952. Testing message diffusion from person to person. *Public Opinion Quarterly* 16 : 247–62.

——, 1953. Testing message diffusion in controlled experiments. *American sociological Review* 18 : 410–16.

——, 1956. A test of message diffusion by chain tags. *American Journal of Sociology* 61 : 425–32.

——, 1958–59. Formulas for spreading opinions. *Public Opinion Quarterly* 22 : 537–54.

DODWELL, H. H., ed., 1932. *The Cambridge history of India.* Vol. VI. London: Cambridge University Press.

DOOB, LEONARD W., 1941. War reactions of a rural Canadian community. *Journal of abnormal and social Psychology* 36 : 200–23.

DUBNOW, SIMON M., 1920. *History of the Jews in Russia and Poland.* Vol. III. Philadelphia: Jewish Publication Society of America.

EDWARDS, LYFORD P., 1927. *The natural history of revolution.* Chicago: University of Chicago Press.

EISSLER, RUTH S., 1949. Riots: observation in a home for delinquent girls. *Psychoanalytic Study of the Child* 3–4 : 449–60.

ELLIOTT, HARRISON S., 1938. *The process of group thinking.* New York: Association Press.

EMERSON, RICHARD M., 1954. Deviation and rejection: an experimental replication. *American sociological Review* 19 : 688–93.

ERASMUS, CHARLES J., 1952. Changing folk beliefs and the relativity of empirical knowledge. *Southwestern Journal of Anthropology* 8 : 411–28.

ERBE, WILLIAM, 1962. Gregariousness, group membership, and the flow of information. *American Journal of Sociology* 67 : 502–16.

ERICKSON, M. N., 1939. An experimental investigation of the possible anti-social uses of hypnosis. *Psychiatry* 2 : 391–414.

FARAGO, LADISLAS, ed., 1942. *German psychological warfare.* New York: G. P. Putnam's Sons.

FECHTER, PAUL, 1934. Gerüchte. *Deutsche Rundschau* 241 : 134–38.

FEDER, ALFRED L., 1924. *Lehrbuch der geschichtlichen Methode.* Regensburg: Josef Kösel & Friedrich Pustet.

FESHBACH, SEYMOUR, and ROBERT D. SINGER, 1957. The effects of fear arousal and suppression of fear upon social perception. *Journal of abnormal and social Psychology* 55 : 283–88.

FESTINGER, LEON, 1950. Informal social communication. *Psychological Review* 57 : 271–82.

——, 1954. A theory of social comparison processes. *Human Relations* 7 : 117–40.

——, 1957. *A theory of cognitive dissonance.* Evanston: Row, Peterson.

——, DORWIN CARTWRIGHT, KATHLEEN BARBER, JULIET FLEISCHL, JOSEPHINE GOTTSDANKER, ANNETTE KEYSEN, and GLORIA LEAVITT, 1948. A study of a rumor: its origin and spread. *Human Relations* 1 : 464–86.

FESTINGER, LEON, HAROLD B. GERARD, BERNARD HYMOVITCH, HAROLD H. KELLEY, and BERT RAVEN, 1952. The influence process in the presence of extreme deviates. *Ibid.* 5 : 327–46.

FESTINGER, LEON, STANLEY SCHACHTER, and KURT BACK, 1950. *Social pressures in informal groups.* New York: Harper & Bros.

FESTINGER, LEON, and JOHN THIBAUT, 1951. Interpersonal communication in small groups. *Journal of abnormal and social Psychology* 46 : 92–99.

FIELD, LOUISE F., 1919. Sleeping heroes. *Contemporary Review* 115 : 444–50.

FIRTH, RAYMOND, 1956. Rumor in a primitive society. *Journal of abnormal and social Psychology* 53 : 122–32.

FISCHER, GUIDO, 1961. Das Gerücht und seine Bekämpfung im Betrieb. *Mensch und Arbeit* 13 : 36–38.

FISHER, SYDNEY G., 1912. The legendary and myth-making process in histories of the American revolution. *Proceedings of the American Philosophical Society* 51 : 53–76.

FLEMING, PETER, 1959. *The siege at Peking.* New York: Harper & Bros.

FLUHARTY, VERNON L., 1957. *Dance of the millions: military rule and the social revolution in Colombia.* Pittsburgh: University of Pittsburgh Press.

FOLLETT, MARY P., 1923. *The new state.* New York: Longmans, Green.

FOSTER, JAMES E., 1937. Censorship as a medium of propaganda. *Sociology and social Research* 22 : 57–66.

FRAIBERG, SELMA H., 1947. Studies in group symptom formation. *American Journal of Orthopsychiatry* 17 : 278–89.

FRANK, JEROME D., 1946. Emotional reactions of American soldiers to an unfamiliar disease. *American Journal of Psychiatry* 102 : 631–40.

FRANK, PHILIPP G., ed., 1961. *The validation of scientific theories.* New York: Collier Books.

FRANKL, GEORGE, 1943. Language and affective contact. *The nervous Child* 2 : 251–62.

FREUD, SIGMUND, 1922. *Group psychology and the analysis of the ego.* JAMES STRACHEY, trans., New York: Liveright.

——, 1938. *The basic writings of Sigmund Freud.* A. A. BRILL, ed. and trans., New York: Modern Library.

FRIEDRICH, CARL J., 1943. Issues of informational strategy. *Public Opinion Quarterly* 7 : 77–89.

FRITZ, CHARLES E., and ELI S. MARKS, 1954. The NORC studies of human behavior in disaster. *Journal of social Issues* 10 : 26–41.

FRITZ, CHARLES E., and HARRY B. WILLIAMS, 1957. The human being in disasters: a research perspective. *Annals of the American Academy of Political and Social Science* 309 : 42–51.

GENNEP, ARNOLD VAN, 1910. *La formation des légendes.* Paris: Ernest Flammarion.

GILLY, ADOLFO, 1965. The guerrilla movement in Guatemala. *Monthly Review: an independent socialist Magazine* 17 : 9–40

GLASER, BARNEY G., and ANSELM L. STRAUSS, 1965. Discovery of substantive theory: a basic strategy underlying qualitative research. *American behavioral Scientist* 8 : 5–12

GLOVER, EDWARD, 1940. *The psychology of fear and courage.* London: Penguin Books.

GOFFMAN, ERVING, 1957. Alienation from interaction. *Human Relations* 10 : 47–60.

GORPHE, FRANÇOIS, 1927. *La critique du témoignage.* Paris: Librairie Dalloz.

GRANT, VICTOR, 1946. Who started that rumor? He did. *Magazine Digest* 32 (May) : 38–44.

GRAUX, LUCIEN, 1918–20. *Les fausses nouvelles de la grande guerre.* Paris: L'Édition française illustrée.

GREENBERG, BRADLEY S., 1964. Diffusion of news of the Kennedy assassination. *Public Opinion Quarterly* 28 : 225–32.

GROSSER, GEORGE H., HENRY WECHSLER, and MILTON GREENBLATT, eds., 1964. *The threat of impending disaster.* Cambridge: M.I.T. Press.

GUÉRARD, ALBERT L., 1924. *Reflections on the Napoleonic legend.* New York: Charles Scribner's Sons.

GUETZKOW, HAROLD, and JOHN GYR, 1954. An analysis of conflict in decision-making groups. *Human Relations* 7 : 367–82.

GURFEIN, M.I., and MORRIS JANOWITZ, 1946. Trends in Wehrmacht morale. *Public Opinion Quarterly* 10 : 78–84.

HALDANE, RICHARD B. H., 1914. *The meaning of truth in history*. London: University of London Press.

HALL, MAX, 1965. The great cabbage hoax: a case study. *Journal of personality and social Psychology* 2 : 563–69.

HALL, WILLIAM E., 1936. *Reporting news*. Boston: D.C. Heath.

HAMBLIN, ROBERT L., and JAMES A. WIGGINS, 1957. Suggestibility, imitation, and recall during a crisis. *Midwest Sociologist* 20 : 26–32.

HAMPSON, NORMAN, 1963. *A social history of the French Revolution*. London: Routledge & Kegan Paul.

HART, BERNARD, 1916. The psychology of rumour. *Proceedings of the Royal Society of Medicine* 9 (Psychiatry) : 1–26. Reprinted in *Psychopathology: its development and its place in medicine*. London: Cambridge University Press, 1927. Pp. 94–124.

HARTGENBUSCH, HANNS G., 1933. Untersuchungen zur Psychologie der Wiedererzählung und des Gerüchtes. *Psychologische Forschung* 18 : 251–85.

HARTMANN, GEORGE W., 1948. The "black hole" of Calcutta: fact or fiction. *Journal of social Psychology* 27 : 17–35.

HARVEY, GEORGE, 1915. The mystery of myths. *North American Review* 201 : 825–27.

HAWORTH, PETER, ed., 1928. *Rumours and hoaxes*. Oxford: Basil Blackwell.

HEBB, DONALD O., 1946. Emotion in man and animal: an analysis of the intuitive processes of recognition. *Psychological Review* 53 : 88–106.

HECKER, JUSTUS F. C., 1859. *The epidemics of the Middle Ages*. B. G. BABINGTON, trans. London: Trübner.

HEMPEL, CARL G., 1952. Problems of concept and theory formation in the social sciences. In *Science, language, and human rights*. Philadelphia: University of Pennsylvania Press. Pp. 65–86.

HERSEY, JOHN, 1946. *Hiroshima*. New York: Alfred A. Knopf.

HERSHEY, ROBERT, 1956. Heed rumors for their meaning. *Personnel Journal* 34 : 299–301.

HIGHAM, T. M., 1951. The experimental study of the transmission of rumour. *British Journal of Psychology* 42 : 42–55.

HOCART, ARTHUR M., 1916. The common sense of myth. *American Anthropologist* 18 : 307–18.

HOCHBAUM, GODFREY M., 1954. The relation between group members' self confidence and their reactions to group presssures to uniformity. *American sociological Review* 19 : 678–87.

HOFSTADTER, RICHARD, 1944. *Social Darwinism in American thought*. Philadelphia: University of Pennsylvania Press.

HOLT, PAT M., 1964. *Colombia today—and tomorrow*. New York: Frederick A. Praeger.

HÖSCH-ERNST, LUCY, 1915. Die Psychologie der Aussage und ihre Beziehung auf die Gegenwart. *Internationale Rundschau* 1 : 15–33.

HOVLAND, CARL I., IRVING L. JANIS, and HAROLD H. KELLEY, 1953. *Communication and persuasion*. New Haven: Yale University Press.

HOVLAND, CARL I., ARTHUR A. LUMSDAINE, and FRED D. SHEFFIELD, 1949. *Experiments in mass communication*. Princeton: Princeton University Press.

HOVLAND, CARL I., and WALTER WEISS, 1951. Influence of source credibility on communication effectiveness. *Public Opinion Quarterly* 15 : 635–50.

HUDSON, BRADFORD B., 1954. Anxiety in response to the unfamiliar. *Journal of social Issues* 10 : 53–60.

HUGHES, HELEN M., 1940. *News and the human interest story*. Chicago: University of Chicago Press.

HULL, CLARK L., 1933. *Hypnosis and suggestibility*. New York: Appleton-Century-Crofts.

HYMAN, HERBERT H., and PAUL B. SHEATSLEY, 1947. Some reasons why information campaigns fail. *Public Opinion Quarterly* 11 : 413–23.

INKELES, ALEX, 1950. *Public opinion in Soviet Russia*. Cambridge: Harvard University Press.

INTERNATIONAL CONFERENCE ON THE HISTORY OF THE RESISTANCE MOVEMENTS, 1960. *European resistance movements, 1939–1945*. New York: Pergamon Press.

IRVING, JOHN A., 1943. The psychological analysis of wartime rumor patterns in Canada. *Bulletin of the Canadian psychological Association* 3 : 40–44.

IRWIN, WILL, 1911. What is news? *Collier's* 46 (March 18) : 16–18.

———, 1936. *Propaganda and the news*. New York: McGraw-Hill.

JACOBSON, DAVID J., 1948. *The affairs of dame rumor*. New York: Rinehart.

JAFFA, S., 1903–04. Ein psychologisches Experiment im kriminalistischen Seminar der Universität Berlin. *Beiträge zur Psychologie der Aussage* 1 : 79–99.

JAMES, WILLIAM, 1890. *The principles of psychology*. New York: Henry Holt.

———, 1897. *The will to believe and other essays in popular philosophy*. New York: Longmans, Green.

JANIS, IRVING L., 1951. *Air war and emotional stress*. New York: McGraw-Hill.

———, 1954. Personality correlates of susceptibility to persuasion. *Journal of Personality* 22 : 504–18.

———, 1959. Decisional conflicts: a theoretical analysis. *Journal of Conflict Resolution* 3 : 6–27.

———, ARTHUR A. LUMSDAINE, and ARTHUR I. GLADSTONE, 1951. Effects of preparatory communications on reactions to a subsequent news event. *Public Opinion Quarterly* 15 : 487–518.

JENNESS, ARTHUR, 1932. The role of discussion in changing opinion regarding a matter of fact. *Journal of abnormal and social Psychology* 27 : 279–96.

JOHNSON, DONALD M., 1945. The "phantom anesthetist" of Mattoon: a field study of mass hysteria. *Ibid.* 40 :175–86.

JOHNSON, WENDELL, and CAROLYN B. WOOD, 1944. John told Jim what Joe told him: a study of the process of abstracting. *Etc.: a Review of general Semantics* 2 : 10–28.

JONES, EDWARD E., and RIKA KOHLER, 1958. The effects of plausibility on the learning of controversial statements. *Journal of abnormal and social Psychology* 57 : 315–20.

JONG, LOUIS DE, 1956. *The German fifth column in World War II*. C. M. GEYL, trans., Chicago: University of Chicago Press.

JUNG, CARL G., 1910. Ein Beitrag zur Psychologie des Gerüchtes. *Zentralblatt für Psychoanalyse* 1 : 81–90. Reprinted in *Collected papers on analytical psychology*. CONSTANCE E. LONG, trans., New York: Moffat Yard, 1916. Pp. 176–90.

———, 1959. A visionary rumour. *Journal of analytical Psychology* 4 : 5–19.

KALLICH, MARTIN, and ANDREW MACLEISH, eds., 1962. *The American revolution through British eyes*. Evanston: Row, Peterson.

KARIUKI, JOSIAH M., 1964. *Mau Mau detainee*. Baltimore: Penguin Books.

KATZ, ELIHU, 1957. The two-step flow of communication: an up-to-date report on an hypothesis. *Public Opinion Quarterly* 21 : 61–78.

———, and PAUL F. LAZARSFELD, 1955. *Personal influence*. Glencoe: Free Press.

KAUS, GINA, 1935. *Catherine: the portrait of an empress*. JUNE HEAD, trans. New York: Literary Guild.

KELLAND, CLARENCE B., 1930. Panic: how men and women act when facing terror. *American Magazine* 109 (March) : 44–45, 92–95.

KELLER, ALBERT G., 1915. *Societal evolution*. New York: Macmillan.

KELLEY, HAROLD H., and JOHN W. THIBAUT, 1954. Experimental studies of group problem solving and process. In G. LINDZEY, ed., *Handbook of social psychology*. Vol. II. Cambridge: Addison-Wesley. Pp. 735–85.

KELLOCK, HAROLD, 1928. *Parson Weems and the cherry tree*. New York: Century.

KELLY, FRANK K., and MICHAEL ROSSMAN, 1944. The "G.I." and the rumor. *Infantry Journal* 54 (February) : 37–38.

KELMAN, HERBERT C., 1950. Effects of success and failure on "suggestibility" in the autokinetic situation. *Journal of abnormal and social Psychology* 45 : 267–85.

KERCKHOFF, ALAN C., KURT W. BACK, and NORMAN MILLER, 1965. Sociometric patterns in hysterical contagion. *Sociometry* 28 : 2–15.

KETCHUM, J. DAVIDSON, 1965. *Ruhleben: a prison camp society*. Toronto: University of Toronto Press.

KILLIAN, LEWIS M., 1956. *An introduction to methodological problems of field studies in disasters*. Washington, D. C.: National Research Council.

KIMURA, YUKIKO, 1947. Rumor among the Japanese. *Social Process in Hawaii* 11 : 84–92.

KIRKPATRICK, CLIFFORD, 1932. A tentative study in experimental social psychology. *American Journal of Sociology* 38 : 194–206.

KISHLER, JOHN P., KENNETH W. YARNOLD, JEAN M. DALY, FRANK I. MC-CABE, and JESSE ORLANSKY, 1960. The use of rumor in psychological warfare. In WILLIAM E. DAUGHERTY and MORRIS JANOWITZ, eds., *A psychological warfare casebook*. Baltimore: Johns Hopkins Press. Pp. 657–66.

KLEILER, FRANK M., 1954. Putting the "grapevine" to work. *New York Times Magazine*. (October 31) : 19, 33.

KLINEBERG, OTTO, 1938. Emotional expression in Chinese literature. *Journal of abnormal and social Psychology* 33 : 517–20.

KNAPP, PETER H., ed., 1963. *Expression of the emotions in man*. New York: International Universities Press.

KNAPP, ROBERT H., 1944. A psychology of rumor. *Public Opinion Quarterly* 8 : 23–37.

———, 1948. *Serial reproduction and related aspects of rumor*. Unpublished Doctoral Dissertation, Harvard University.

KOHN-BRAMSTEDT, ERNST, 1945. *Dictatorship and political police*. London: Kegan Paul, Trench, Trübner.

KORBEL, JOSEF, 1954. *Danger in Kashmir*. Princeton: Princeton University Press.

KRANZBERG, MELVIN, 1950. *The siege of Paris, 1870–1871.* Ithaca: Cornell University Press.

KRIESBERG, MARTIN, 1949. Cross-pressures and attitudes. *Public Opinion Quarterly* 13 : 5–16.

KRIM, ALAINE, 1953. A study in non-verbal communications: expressive movements during interviews. *Smith College Studies in social Work* 24 : 41–80.

KRIS, ERNST, and HANS SPEIER, 1944. *German radio propaganda.* London: Oxford University Press.

KRUGLAK, THEODORE E., 1962. *The two faces of TASS.* Minneapolis: University of Minnesota Press.

KUBIE, LAWRENCE S., and SYDNEY MARGOLIN, 1944. The process of hypnotism and the nature of the hypnotic state. *American Journal of Psychiatry* 100 : 611–22.

KUBO, JUDY, 1945. The Negro soldiers in Kahuku. *Social Process in Hawaii* 9 : 28–32.

KUHN, THOMAS S., 1962. *The structure of scientific revolutions.* Chicago: University of Chicago Press.

KULISCHER, EUGEN, 1906. Das Zeugnis von Hörensagen. *Zeitschrift für das privat- und öffentliche Recht der Gegenwart* 24 : 169–233.

LANDAU, H. G., and ANATOL RAPOPORT, 1953. Contributions to the mathematical theory of contagion and spread of information. *Bulletin of mathematical Biophysics* 15 : 173–83.

LANG, KURT, and GLADYS LANG, 1961. *Collective dynamics.* New York: Thomas Y. Crowell.

LANGENHOVE, FERNAND VAN, 1916. *The growth of a legend.* E. B. SHERLOCK, trans., New York: G. P. Putnam's Sons.

LANGER, SUSANNE K. 1944. The lord of creation. *Fortune* 19 : 127–28, 139–54.

LANGLOIS, CHARLES V., and CHARLES SEIGNOBOS, 1898. *Introduction to the study of history.* G. G. BERRY, trans., London: Duckworth.

LANZ, HENRY, 1936. Metaphysics of gossip. *International Journal of Ethics* 46 : 492–99.

LANZETTA, JOHN T., 1955. Group behavior under stress. *Human Relations* 8 : 29–52.

LAPIERE, RICHARD T., 1938. *Collective behavior.* New York: McGraw-Hill.

LARDNER, JOHN, 1943. The front is a rumor factory. *Newsweek* 22 (December 20) : 27.

LARGUIER DES BANCELS, J., 1906. La psychologie judiciaire: le témoignage. *L'Année psychologique* 12 : 157–232.

LARSEN, OTTO N., 1954. Rumors in a disaster. *Journal of Communication* 4 : 111–23.

———, and RICHARD J. HILL, 1954. Mass media and interpersonal communication in the diffusion of a news event. *American sociological Review* 19 : 426–33.

———, 1958. Social structure and interpersonal communication. *American Journal of Sociology* 63 : 497–505.

LASSWELL, HAROLD D., 1927. *Propaganda technique in the World War.* New York: Alfred A. Knopf.

———, 1933a. Agitation. *Encyclopedia of the social sciences.* Vol. I. New York: Macmillan. Pp. 487–88.

———, 1933b. Propaganda. *Ibid.* Vol. XII, pp. 521–28.

———, 1935. *World politics and personal insecurity.* New York: McGraw-Hill.

LAZARSFELD, PAUL F., BERNARD BERELSON, and HAZEL GAUDET, 1944. *The people's choice.* New York: Duell, Sloan & Pearce.

LEA, HENRY C., 1888. *A history of the inquisition of the Middle Ages.* Vol. I. New York: Harper & Bros.

LEAKEY, LOUIS S. B., 1952. *Mau Mau and the Kikuyu.* London: Methuen.

LEBON, GUSTAVE, 1896. *The crowd: a study of the popular mind.* London: T. Fisher Unwin.

———, 1911. *Les opinions et les croyances: genèse-évolution.* Paris: Ernest Flammarion.

LEE, ALFRED M., 1945. Public opinion in relation to culture. *Psychiatry* 8 : 49–61.

LEFEBVRE, GEORGES, 1932. *La grande peur de 1789.* Paris: Armand Colin.

———, 1934. Foules révolutionaires. *Annales historiques de la révolution française* 11 : 1–26.

———, 1947. *The coming of the French Revolution.* R. R. PALMER, trans., Princeton: Princeton University Press.

LEFFORD, ARTHUR, 1946. The influence of emotional subject matter on logical reasoning. *Journal of general Psychology* 34 : 127–51.

LEGALLIENNE, RICHARD, 1912. The psychology of gossip. *Munsey's Magazine* 48 (October) : 123–27.

LEIGHTON, ALEXANDER H., 1945. *The governing of men.* Princeton: Princeton University Press.

LEMKIN, RAPHAEL, 1944. *Axis rule in occupied Europe.* Washington, D. C.: Carnegie Endowment for International Peace.

LEWIN, KURT, 1952. Group decision and social change. In G. E. SWANSON et al., eds., *Readings in social psychology.* New York: Henry Holt. Pp. 459–73.

LEWIS, LLOYD, 1929. *Myths after Lincoln*. New York: Harcourt, Brace.

LIND, ANDREW W., 1946. *Hawaii's Japanese*. Princeton: Princeton University Press.

LINDBERG, JOHN S., 1930. *The background of Swedish emigration to the United States*. Minneapolis: University of Minneapolis Press.

LINDEMAN, EDWARD C., 1933. Discussion. *Encyclopedia of the social sciences*. Vol. V. New York: Macmillan. Pp. 166–67.

LINEBARGER, PAUL M. A., 1948. *Psychological warfare*. Washington, D. C.: Infantry Journal Press.

LIONBERGER, HERBERT F., 1954. The relation of informal social groups to the diffusion of farm information in a northeast Missouri farm community. *Rural Sociology* 19 : 233–43.

LIPPMANN, WALTER, 1922. *Public opinion*. New York: Harcourt, Brace.

———, 1925. *The phantom public*. New York: Harcourt, Brace.

LITERARY DIGEST, 1917. Declaring war on lie mongers. 55 (December 15) : 11–12.

———, 1931. Whispering reds as bank wreckers. 108 (January 10) : 10.

LITTELL, ROBERT, and JOHN J. MCCARTHY, 1936. Whispers for sale. *Harper's Magazine* 172 : 364–72.

LOEWENBERG, RICHARD D., 1943. Rumors of mass poisoning in times of crisis. *Journal of criminal Psychopathology* 5 : 131–42.

LOMER, GEORG, 1913. Über den klatsch. *Psychiatrisch-neurologische Wochenschrift* 15 (July 5) : 171–75.

LORD, WALTER, 1957. *Day of infamy*. New York: Henry Holt.

LORENZ, MARIA, 1955. Expressive behavior and language patterns. *Psychiatry* 18 : 353–66.

LOWE, HERBERT, 1941. The psychology of rumour. *Medical Press and Circular* 206 : 219–21.

LYONS, EUGENE, 1935. Stifled laughter. *Harper's Magazine* 170 : 557–67.

MCCLEERY, RICHARD, 1960. Communication patterns as bases of systems of authority and power. In D. R. CRESSEY, ed., *Theoretical studies in social organization of the prison*. New York: Social Science Research Council. Pp. 49–77.

MCCORMICK, ELSIE, 1942. Boston's fight against rumors. *American Mercury* 55 : 275–81.

MCDAVID, JOHN, 1959. Personality and situational determinants of conformity. *Journal of abnormal and social Psychology* 58 : 241–46.

MCGINNIS, H. C., 1942. Dame rumor our enemy. *Catholic Digest* 6 : 94–97.

MCGREGOR, DOUGLAS, 1938. Major determinants of the prediction of social events. *Journal of abnormal and social Psychology* 33 : 179–204.

MACHOVER, SOLOMON, and ANITA SCHWARTZ, 1952. A homeostatic effect of mood on associative abstractness and reaction time. *Journal of Personality* 21 : 59–67.

McHUGH, ROGER J., 1957. The famine in Irish oral tradition. In ROBERT D. EDWARDS and T. DESMOND WILLIAMS, eds., *The great famine: studies in Irish history, 1845–52.* New York: New York University Press. Pp. 391–436.

MACKAY, CHARLES, 1932. *Extraordinary popular delusions and the madness of crowds.* Boston: L. C. Page.

McKELWAY, ST. CLAIR, 1940. *Gossip: the life and times of Walter Winchell.* New York: Viking Press.

MAJDALANY, FRED, 1963. *State of emergency: the full story of the Mau Mau.* Boston: Houghton Mifflin.

MALINOWSKI, BRONISLAW, 1925. Magic, science, and religion. In JAMES NEEDHAM, ed., *Magic, science, and reality.* New York: Macmillan.

——, 1935. *Coral gardens and their magic.* Vol. II. London: George Allen & Unwin.

MANNHEIM, KARL, 1936. *Ideology and utopia.* LOUIS WIRTH and EDWARD SHILS, trans. New York: Harcourt, Brace.

MARSHALL, SAMUEL L. A., 1947. *Men against fire.* Washington, D. C.: Infantry Journal Press.

MARSTON, WILLIAM M., 1924. Studies in testimony. *Journal of the American Institute of Criminal Law and Criminology* 15 : 5–31.

MARTIN, ROBERT B., 1962. *Enter rumour: four early Victorian scandals.* New York: W. W. Norton.

MARTZ, JOHN D., 1962. *Colombia: a contemporary political survey.* Chapel Hill: University of North Carolina Press.

MARUYAMA, MAGOROH, 1963. The second cybernetics: deviation-amplifying mutual causal processes. *American Scientist* 51 : 164–79.

MASLOW, ABRAHAM H., 1949. The expressive component of behavior. *Psychological Review* 56 : 261–72.

MATSUMOTO, HIROSHI, 1935. Toron no Kado to sono Toronshudan no Sei-in no Iken ni Oyobosu Eikyo. *Japanese Journal of Psychology* 10 : 79–106.

MEAD, GEORGE H., 1932. *The philosophy of the present.* ARTHUR E. MURPHY, ed. Chicago: Open Court.

——, 1934. *Mind, self, and society.* CHARLES W. MORRIS, ed. Chicago: University of Chicago Press.

MEDALIA, NAHUM Z., and OTTO N. LARSEN, 1958. Diffusion and belief in a collective delusion: the Seattle windshield pitting epidemic. *American sociological Review* 23 : 180–86.

MEHTA, ASOKA, 1946. *1857: the great rebellion.* Bombay: Hind Kitabs.

MENZEL, HERBERT, 1957. Public and private conformity under different conditions of acceptance in the group. *Journal of abnormal and social Psychology* 55 : 398–402.

MERRILL, FRANCIS E., and CARROLL D. CLARK, 1934. The money market as a special public. *American Journal of Sociology* 39 : 626–36.

MERTON, ROBERT K., 1948. Self-fulfilling prophecy. *Antioch Review* 8 : 193–210.

MICELI, V., 1899. La psicologia della folla. *Rivista italiana di sociologia* 3 : 166–95.

MICHEL, O. H., 1907. Über das Zeugnis von Hörensagen bei Kindern. *Zeitschrift für angewandte Psychologie* 1 : 421–25.

MIDDLETON, RUSSELL, 1960. Ethnic prejudice and susceptibility to persuasion. *American sociological Review* 25 : 679–86.

MILLARD, OSCAR E., 1938. *Underground news.* New York: R. M. McBride.

MILLER, DELBERT C., 1945. How our community heard about the death of President Roosevelt. *American sociological Review* 10 : 691–94.

MILLER, HENRY W., 1930. *The Paris gun.* New York: Jonathan Cape & Harrison Smith.

MILLS, C. WRIGHT, 1939. Language, logic, and culture. *American sociological Review* 4 : 670–80.

MIOTTO, ANTONIO, 1937. *Introduzione alla psicologia della folla.* Florence: La Nuova Italia.

———, 1953. *Psicologia della propaganda.* Florence: Editrice Universitaria.

MOLL, ALBERT, 1890. *Hypnotism.* London: Walter Scott.

MOORE, ELON H. 1935. Elements of error in testimony. *Journal of applied Psychology* 19 : 447–62.

MOORE, OMAR K., and SCARVIA B. ANDERSON, 1954. Search behavior in individual and group problem solving. *American sociological Review* 19 : 702–14.

MOORE, WILBERT E., and MELVIN M. TUMIN, 1949. Some social functions of ignorance. *Ibid.* 14 : 787–95.

MORGAN, EDMUND M., 1927. The relation between hearsay and preserved memory. *Harvard Law Review* 40 : 712–32.

———, 1935. Hearsay and non-hearsay. *Ibid.* 48 : 1138–60.

MORGAN, EDWARD P., 1962. Washington's No. 1 hostess: dame rumor. *New York Times Magazine* (February 11) : 29, 39–42.

MORLEY, CHRISTOPHER D., 1919. *Mince pie.* New York: George H. Doran.

MOTT, FRANK L. 1952. *The news in America.* Cambridge: Harvard University Press.

MULLER, HERMANN J., 1949. The Darwinian and modern conceptions of natural selection. *Proceedings of the American Philosophical Society* 93 : 459–70.

MUNSON, EDWARD L., 1921. *The management of men.* New York: Henry Holt.

MÜNSTERBERG, HUGO, 1908. *On the witness stand.* New York: McClure.

MURRAY, HENRY A., 1933. The effect of fear upon estimates of the maliciousness of other personalities. *Journal of social Psychology* 4 : 310–29.

MUSCIO, BERNARD, 1916. The influence of the form of a question. *British Journal of Psychology* 8 : 351–89.

NATIONAL RESEARCH COUNCIL, 1943. *Psychology for the fighting man.* New York: Penguin Books.

NEWSWEEK, 1953. Result of a rumor. 41 (April 27) : 85.

NOHL, JOHANNES, 1960. *The black death: a chronicle of the plague.* C. H. CLARKE, trans. New York: Ballantine Books.

OBRDLIK, ANTONIN J., 1942. Gallows humor—a sociological phenomenon. *American Journal of Sociology* 48 : 709–16.

ODUM, HOWARD W., 1943. *Race and rumors of race.* Chapel Hill: University of North Carolina Press.

O'HIGGINS, HARVEY, 1918. *The German whisper.* Washington, D. C.: Committee on Public Information.

OMAN, CHARLES W. C., 1918. Rumour in time of war. *Transactions of the Royal Historical Society* 1 (4th series) : 1–27. Reprinted in *The unfortunate Colonel Despard and other studies.* London: Edward Arnold, 1922. Pp. 49–70.

OPPENHEIM, ROSA, 1911. Zur Psychologie des Gerüchtes. *Zeitschrift für angewandte Psychologie* 5 : 344–55.

ORLOV, ALEXANDER, 1963. *Handbook of intelligence and guerrilla warfare.* Ann Arbor: University of Michigan Press.

ORNE, MARTIN T., 1959. The nature of hypnosis: artifact and essence. *Journal of abnormal and social Psychology* 58 : 277–99.

OSBORNE, HAROLD, 1952. *Indians of the Andes: Aymaras and Quechuas.* Cambridge: Harvard University Press.

OSGOOD, CHARLES E., and PERCY H. TANNENBAUM, 1955. The principle of congruity in the prediction of attitude change. *Psychological Review* 62 : 42–55.

OTTO, M. C., 1918. Testimony and human nature. *Journal of the American Institute of Criminal Law and Criminology* 9 : 98–104.

PADFIELD, HARLAND, and CARL GORHAM, 1957. Silly little rabbit. *Journal of the National Education Association* 46 : 533.

PARK, ROBERT E., 1923. Negro race consciousness as reflected in race literature. *American Review* 1 : 505–17.

——, 1927. Human nature and collective behavior. *American Journal of Sociology* 32 : 733–41.

——, 1933. Collective behavior. *Encyclopedia of the social sciences.* Vol. III. New York: Macmillan. Pp. 631–33.

——, 1940. News as a form of knowledge. *American Journal of Sociology* 45 : 669–86. Reprinted in E. C. HUGHES *et al.,* eds., *Society.* Glencoe: Free Press, 1955. Pp. 71–88.

——, 1941. Morale and the news. *American Journal of Sociology.* 47 : 360–77.

PARSONS, ELSIE C., 1936. *Mitla: town of the souls.* Chicago: University of Chicago Press.

PARSONS, TALCOTT, 1938. The role of ideas in social action. *American sociological Review* 3 : 652–64.

——, 1942. Propaganda and social control. *Psychiatry* 5 : 551–72.

PAYNE, ROBERT, 1964. Mayerling remains a mystery. *New York Times Magazine* (January 26) : 34–35.

PETERSON, WARREN, and NOEL P. GIST, 1951. Rumor and public opinion. *American Journal of Sociology* 57 : 159–67.

PINGAUD, ALBERT, 1916. La guerre vue par les combattans allemands. *Revue des deux mondes* 36 : 145–67, 642–61.

POLLARD, A. F., 1915. Rumour and historical science in time of war. *Contemporary Revue* 107 : 321–30.

PONSONBY, ARTHUR, 1928. *Falsehood in war-time.* London: George Allen & Unwin.

POSTMAN, LEO, 1951. Toward a general theory of cognition. In J. H. ROHRER and M. SHERIF, eds., *Social psychology at the crossroads.* New York: Harper & Bros. Pp. 242–72.

—— and JEROME S. BRUNER, 1948. Perception under stress. *Psychological Review* 55 : 314–23.

——, 1952. Hypothesis and the principle of closure: the effect of frequency and recency. *Journal of Psychology* 33 : 113–25.

POWDERMAKER, HORTENSE, 1943. The channeling of Negro aggression by the cultural process. *American Journal of Sociology* 48 : 750–58.

PRASAD, JAMUNA, 1935. The psychology of rumour: a study relating to the great Indian earthquake of 1934. *British Journal of Psychology* 26 : 1–15.

——, 1950. A comparative study of rumours and reports in earthquakes. *Ibid.* 41 : 129–44

PRIESTLEY, J. B., 1926. My revue. *Saturday Review* 141 : 711–12.

PRINCE, SAMUEL H., 1920. *Catastrophe and social change.* New York: Columbia University Press.

PURCELL, VICTOR, 1963. *The Boxer uprising: a background study.* New York: Cambridge University Press.

PUTNEY, SNELL W., and MERVYN L. CADWALLADER, 1954. An experiment in crisis interaction. *Research Studies of the State College of Washington* 22 : 94–102.

QUARANTELLI, ENRICO L., 1960. Images of withdrawal behavior in disasters: some basic misconceptions. *Social Problems* 8 : 68–79.

RAMNOUX, CLÉMENCE, 1948. Expérience sur la transmission des légendes. *Psyché: revue internationale de psychoanalyse et des sciences de l'homme* 3 : 310–23.

RAPOPORT, ANATOL, 1953. Spread of information through a population with socio-structural bias. *Bulletin of mathematical Biophysics* 15 : 523–33, 535–46.

—— and LIONEL I. REBHUN, 1952. On the mathematical theory of rumor spread. *Ibid.* 14 : 375–83.

RAVEN, BERTRAM H., 1959. Social influence on opinions and the communication of related content. *Journal of abnormal and social Psychology* 58 : 119–28.

REMINI, ROBERT V., 1963. *The election of Andrew Jackson.* Philadelphia: J. B. Lippincott.

RICHARDSON, DOW, 1943. Rumormongers. *Catholic Digest* 7 : 41–43.

RIEZLER, KURT, 1944a. The social psychology of fear. *American Journal of Sociology* 49 : 489–98.

——, 1944b. What is public opinion? *Social Research* 11 : 397–427.

——, 1951. *Man: mutable and immutable.* Chicago: Henry Regnery.

RIVERS, W. H. R., 1912. The sociological significance of myths. *Folk-Lore* 23 : 307–31.

ROLPH, C. H., 1944. Rumours. *New Statesman and Nation* 27 : 122–23.

ROMMETVEIT, RAGNAR, 1952. Det psykologiske grunnlaget for ryktedaning og ryktespreiing. *Norsk Pedagogisk Tidsskrift* 36 : 1–11 (*Psychological Abstracts,* 26 : 6187).

ROOS, ALLAN J. 1943. The scuttle butt afloat: a study in group psychology. *Archives of Neurology and Psychiatry* 50 : 472–74.

RORETZ, KARL VON, 1915. Zur Psychologie des Gerüchtes. *Österreichische Rundschau* 44 : 205–12.

ROSE, ARNOLD M., 1940. *A study of rumor.* Unpublished Master's Thesis, University of Chicago.

———, 1946. Popular logic: a methodological suggestion. *American sociological Review* 11 : 590–92.

———, 1951. Rumor in the stock market. *Public Opinion Quarterly* 15 : 461–86.

ROSSI, PASQUALE, 1902. *I suggestionatori e la folla.* Turin: Fratelli Bocca.

———, 1905. Dell'attenzione colletiva e sociale. *Manicomio: archivio di psichiatria e scienze affini* 21 : 248–53.

ROSTEN, LEO C., 1937. *The Washington correspondents.* New York: Harcourt, Brace.

ROWSE, ARTHUR E., 1957. *Slanted news.* Boston: Beacon Press.

RUCH, FLOYD L., and KIMBALL YOUNG, 1942. Penetration of Axis propaganda. *Journal of applied Psychology* 26 : 448–55.

RUESCH, JURGEN, and WELDON KEES, 1956. *Nonverbal communication.* Berkeley: University of California Press.

RUESCH, JURGEN, and A. RODNEY PRESTWOOD, 1949. Anxiety: its initiation, communication, and interpersonal management. *Archives of Neurology and Psychiatry* 62 : 527–50.

RUSSIAN INSTITUTE, COLUMBIA UNIVERSITY, 1956. *The anti-Stalin campaign and international Communism.* New York: Columbia University Press.

SADY, RACHEL R., 1947. *The function of rumors in relocation centers.* Unpublished Doctoral Dissertation, University of Chicago.

SAPIR, EDWARD, 1927. Language as a form of human behavior. *English Journal* 16 : 421–33.

———, 1949. *Selected writings in language, culture, and personality.* DAVID MANDELBAUM, ed. Berkeley: University of California Press.

SAVARKAR, VINAYAK D., 1947. *The Indian war of independence, 1857.* Bombay: Phoenix Publications.

SCHACHTER, STANLEY, 1951. Deviation, rejection, and communication. *Journal of abnormal and social Psychology* 46 : 190–207.

———, and HARVEY BURDICK, 1955. A field experiment on rumor transmission and distortion. *Ibid.* 50 : 363–71.

SCHALL, HERBERT M., BERNARD LEVY, and M. E. TRESSELT, 1950. A sociometric approach to rumor. *Journal of social Psychology* 31 : 121–29.

SCHÖNE, WALTER, 1936. *Das Gerücht.* Leipzig: Robert Noske.

SCHRAMM, WILBUR, ed., 1959. *One day in the world's press.* Stanford: Stanford University Press.

SCHUBERT, PAUL, and LANGHORNE GIBSON, 1932. *Death of a fleet, 1917–1919.* New York: Coward-McCann.

SCHUETZ, ALFRED, 1942. Scheler's theory of inter-subjectivity and the general thesis of the alter ego. *Philosophy and phenomenological Research* 2 : 323–47.

SEARS, CLARA E., 1924. *Days of delusion*. Boston: Houghton Mifflin.

SEIGNOBOS, CHARLES, 1901. *La méthode historique appliquée aux sciences sociales*. Paris: Félix Alcan.

SELLERS, EDITH, 1918. On fighting against lying rumors. *Living Age* 298: 281–86.

SELYE, HANS, 1956. *The stress of life*. New York: McGraw-Hill.

SEN, SURENDRA N., 1957. *Eighteen fifty-seven*. Delhi: Ministry of Information and Broadcasting.

SHANAS, ETHEL, 1937. *The nature and manipulation of crowds*. Unpublished Master's Thesis, University of Chicago.

SHAPIRO, FRED C., and JAMES W. SULLIVAN, 1964. *Race riots: New York, 1964*. New York: Thomas Y. Crowell.

SHEATSLEY, PAUL B., and JACOB J. FELDMAN, 1964. The assassination of President Kennedy. *Public Opinion Quarterly* 28 : 189–215.

SHEPPERSON, GEORGE, and THOMAS PRICE, 1958. *Independent African: John Chilembwe and the Nyasaland rising of 1915*. Edinburgh: Edinburgh University Press.

SHERIF, MUZAFER, and O. J. HARVEY, 1952. A study in ego functioning: elimination of stable anchorages in individual and group situations. *Sociometry* 15 : 272–305.

SHIBUTANI, TAMOTSU, 1944. *Rumors in a crisis situation*. Unpublished Master's Thesis, University of Chicago.

SIDIS, BORIS, 1899. *The psychology of suggestion*. New York: D. Appleton.

SIGHELE, SCIPIO, 1891. *La folla delinquente*. Turin: Fratelli Bocca.

——, 1911. *L'intelligenza della folla*. Turin: Fratelli Bocca.

SIMMEL, GEORG, 1950. *The sociology of Georg Simmel*. KURT WOLFF, ed. and trans. Glencoe: Free Press.

SIMON, ALFRED, 1915. Die Strafbarkeit der Verbreitung falscher Gerüchte. *Zeitschrift für die gesamte Strafrechtswissenschaft* 36 : 792–97.

SINHA, DURGANAND, 1952. Behaviour in a catastrophic situation: a psychological study of reports and rumours. *British Journal of Psychology* 43 : 200–09.

——, 1954a. Psychological study of catastrophes. *Patna University Journal* 8 : 51–60.

——, 1954b. Rumours as a factor in public opinion during election. *Eastern Anthropologist* 8 : 63–72.

SMELSER, NEIL J., 1963. *Theory of collective behavior*. New York: Free Press of Glencoe.

SMITH, CARL O., and STEPHEN B. SARASOHN, 1946. Hate propaganda in Detroit. *Public Opinion Quarterly* 10 : 24–52.

SMITH, EMORY, 1930. The fallibility of eye-witness testimony. *American Journal of police Science* 1 : 487–95.

SMITH, GEORGE H., 1947. Beliefs in statements labeled fact and rumor. *Journal of abnormal and social Psychology* 42 : 80–90.

SMITH, HELENA H., 1943. The same old rumors. *Collier's* 111 (April 10) : 43, 52.

SMITH, THOMAS V., 1937. Custom, gossip, legislation. *Social Forces* 16 : 24–34.

SNEE, T. J., and D. E. LUSH, 1941. Interaction of the narrative and interrogatory methods of obtaining testimony. *Journal of Psychology* 11 : 229–36.

SOROKIN, PITIRIM A., 1942. *Man and society in calamity.* New York: E. P. Dutton.

SPILLIUS, JAMES, 1957. Natural disaster and political crisis in a Polynesian society. *Human Relations* 10 : 3–27.

STEPHENS, H. MORSE, 1902. *A history of the French Revolution.* New York: Charles Scribner's Sons.

STERN, L. WILLIAM, 1902. *Zur Psychologie der Aussage.* Berlin: J. Guttentag.

———,1939. The psychology of testimony. *Journal of abnormal and social Psychology* 34 : 3–20.

STOETZEL, JEAN, 1963. *La psychologie sociale.* Paris: Flammarion.

STRATTON, GEORGE M., 1928a. Excitement as an undifferentiated emotion. In MARTIN REYMERT, ed., *Feelings and emotions: a Wittenberg symposium.* Worcester: Clark University Press. Pp. 215–21.

———, 1928b. The function of emotion as shown particularly in excitement. *Psychological Review* 35 : 351–66.

STREIT, PEGGY, 1964. Jokes that seep through the iron curtain. *New York Times Magazine* (April 19) : 28, 56.

STREMPEL, HERIBERT VON, 1946. Confessions of a German propagandist. *Public Opinion Quarterly* 10 : 216–33.

STYCOS, J. MAYONE, 1952. Patterns of communication in a rural Greek village. *Ibid.* 16 : 59–70.

SUMNER, WILLIAM G., 1906. *Folkways.* Boston: Ginn.

SWIFT, EDGAR J., 1918. *Psychology in the day's work.* New York: Charles Scribner's Sons.

TARDE, GABRIEL, 1901. *L'Opinion et la foule.* Paris: Félix Alcan.

TAYLOR, EDMOND, 1940. *The strategy of terror.* Boston: Houghton Mifflin.

TEGGART, FREDERICK J., 1941. *The theory and processes of history.* Berkeley: University of California Press.

THOMAS, WILLIAM I., 1909. *Source book for social origins.* Boston: Richard G. Badger.

THOMPSON, GLADYS S., 1950. *Catherine the Great and the expansion of Russia.* New York: Macmillan.

THOMPSON, JAMES W., and BERNARD J. HOLM, 1942. *A history of historical writing.* New York: Macmillan.

THOMPSON, STITH, 1946. *The folktale.* New York: Dryden Press.

THORNDIKE, ROBERT L., 1938. The effect of discussion upon the correctness of group decision. *Journal of social Psychology* 9 : 343–62.

TIME, 1934. Ambergris. 23 (March 19) : 33–34.

——, 1935a. Hysterics. 26 (July 22) : 14.

——, 1935b. Mischief out of misery. 25 (April 1) : 11–13.

——, 1946. Vigil at Nürnberg. 48 (October 28) : 56–58.

——, 1948. How he did it. 52 (July 5) : 15–18.

——, 1953. Hear ye! Hear ye! 62 (November 9) : 98–100.

TINKER, HUGH, 1958. 1857 and 1957: the mutiny and modern India. *International Affairs* 34 : 57–65.

TITIEV, MISCHA, 1949. *Social singing among the Mapuche.* Ann Arbor: University of Michigan Press.

TOCH, HANS H., 1955. Crisis situations and ideological evaluations. *Public Opinion Quarterly* 19 : 53–67.

TORRANCE, E. PAUL, 1957. Group decision-making and disagreement. *Social Forces* 35 : 314–18.

TRANKELL, ARNE, 1958. Was Lars sexually assaulted? *Journal of abnormal and social Psychology* 56 : 385–95.

TREADWELL, MATTIE E., 1954. *The Women's Army Corps.* Washington, D. C.: Government Printing Office.

TRESSELT, MARGARET E., and D. S. SPRAGG, 1941. Changes occuring in the serial reproduction of verbally perceived materials. *Journal of genetic Psychology* 58 : 255–64.

TROTSKY, LEON, 1936. *The history of the Russian revolution.* MAX EASTMAN, trans., New York: Simon & Schuster.

TROTTER, WILFRED, 1917. *Instincts of the herd in peace and war.* New York: Macmillan.

TUMIN, MELVIN, and ARNOLD S. FELDMAN, 1955. The miracle at Sabana Grande. *Public Opinion Quarterly* 19 : 125–39.

TURNBULL, CLIVE, 1948. *Black war.* London: F. W. Cheshire.

TURNER, RALPH H., 1953. The quest for universals in sociological research. *American sociological Review* 18 : 604–11.

———, 1964. Collective behavior. In R. E. L. FARIS, ed., *Handbook of modern sociology.* Chicago: Rand McNally. Pp. 382–425.

———, and LEWIS M. KILLIAN, 1957. *Collective behavior.* Englewood Cliffs, N.J.: Prentice-Hall.

TURNER, RALPH H., and SAMUEL J. SURACE, 1956. Zootsuiters and Mexicans: symbols in crowd behavior. *American Journal of Sociology* 42 : 14–20.

UEMATSU, TADASHI, 1939. Taiken Shogen ni Okeru Denbun no Konniu. *Japanese Journal of Psychology* 14 : 232–43.

U. S. OFFICE OF WAR INFORMATION, 1942. *Intelligence report: rumors in wartime.* Washington, D. C.: Office of War Information.

U. S. PRESIDENT'S COMMISSION ON THE ASSASSINATION OF PRESIDENT KENNEDY, 1964. *Report.* Washington, D. C.: Government Printing Office.

U. S. STRATEGIC BOMBING SURVEY, 1946. *Japan's struggle to end the war.* Washington, D. C.: Government Printing Office.

———, 1947. *The effects of strategic bombing on German morale.* Washington, D. C.: Government Printing Office.

URIS, AUREN, 1954. Rumors can ruin you. *Petroleum Refiner* 33 (September) : 107–08, 385.

VALDES DELIUS, FRANCISCO, 1960. Psico-sociologia del rumor. *Revista mexicana de sociologia* 22 : 77–88. (*Sociological Abstracts,* 11 : A5401).

VALLON, CHARLES, 1918. Les alarmistes: étude médico-légale. *Revue scientifique* 56 : 342–43.

VANSINA, JAN, 1965. *Oral tradition: a study in historical methodology.* H. M. WRIGHT, trans. Chicago: Aldine.

VAUGHAN, ELIZABETH H., 1949. *Community under stress: an internment camp culture.* Princeton: Princeton University Press.

VAUGHAN, WAYLAND F., 1948. *Social psychology.* New York: Odyssey Press.

VICKERY, KATHERINE, and LEE M. BROOKS, 1938. Time-spaced reporting of a "crime" witnessed by college girls. *Journal of criminal Law and Criminology* 29 : 371–82.

WALLACE, ANTHONY F. C., 1956. *Human behavior in extreme situations.* Washington, D. C.: National Research Council.

WATERMAN, T. T., 1914. The explanatory element in the folk-tales of the North American Indians. *Journal of American Folk-lore* 27 : 1–54.

WEBER, MAX, 1946. *Essays in sociology.* HANS H. GERTH and C. WRIGHT MILLS, ed. and trans., New York: Oxford University Press.

WECHSBERG, JOSEPH, 1953. A reporter in Germany: the seventeenth of June. *New Yorker* 29 (August 29) : 33–51.

WECKLER, JOSEPH E., and THEO E. HALL, 1944. *The police and minority groups.* Chicago: International City Managers' Association.

WEIKER, WALTER F., 1963. *The Turkish revolution, 1960–1961.* Washington, D. C.: Brookings Institution.

WEINGARTEN, ERICA M., 1949. A study of selective perception in clinical judgment. *Journal of Personality* 17 : 369–406.

WEINSTEIN, EDWIN A., ROBERT L. KAHN, SIDNEY MALITZ, 1956. Confabulation as a social process. *Psychiatry* 19 : 383–96.

WELLS, W. R., 1941. Experiments in the hypnotic production of crimes. *Journal of Psychology* 11 : 63–102.

WHIPPLE, GUY M., 1909. The observer as reporter: a survey of the psychology of testimony. *Psychological Bulletin* 6 : 153–70.

——, 1918. The obtaining of information: psychology of observation and report. *Ibid.* 15 : 217–48.

WHITE, JOHN B., 1955. *The big lie.* New York: Thomas Y. Crowell.

WHITE, RALPH K., and RONALD LIPPITT, 1960. *Autocracy and democracy: an experimental inquiry.* New York: Harper & Bros.

WIGMORE, JOHN H., 1909. Professor Münsterberg and the psychology of testimony. *Illinois Law Review* 3 : 399–445.

WILLIAMS, WYTHE, and WILLIAM VAN NARVIG, 1943. *Secret sources.* Chicago: Ziff-Davis.

WIRTH, LOUIS, 1940. Ideological aspects of social disorganization. *American sociological Review* 5 : 472–82.

——, 1948. Consensus and mass communication. *Ibid.* 13 : 1–15.

WISH, HARVEY, 1939. Slave insurrection panic of 1856. *Journal of Southern History* 5 : 206–22.

WITTELS, DAVID G., 1942. Hitler's short-wave rumor factory. *Saturday Evening Post* 215 (November 21) : 12–13, 118–23.

WOHLSTETTER, ROBERTA, 1962. *Pearl Harbor: warning and decision.* Stanford: Stanford University Press.

WOLFE, BERNARD, 1949. Uncle Remus and the malevolent rabbit. *Commentary* 8 (July) : 31–41.

WOLFF, KURT H., 1947. A partial analysis of student reactions to President Roosevelt's death. *Journal of social Psychology* 26 : 35–53.

WORK, ROBERT E., 1946. Last days in Hitler's air raid shelter. *Public Opinion Quarterly* 10 : 565–81.

WRIGHT, CHARLES, and C. ERNEST FAYLE, 1928. *A history of Lloyd's.* London: Macmillan.

WRIGHT, EUGENE A., and MICHAEL MITCHELL, 1943. The Jap is not mysterious. *Infantry Journal* 53 (December) : 12–15.

ZAIDI, S. M. H. 1958. An experimental study of distortion in rumour. *Indian Journal of social Work* 19 : 211–15.

ZERNER, ELISABETH H., 1946. Rumors in Paris newspapers. *Public Opinion Quarterly* 10 : 382–91.

——, and Frederic Zerner, 1948. Rumeurs et opinion publique. *Cahiers internationaux de sociologie* 5 : 135–50.

ZIRKLE, CONWAY, 1941. Natural selection before the *Origin of Species*. *Proceedings of the American Philosophical Society* 84 : 71–123.

ZNANIECKI, FLORIAN, 1934. *The method of sociology.* New York: Farrar & Rinehart.

INDEX